Indus Water Conflict and Peace Building : India and Pakistan

Sasmita Swain   Narottam Gaan

Pustak Bharati
Toronto Canada

Book Title : Indus Water Conflict and Peace Building :
India and Pakistan

Authors : Sasmita Swain and Narottam Gaan

Published by :
Pustak Bharati (Books-India)
180 Torresdale Ave, Toronto Canada M2R 3E4
email : pustak.bharati.canada@gmail.com

Abbreviations

ADB- Asian Development Bank

BHP- BagliharHydel Power Project

CBDC- Central Bari Doab Canal

CBM- Confidence Building Measure

CRRID- Centre for Research in Rural and Industrial
   Development

CRS- Common Reporting Standard

CUMECS- cubic meters per second

DC- Dipalpur Canal

GDP- Gross Domestic Product

GEF- Global Environment Facility

HKH- Himalayan-Karakorum-Hindukush

IBWC- International Boundary and Water Commission

ICA- International Court of Arbitration

ICIMOD- International Centre for Integrated Mountain
   Development

ICWE- International Conference on Water and the
   Environment

IDSA- Institute for Defence Studies and Analyses

ILC- International Law Commission

IMF- International Monetary Fund

ISIL- Islamic State of Iraq and the Levant

IOK- Indian occupied Kashmir

IWMI- International Water Management Institute

IWRM- Integrated Water Resource Management

IWT- Indus Water Treaty

IYWC- International Year of Water Cooperation

J&K- Jammu and Kashmir

KHEP- Kishanganga Hydroelectric Project

LOC- Line of Control

MAF- Million Acre Feet

MOU- Memorandum ofUnderstanding

MW- Megawatt

NBI- Nile Basin Initiative

NGO- Non Governmental Organization

NTS- Non Traditional Security

O&M- Operation and Maintenance

PIC- Permanent Indus Commission

PPP- Public Private Partnership

RBO- River Basin Organisation

ROR- Run-of-River

SAARC- South Asian Association for Regional Cooperation

SCARP- Salinity Control and Rehabilitation Projects

TC-ARD- Technical Committee on Agriculture and Rural
        Development

TNP- Tulbul Navigation Project

TWAP- Transboundary Waters Assessment Programme

UN- United Nations

UNECE- United Nations Economic Commission for Europe

UNCED- United Nations Conference on Environment and
        Development

UNESCO- United Nations Educational, Scientific and
        Cultural Organisation

WAPDA- Water and Power Development Authority

WB- World Bank

WMO- World Meteorological Organization

WWAP- World Water Assessment Programme

WWSD- World Summit on Sustainable Development

Contents

		Page No.
	Introduction	i
Chapter-1	Water as a non-traditional security threat, conflict and cooperation	1
Chapter-2	Water sharing between India and Pakistan: Indus-Water Treaty	65
Chapter-3	Issues of conflict on water between India and Pakistan	122
Chapter-4	Resolutioning Water Conflict and Peace Building:Issues and Challenges	189
Chapter-5	Conclusion	248
	Bibliography	273

Introduction

Water is life. It is the lifeblood of our planet, a wonderful element without which the existence of life is impossible on earth. Water is one of the five basic elements with which God has created the entire cosmos. Because of its quintessential aspects, water is in the form of rivers, oceans, springs and streams worshipped as divine mother by the Hindus in India. In every aspect of life water is adored as sacrosanct without which living beings cannot live a moment. Though, water seems over-abundant on the planet earth about three quarters of the earth's area, only 2.5 per cent is fresh water. Out of 1.3 per cent of the freshwater-0.01 per cent of the total water on the earth, is in the form of ice and snow outside Polar Regions. It should be noted that rivers, lakes, soil, vegetation, atmosphere and exploitable underground aquifers constitute the fresh water resources of the world. However, more than a billion people in the world do not have access to safe drinking water. Water scarcity is, therefore, fast emerging as a grave concern, throughout the world.

Water poses both a threat and an opportunity for the UN system. Increasing scarcity of clean fresh water impedes development, undercuts human health, and plays critical roles along the conflict continuum between and within states. While rarely starting a war between states, water allocation is often a key sticking point in ending conflict and undertaking national and regional reconstruction and development. Within states water scarcity can assume an increasingly contentious and violent role when, for example, water-dependent sectors such as irrigated agriculture can no longer sustain farming livelihoods, leading to destabilizing migration flows. Conflict prevention, conflict resolution, and post-conflict reconstruction efforts ignore water at their peril in key regions of the world.

Water has also proven to be a productive pathway for confidence building, cooperation, and arguably, conflict prevention. Cooperative incidents outnumbered conflicts by more than two to one from 1945-1999. The key variable is not absolute water scarcity, but the resilience of the institutions that manage water and its associated tensions. In some cases, water provides one of the few paths for dialogue in otherwise heated bilateral conflicts. In politically unsettled regions, water is often essential to regional development negotiations that serve as de facto conflict-prevention strategies. The UN system and its partners have ripe opportunities to capitalize on water's cooperation promise while undercutting its conflict potential.

Water is an essential commodity, indispensable for the well-being of humanity, the environment, and the economy. Households, agriculture, industry, electricity generation, and ecosystems all require it in timely and adequate quantities and quality, so stakeholders must balance competing interests. The hydrologic cycle connects not only different sectors, but also different regions and countries, which share the impacts of water use and water pollution across national borders. Dependence on the same water resources can create communities out of diverse groups of users and stakeholders, transcending conflicting economic interests and fostering cooperative management, thereby generating advantages for all participants. Some researchers have identified cooperation over water resources as a highly promising approach to peace building because riparian countries are willing to enter into lengthy and complex negotiations so as to benefit from mutual development of water resources.

Through history, humankind has found ways to deal with water scarcity and cooperated to manage shared water resources. Water has helped pave the way for greater trust and cooperation and also helped prevent conflicts in heavily disputed river basins. On balance, international water disputes are usually resolved in a cooperative manner, even between hostile states and even when other contentious issues erupt into conflict. The bitterest enemies have entered into water treaties or are negotiating such agreements. The institutions they have established have often proved to be surprisingly stable, even when political relations are highly strained (e.g., the Mekong River Commission comprising Cambodia, Laos, Thailand, and Vietnam; "picnic table talks" between Israel and Jordan; and the Indus Commission between India and Pakistan). In some cases, water problems offer one of the few chances for cooperative dialogue in otherwise heated bilateral conflicts. In other political hotspots, water is a key component of regional development negotiations, which are indirect strategies of conflict prevention.

Water, on the other hand, is a vital component for economic development. With the growth in the national economies of the developing world, there is an upward swing in the standard of living- urbanization and industrialization- which demands more fresh water. In addition, the ever expanding population and climatic vagaries are further intensifying this problem. The United Nation (UN) estimates that "the number of people living in water stressed countries will increase from about 783 million today to more than three billion by 2035" (UNESCO). In short, water has become a major concern all over the world. As a matter of fact, many countries are facing water disputes due to water scarcity. Similarly, India and Pakistan have been facing such problems since their independence in 1947. The new political boundary between these two countries had divided the Indus River system by leaving the irrigation 'head-works' in one country and the canals as well as the irrigation land in another country. Thus, the Indus basin emerged as a potential conflict between India and Pakistan.

To resolve the conflict, India and Pakistan signed a Standstill Agreement on December 20, 1947. This agreement maintained the status quo till March 31, 1948. Two days before the superannuation of this agreement, Pakistan requested India for its extension but it declined. As a result, India stopped the water flowing towards Pakistan on April 1, 1948. This posed a grave threat to Pakistan.

However, India and Pakistan soon started negotiations on the resumption of water between April and May 1948. The first round of talks opened up on April 15 at Shimla in India. This round failed to break the deadlock between them. The second round was held in New Delhi on May 4 the same year, where both the parties successfully signed an agreement called "Delhi Agreement". India, after agreeing to resume the flow of water, asserted that Pakistan had no right to the waters of the Eastern Rivers of Sutlez, Beas and Ravi. It stressed that Pakistan recognize India's rights to all the rivers and demanded that Karachi had to pay for the waters. Despite New Delhi's restoration of the water supply to the Central Bari Doab Canal (CBDC) and the Dipalpur Canal (DC), Pakistan later rejected the agreement, reasoning that it was against its national interest. Therefore, the uncompromising stance of both the parties resulted in the failure of the negotiations.

Moreover, environmental and ecological changes call for re-consideration of Indus Water Treaty. Projections of climate change on water resources have important implications for both water scarce and flood prone regions, as many indicate dry regions becoming drier and wet regions becoming wetter. Within the next 50 years, however, experts believe there will be a 30 to 40 percent drop in glacial melt because the glaciers will have receded. In this regard, the canal withdrawals in Indus Irrigation System more or less stagnated in 1979 after construction of Tarbela Dam, have now declined to around 103 MAF, partly due to silting of the reservoirs.

Indus Water Treaty was signed to protect the interests of Pakistan and India. Pakistan gave off the right of three Eastern Rivers for the sake of complete and unhindered use of Western Rivers. India got the benefit of the three Eastern Rivers in full, but Pakistan's usages of the waters of three Western Rivers is yet on stake because India has started work on many projects at the cost of Pakistani concerns.

The challenge to the treaty came regarding the construction of the Wullar Barrage, as it is called by Pakistan, or Tubul Navigation project as termed by India. There is controversy on the explanations of the specific provisions of the Indus Water Treaty. The 330 MW Kishanganga Hydroelectric Projects that is located about 160 kilometers upstream of Muzaffarabad and involves diversion of Kishanganga or Neelum River to a tributary, Bunar Madumati Nullah of the River Jhelum through a 22-kilometer tunnel, is another controversial water issue between the two countries which could not have been resolved under Indus Water Treaty. Located on the River Chenab in Doda district, the Baglihar Hydropower Project is one of the nine major hydroelectric projects identified by India on the Chenab. Pakistan protested over the design of the dam in 1992 and demanded a halt to its construction.

During 2006 to 2011 Pakistan's concerns over another controversial project Nimoo Bazgo near village Alchi in the district Leh in Kashmir could not be highlighted due to the alleged negligence of Pakistans Indus Water Commissioner Jamaat Ali Shah. Citing Ali's alleged secret compliance with India Pakistan initiated a probe against him. However, during the inspection, the Pakistani team learnt that more than 80 percent of the work on the dam had been completed and the expected date of inauguration is July 2012.

India is third after US and China in dam building and has constructed 4365 dams. Also India is considering making 62 more hydroelectric dams on Pakistani rivers, which will enable India to close down the two Pakistani rivers Jhelum and Chenab hence turning Pakistan barren. India is also accused of water theft by using Pakistan's share of water through tunnels. In the meantime, India is also negotiating a dam on river Kabul with Afghanistan for setting up Kama Hydro-Electric Project which will utilize 0.5 MAF of Pakistani water. Pakistan is of the view that India is withholding the waters and terms it as a violation of the Indus Water Treaty, while the Indians always come up with the answer that Pakistan's assumption that India withholding its water is wrong and says that it is the flow of water that has decreased in the respective rivers causing lesser flow of water to Pakistan due to the global climate change, which Pakistan calls as water theft by India.

Haroon Ur Rashid, a Pakistani columnist thinks: "a possible tension between the two nations was feared to erupt on water sharing of the Indus Water". Pakistan's policy towards Kashmir is deeply influenced by the water factor and it does not seem possible in the long run for Pakistan to change its policy on Kashmir. This blame game is coming along for the last 63 years and has yet brought no significant progress to any side, especially affecting Pakistan. What is needed now is an urgent resumption of dialogues between the two countries, the dialogues should be aimed particularly at the water dispute and both countries should try to resolve the conflict peacefully as water is the most important necessity on earth.

The following questions crop up in the mind of researchers, scholars, policy makers, experts, environmenttalists and laymen while studying the water issue between India and Pakistan.

- How and why does cooperation in water resources not lend itself to the prevention of armed conflicts and to peace building between India and Pakistan?
- Which do political and social factors not favor the evolution of environmental cooperation into a wider social and political peace process?
- Which conditions facilitate or hinder this development?

- Is it possible to estimate the impact of trans-boundary environmental cooperation on peace building and conflict prevention in the context of climate change?

References:

- Arora R.K., 2007, "The Indus Water Regime", New Delhi; Mohit publication.
- Carius Alexander, Geoffrey D. Dabelko and Aaron T. Wolf, 2004, policy brief, The United Nations and Environmental Security, Water, Conflict and Cooperation.
- Conca Ken, "Governing Water: Contentiou Transnational Politics and Global Institution Building", 2005, Cambridge, MA:MIT press.
- Dinar Ariel, Dinar Shlomi, McCaffrey Stephen, and McKinney Daene, "Bridge over Water: Understanding Transboundary Water Conflict, Negotiation and Cooperation", 2007, Singapore: World Scintific.
- Gulhati N.D, 1973, "Indus Water Treaty: An Exercise in International Mediation; Bombay: Allied publishers.
- Kalpakian Jack, 2004, "Identity, Conflict, and Cooperation in International River System", Aldershot, UK: Ashgate.
- Kameri-Mbote Patricia, January 2007, No4, "Water Conflict and cooperation: Lessons from the Nile River Basin", environmental change and security program special report.
- KhagramSanjeev, 2004, "Dams and Development: Transnational Struggles for Water and Power", Ithaca: Cornell University Press.
- Malik A. Bashir, 2007 "Indus Water Regime", New Delhi; Mohit Publications.
- Michel A. Aloys, 1967, "The Indus Rivers: A Study of the Effects of Partition", New Haven and London: Yale University Press.

- Miner Mary, "Water Sharing Between India and Pakistan: a critical evaluation of the Indus Water Treaty", Water International 34, no.2 (May 2009); 204-216.
- Sinha K. Uttam, "India and Pakistan: Introspecting the Indus Treaty", strategic Analysis 32, No.6 (October,2008) 961-967; Sinha, "50 years of the Indus Water Treaty: An Evaluation", Strategic Analysis 34, no.5 (August,2010), 667-670; "Water a Pre-eminent Issue between India and Pakistan", Strategic Analysis 34, No.4 (June,2010) 482-485, "Will the Indus Water Treaty Survive" Strategic Analysis 36, No.5 (September,2012) 735-752.
- Stone R. David, "The United States and the Negotiation of the Indus Water Treaty", U.S.I. Journal 140, no.579 (January-March,2010):75-87.
- United Nations Educational, Scientific and Cultural Organization (UNESCO), 2009, "Valuing Water", UNESCO World Water Assessment Programmers.

Chapter-I

Water as a non-traditional security threat: potential for conflict and cooperation

Introduction

The traditional concept of security as defined by the school of realism and neo-realism is understood and weaved around state and is associated with military establishment. In other words, it is state centric and the protection of its territorial boundary and sovereignty lies solely on the state's military capability. The security of the state is held equivalent with that of the people. If the state is secured, the citizens living within the territorial boundary of the state are also secured. According to the traditional paradigm represented by realism and neo-realism, in an anarchical international system, the states are bound to be dependent on their own military strength and capability to protect them against the threat stemming from other states. The states are the sole decider of defining what a security threat is and of the means by which the threats can be nullified.

Thus, the international system is a dreary picture of conflict and wars between states on the issue of threats to their existence, survival and interests. This kind of established thinking dominated the foreign policy and security concerns of modern states, especially during the cold war. The consequences of this are the continued arms rule both convential and nuclear and competition among the states for superiority in military and defence. The world has been turned into a landscape of warfare and the scene of piling of weapons. The greatest military threat appeared to be from the nuclear weapons is demonstrated in the Second World War by America's dropping of nuclear bombs on Japan's two cities with millions of people dead.

After the Second World War, there has not been yet the

third world war, but the threat from it looms large. Apart from the danger of the nuclear weapons, millions of people lost their lives not because of war, but because of poverty, malnutrition, fatal diseases, environmental scarcity of resources, natural calamities and other factors. This loss of human life is not necessarily in all cases attributed to the state. The rise of non-state centric sources of security threats created an intellectual and academic resolution in the western hemisphere about the need to redefine security. In their strides to redefine security, environmental security and human security gain importance.

The threats to human lives from the source other than the states are held as non-traditional security threats. These are non-traditional in the sense that their origin is not necessarily state centric and the response to these threats are not necessarily military. For example, the consequences of environmental security are not confined to a particular state and are transboudary. Environmental security cannot be understood in a traditional self-versus others syndrome. Environmental crisis, as instantiated by climate change can have far reaching consequences on the survival and existence of humanity on this earth. The solution lies not in nuclear weapon or missiles, but in cooperative efforts of all the nations in the world with the help of epistemic knowledge community of scientists, technocrats and doctors.

With the rise of non-traditional security threats, the relevance of realism and neo-realism paradigm of understanding security solely in state-centric and military terms, has been questioned.

Water management is a heterogeneous issue with linkages to different sectors of national economy including the agricultural, industrial, domestic and household, power, environment, fisheries and transportation. Because, water is a shared and community resource, it has often led to disputes between different states and also with the neighboring countries and that adds to the problems of water resource management in countries.

Transboundary water disputes can be defined broadly, occurring whenever demand for water is shared by any sets of interests, is they political, economic, environmental, or legal. Conflicts over shared water resources occur at multiple scales, from sets of individual irrigators, to urban versus rural uses, to users located in different political jurisdictions—the traditional definition of transboundary. Transboundary waters share certain characteristics that make their management especially complicated, most notable of which is that these basins require a more complete appreciation of the political, cultural, and social aspects of water, and that the tendency is for regional politics to regularly exacerbate the already difficult task of understanding and managing complex natural systems (Wolf 2003).

Conflicts over water-a precious resource, the supply of which is growing sparser and the demand for which is ever mounting-have been much talked about by experts. Growing populations and extending development would render conflicts between water-rich and water-scarce nations inevitable. Upstream states that control the flow of water to downstream states would use this valuable resource as a key diplomatic and strategic tool to coerce the downstream nations into submitting to their demands. According to the 2002 United Nations World Water Development Report, there were 507 conflictive events over water during the previous fifty years. Thirty-seven among these involved violence, of which 21 consisted of military acts (18 between Israel and its neighbors). "Some of the most vociferous enemies around the world have negotiated water agreements [concerning international rivers] or are in the process of doing so," the report said. Global warming would act as a catalyst to water-conflict scenarios, with decreasing rainfall and increasing evaporàtion in some areas that have made the regular climate patterns erratic. Intermittent phases of flooding and droughts causing massive human suffering would pressure governments into turning off the taps to their neighbours.

The UN has recorded that the world's 263 trans-boundary lake and river basins include the territory of 145 countries and cover nearly half of the Earth's land surface. In the Mediterranean region as much as 80 percent of water resources are shared between two or more countries, whereas in the Balkan region this rate rises up to 90 percent.

The importance of trans-boundary waters climaxes as globally we face climate change and drought, amongst other environmental problems. The possibility that conflicts will arise between countries over the use of water is a real threat to our planet. The only way to avoid this is cooperation. According to UN data over the last 60 years there have been more than 200 international water agreements and only 37 cases of reported violence between states over water.

Although water is a potential source of conflict, there are many good examples of peaceful cooperation. The Indus Water Treaty, signed between Pakistan and India in 1960, has survived three major conflicts and remains valid today (Sarvat N.Hanif 2013).

International transboundary water issues are increasengly being viewed through the lens of security studies, which are guided by an appreciation of the mutually destabilizing forces of poverty and political instability. The process of poverty alleviation is often hampered in regions where human security is at risk. As a consequence, much of the thinking about the concept of "environmental security" has moved beyond a presumed causal relationship between environmental stress and violent conflict to a broader notion of "human security" – a more inclusive concept focusing on the intricate sets of relationships between environment and society.

Within this framework, water resources–including scarcity, distribution, and quality – have been named as the factor most likely to lead to intense political pressures, while threatening the processes of sustainable development and environmental protection. Water ignores political boundaries, evades institutional classification, and eludes legal generalizations. Worldwide, water demands are increasing, groundwater levels are dropping, water bodies are increasingly contaminated, and delivery and treatment infrastructure is aging (Wolf 2003).

Environmental Security and Conflict

The state-centric and military perspective of security has lost both practical relevance and intellectual credibility in the context of a number of historic forces and events in the contemporary age. These include the end of cold war, global integration of national economies, erosion of national identities and cultures, the shift in priority from military rivalry to economic competition, and the diminishing role of state as the dominant actor in international politics. On the other hand, diverse new issues have emerged ranging from poverty to refugee crises, information privacy to cyber-terrorism, environmental problems to natural disasters – which require non-state and non- military policies and strategies. These newly emerging security concerns have been characterized as non-traditional, and are now considered a major component of what is christened as comprehensive security. Among these emergent problems replacing the threat of East-West ideological divide, military aggression and struggle for global preponderance is the global environmental crisis. It looms large in terms of global warming, sea level rise, acid rain, greenhouse effect, diminishing capacity of the agricultural system, depletion of earth's finite resources, punching holes in the ozone layer, and biodiversity loss. Simply put, the global agenda has expanded since the demise of cold war as has the need for urgent attention to these problems for solution. It is thus seen that "welfare not warfare, will shape the rules and global threats like ozone holes and pollution will dictate the agenda."(Joffe J, 1992:35). It is within this context that the environmental question has gained worldwide significance as a security issue. In fact, environmental security stands out as perhaps the most widely debated issue especially due to its all pervasive nature, cross national scope and inter-generational implications (Haque M. Shamsul, 2002:24).

While many of the past, present and future causes of conflict and war may seem to have little or no direct connection with the environment or with resources, a strong argument can be made for linking certain resource and environmental problems with the prospects for political frictions and tensions, or even war and peace. At the centre of ongoing debate is the assertion that resource scarcity and certain forms of environmental degradation are important factors contributing to political instability or violent conflict at local, regional and interstate levels. There is a growing perception that local, regional and global environmental deficiencies or resource scarcities will increasingly produce conditions that may lead to conflict (Gleick Peter H, 1998: 105-106).

This conceptual shift towards environmental security in the context of collapse of the Soviet Union and diminution of security threats associated with cold war, pitchforked into the mainstream security debates urging the policymakers to cast about for a new security focus. Despite contentious debates within the field of environmental security, a wide variety of recent comments by senior diplomats and policy makers are symptomatic of the recognition that issues related to environmental security have ascended to the highest levels.

In 1987, the General Secretary of the Soviet Union,

Mikhail Gorbachev stated:

[The World] is not secure in the direct meaning of the word when currents of poison flow along river channels, when poison rains pour down from the sky, when an atmosphere polluted with industrial and transport waste chokes cities and whole regions, when the development of atomic engineering is justified by unacceptable risks...The relationship between man and the environment has become menacing. Problems of ecological security affect all the rich and the poor (Gorbachev M, 1987:3257).

In November 1989, British Prime Minister Margaret Thatcher gave a speech to the United Nations General Assembly-saying:

While the conventional political dangers – the threat of global annihilation, the fact of regional war- appear to be receding, we have all recently become aware of another insidious danger. It is as menacing in its way as these more accustomed perils with which international diplomacy has concerned itself for centuries. It is the prospect of irretrievable damage to the atmosphere, to the oceans, to earth it (Gleick, 1998:106).

In April 1997, as United States Secretary of State, Ms Albright went on to say:

Not so long ago, many believed that the pursuit of clean air, clean water, and healthy forests was a worthy goal, but not part of our national security. Today environmental issues are part of the mainstream of American foreign Policy (US Department of State, 1997).

It was in this backdrop of future non-military threats that a number of studies and research institutions undertook works to determine if and how environmental factors were related to the intra and interstate conflicts or violence that appeared to be surfacing around the globe (Gurr Ted, 1993).

Water Security : Definition

The meaning of the term "water security" varies according to the context and discipline from which it is being viewed. Water security can be defined as the allocation rules that ensure adequate and desired quantities of water or it can be defined as nation's ability to protect its inhabitants from droughts and floods. In the context of transboundary waters, nations have historically defined water security on the basis on securely attaining specific quantities of water every year. According to this definition, water security is measured on the basis of water stress-ratio of water use to availability and water shortage-number of people that have to share each unit of blue water resource. This definition puts human needs at the centre of water security. However, the contemporary definition of water security has been evolving in academic and policy literature. Based on the contemporary under-standing that water crosses various domains and scales it intersects natural, political and social domains at spatial, temporal, judicial and institutional scales and it is important to define water security in a more integrated manner to include access, affordability of water, human needs that encompasses food, energy, sanitation, health and environmental security. The current governance structure at the border of India and Pakistan is based on dividing and allocating water resources and the dispute resolution mechanisms that are put in place are meant to resolve problems relating to water quantity. As the existing governance mechanism was developed in 1960s, it is understandable that the platforms put in place for governance was based on the definition of water security at that time (Kaushik, 2017).

The emergence of many territorial sovereign states following the norms of Westphalian tradition, intersected with the eco-geographical regions, the result was the rivers and water resources were divided among them giving rise to conflict over access to the water resources. Most of the conflict between upper riparian and lower riparian states can be attributed to this artificial decisions of the rules in term of equitable distributing water resources.

Water as a non-traditional national security

The traditional notion of 'national security' (defined as protection of the state's sovereignty and territorial integrity from external military threats) is still of major importance. However, states as well as non-states actors have also raised broader, contemporary concepts that go well beyond external military threats, including human and environmental security. As one observer points out, at the World Commission on Environment and Development: "Today we cannot secure security for one state at the expense of the other. Security can only be universal, but security cannot only be political or military, it must be as well ecological, economical, and social. It must ensure the fulfilment of the aspirations of humanity as a whole" (Haefner, 2013).

Environmental security is central to national security, comprising the dynamics and interconnections among the natural resources, the social structure of the state, and the economic drivers for local and regional stability. Interconnectedness is one of the major characteristics of environmental causes and consequences, and can trigger conflict between states or within a state as a result of environmental degradation (Elliott, 2003, p. 47). As a result, it can threaten the security of a state, its people or even a whole region. This is supported by China and ASEAN which share the perspective that if economic stability and growth falter, regime survival could be in danger (Arase, 2010).

The environment and security can be linked in different ways through traditional or non-traditional lenses (Goh, 2006). The traditional notion of security links environmental degradation with conflict and contributes to potential interstate conflict. The non-traditional realm of security

focuses on the relationship between environmental degradation and social welfare relating to the effects of
environmental scarcity and degradation on the well-being of
communities and individuals (Goh, 2006, p. 229). This
includes a focus on human security, which is increasingly
defined as the security of individuals as human beings
instead of only being a citizen within a specific territorial
entity (Graeger, 1996). Although non-state actors are the
drivers behind Non Traditional Security (NTS), this research
uses the traditional way and focuses on the state level and the
negotiation process. However, this is intertwined with the
NTS aspect because states need to provide clear and
sufficient water for their citizens, economies and industries.
Those in the Copenhagen School argue that war and force
are not the only core elements of security studies and use a
broader definitional catchment in conceptualising security by
including many different types of threats.

This leads to another often discussed point in
environmental security focusing on the inclusiveness or
exclusiveness of water security, energy security, food
security and others in the area of environmental security and
its implications. To add another large field such as water or
energy security into environmental security broadens the
topic and makes it more bulky and difficult. However, for
this research on a transboundary river it is important and
necessary because of the rapid growing demand of
developing countries such as China and possible conflict
between water resources and energy demand. Gleick argues
that the regional level plays an important role as conflicts are
more likely to occur on local or regional levels in developing
countries because common property resources may be more
critical to survival and less easily to replace or supplement
(Haefner 2013).

This is visible on the Mekong as water governance is
closely related to the environmental effects, especially
regarding water quality and water flow. For instance,

damming on the upstream river not only reduces the water flow influencing the problem of water scarcity or allocation in the downstream countries, but also influences the water and soil quality (Lowi, 1999). This is also supported by the study of Phillips which illustrates the significance of environmental related indicators for all riparian states in the Mekong basin ranked on a scale from 1-5 with 5 indicating a high importance for the country. The result is that environmental issues play a significant role for all countries and that the most pressing ones basin wide are water quality, biodiversity and the flow regime (including base flow) which would be affected by the planned regional hydropower projects affecting all countries but severely the most downstream countries Cambodia and Vietnam (Phillips et al, 2006, p.128-129).

Whether water scarcity or security can be seen as a national security threat in addition to an environmental threat depends on several factors. According to Lowi these include water dependency on one special river and the physical location on the river, relating to the upstream-downstream phenomenon. Further factors are the countries climate and condensation, the demand of a growing population and the political relations within the given country and the region (Lowi, 1999, p. 380). For instance, China's role as the most powerful country on the upstream on the Mekong River with several other water resources is different to the role of the most downstream country, Vietnam, with a rapidly growing population and a strong focus on agriculture as one of the largest exporters of rice (it was the world's second largest rice exporter in 2012) (Fernquest, 2012). Similarly, for instance, Cambodia depends about 82 % on water originating from outside their borders, which shows that water scarcity could develop into a national security threat (Gleick, 1993: 103). Growing energy demand is one of the other major aspects in the subregion and often conflict through hydropower developments with environmental challenges. Food and energy depend on access to water and add to the dilemma on transnational river basins such as the Mekong River (Schneider, 2011).

Linking water challenges and security

Water as a security concern is beginning to gain attention worldwide. Researchers and international organisations are developing specific indicators to consider watershed that could be vulnerable to ecological stress and resultant conflicts. The first comprehensive study to examine "basins at risk" for conflicts over freshwater resources was published in 2003 by Yoffee, Wolf, and Giordano, in which they identified the following key criteria to delineate high-risk area:

- High population density (more than 100 people per square kilometre)
- Low per capita gross domestic product (less than US$765 per person)
- Overall unfriendly relations between constituents sharing the resource
- Politically active minority groups
- Proposed large dams or other water development projects
- Limited or no freshwater treaties

Even though this analysis did not consider some of the more contemporary areas of concern such as climate change, 9 out of 12 of the basins at risk are located within Asia.

Much of the popular reporting on water security has been polarized between those who believe that conflicts can arise over water scarcity and those who view such an approach to be sensationalistic and point to the paucity of "water war". Indeed, the ambivalence toward water as a potential source of conflict as well as an agent of cooperation has been the subject of considerable research. The absence of major conflicts over water suggests that we should consider the cooperative aspects of hydro politics more seriously. At the same time, we must recognize that the past may not be an adequate basis from which to draw conclusions about the potential for future conflicts arising from water security issues.

Water management is confronted with many challenges, most notably rising demand and pollution, and the impacts of climate change. In the context of these developments, water is linked to security in three broad ways. Firstly, conflict over the resource itself can induce socio-political destabilisation. Secondly, water can become intertwined in non-resource related conflicts. For example, parties can use water as a military tool and attempt to control access to the resource or limit the quantity or quality available to other parties. Thirdly, lacking water provision can significantly impact human security, and thereby contribute to the destabilisation of societies, increased migration, and heightened resource competition.

Water conflict on the local, national, international, and global levels

Water conflict can be studied at Fournier dependent levels.

Conflict at the Local level

It occurs between various societal groups competing for water in a specific area, or between a state and its citizens in a specific area. For examples, the conflict our water ranges from tribal tension over access to a water point, to entire communities being displaced by the construction of a dam, project or industry to a general population's response to the poor governance of their water services. At the local level, such tension over water use, its availability, and allocation, can contribute to low-scale violence, which can escalate into instability within states and across sub- regions. The tension between citizens and state authorities and initial forms of conflict are frequently manifested in acts of civil disobedience, which may escalate into acts of sabotage and violent protest if adequate participatory decision-making is not achieved. Violent repression by the state in response to citizen protests has not been uncommon.

National conflict

It occurs between different interest groups in relation to national policies affecting water management. The hostilities generated by inadequate or even contradictory national regulations governing competing sectors and priorities, from farming to industry, environmental protection to municipal water supplies can come under this. Such conflicts stem from a lack of integrated water resources management at the national level. In most cases these conflicts are resolved through courts or political processes. But where governments are weak or corrupt, water scarcity, its poor management may play as an catalyst to exacerbate and the discontent among the people which may escalate into violent conflict.

International conflict

This occurs between states over the use of shared water resources. This encompasses tension and threatened hostilities between upstream and downstream states over the use of shared rivers, as well as other transboundary bodies of surface water and underground aquifers. Such tensions between countries may hinder sustainable development, indirectly pushing people into poverty, migration, and social instability. It also has the potential to exacerbate other non-water related violent conflicts.

Global disputes occur

This is between marginalized and affluent populations, in which conflicts result when resources are distributed inequitably favouring the privileged ones at the cost of the marginalised people in the society. One such example is the conflict over securing land exclusively by the rich for example; conflict arises as global freshwater and land resourcesment to agricultural production to the markets and market-friendly governmental policies. The demands of increasing affluence (e.g. grain-based bio fuels for cars and trucks to mitigate emission of CO2 and water-intensive crops for export) ignore the basic human needs of impoverished local populations (Jason Gehrig).

The potential effects of climate change on international water security

Global climate change could alter the international water security landscape in many ways. Present climate models predict increased drought in some areas of the world, and increased flooding in others, coupled with an accelerating variability in the timing, amount, and areal distribution of precipitation. These stressors could increase local violence and aggressive political actions regarding water and food supply which depends on irrigation.

Melting of glacial ice, a vast reserve of fresh water, and associated changes in ocean temperature, salinity and circulation have been cited as factors in regional drought, but global warming could destabilize international security in unexpected ways. For example, according to scientists at NASA and the University of Colorado's National Snow and Ice Data Center, although the summer Arctic ice pack typically reaches a minimum in mid-September, in September of 2012 the existing ice extent reached the lowest value in 33 years since satellite imagery of the pack began, having melted at rates up to an unprecedented 38,600 to 57,900 estimated square miles per day in the summer of 2012, which is over double the climatological rate (World Meteorological Organization 2012). Worldwide, August of 2012 was the 4th hottest month on record. With the observed shrinking of the Arctic icecap, the northmost oceans are opening up to increased commerce and development, with oil, fishing, mining and shipping interests expanding into the region (Kramer 2011), sometimes in the absence of complete governing regulations for such expansion. These interests may become the beneficiaries of more accessible open water, sea lanes, and sea floor, but also competitors, increasing legal and political complexities. The combination of these transformations in the quality and areal distribution of water could portend instabilities and be a precursor to open hostilities (Kreamer, 2012).

Water-related conflict: what, where, and how?

Water-related violence often occurs on the local rather than international level, and the intensity of conflict is generally inversely related to geographic scale (Wolf, 1999). Even if international disputes over water-related issues do not typically cause violent conflict, they have led to interstate tensions and significantly hampered development, such as along the Nile, Mekong, Euphrates, Amu Darya, Syr Darya, and Ganges rivers. And while conflicts often remain local, they can also impact stability at the national and regional levels. Existing territorial or political conflict are escalated further by the issues of water conflict.

The Basins at Risk project's analytical tool helps identify areas where hydrological and political conditions suggest a higher likelihood of conflict over water (Wolf et al., 2003). Based on extensive analysis of the world's 263 international river basins, the project hypothesizes that "the likelihood of conflict rises as the rate of change within the basin exceeds the institutional capacity to absorb that change." Sudden physical changes or reduced institutional capacity are more conducive to disputes. Key examples include uncoordinated development of major projects that affect flow (e.g., dams) in the absence of a treaty or commission; basins that suddenly become "internationalized," as occurred in post-Soviet Central Asia; and general animosity among parties. This approach provides a set of indicators for monitoring potential hot spots, thus allowing us to get ahead of the "crisis curve" and promote institutional capacity in advance of intractable conflict. There are three major linkages between conflict and water (ibid).

1. Access to adequate water supplies

Conflict is most likely to occur over water when disputes involve access to water of adequate quantity and quality. Even when water supplies are not severely limited, allocation of water among different users and uses (urban residents and agriculture, for example) can be highly contested. Degraded water quality which can pose serious threats to health, and aggravate security is also a source of potential violent disputes. Finally, when water supplies for broadly irrigated regions decline either in terms of quantity or quality, those declines can spur migrations that could politically destabilize the receiving cities or neighbouring countries.

2. Water, livelihood loss, and civil conflict

Importance of water in sustaining human livelihoods can indirectly link it to conflict. Water is a basic resource for agriculture, which is traditionally the largest source of livelihoods. If this livelihood is no longer available, people are often forced to search for job opportunities in the cities or turn to other, sometimes illicit, ways to make a living. Migration—induced by lack of water, sudden droughts and floods, infrastructure construction (e.g., dams), pollution, disasters, or loss of livelihood—can produce tensions between local and incoming communities, especially when it increases pressure on already scarce resources. And poverty due to loss of livelihood has been identified as a common denominator of the causes of conflict in most of the civil wars that emerged in Africa, South Asia, and Latin America during the last decade (Ohlsson, 2000).

3. Water management and conflict

Apart from lack of adequate sources of water, lack of proper institutional and legal mechanisms for equitable distribution of water among all sections of the society, lack of transparency in distribution, and lack of development of infrastructures for making the water sustainable and other environmental and technical measures for turning the inadequacy of water into one of adequacy, lead to violent conflict.

Water management highly complex issue is having political connotation. Balancing competing interests over water allocation and managing water scarcity is a very delicate act that requires strong institutions. A reliable database, including meteorological, hydrological, and socio-economic and environmental data, is a fundamental tool for efficient and effective management of water resources. Yet, reliable information is often difficult to obtain, especially in developing countries. Further, disparities among riparian's capacity to generate, interpret, and legitimize data can lead to mistrust and thus hinder cooperative action.

Overlapping, repetitive and competing responsibilities among government bodies make water management very difficult and complex. Disaggregated decision-making often produces divergent management approaches that serve contradictory objectives and lead to competing claims from different sectors. And such claims are even more likely to contribute to disputes in countries where there is no formal system of water-use permits, or where enforcement and monitoring are inadequate. Controversy also often arises when management decisions are formulated without sufficient participation by local communities and water users, thus failing to take into account local rights and practices. Protests are especially likely when the public suspects that water allocations are diverting public resources for private gain or when water use rights are assigned in a secretive and possibly corrupt manner, as demonstrated by the violent confrontations in 2000 following the privatization of the water utility in Cochabamba, Bolivia.

Conflict of Approaches to Water

In trying to understand the various actors and their approaches on the issue of trans-boundary water, it is important to recognise at the outset that there are plurality of actors in the water sector—the state which includes governments, bureaucracy and the state machinery, who can also be termed the "managers" and the market; civil society organisations, activist groups, environmental movements; donors and funding groups; water communities or water users; and knowledge institutions. Each group is characterised with its own strategies and approaches, and within each group there are differences and variations. These approaches are as followed.

1.State/Strategic Approach: The state or the government departments have long been the major actors when it came to water issues. With regard to trans-boundary Rivers, the state approach has been one of strategic and centralised control. In practice, this has meant high-handed approach and securitisation of water. This is quite evident in the way water is 'managed' and hydro politics played out between India-Pakistan, Bangladesh-India, and sometimes between Nepal-India and in the way some of the other conflicts, such as those existing between India and Pakistan, superimpose themselves over watery spaces. One can also draw comparisons of national security and other aspects of high politics getting linked to water management in parts of West Asia.

2.Market/Economic Good Approach: The market approach is based on the understanding that given the problems that nation states have had in sharing their water resources, the mechanisms for governance of water must be left to the market and economic instruments. It includes a wide range of actors who argue for water markets, privatisation of water, tradable water rights, accounting for the economic value of water, public–private partnership. It is supported by

19

Institutions such as the World Bank, Asia Development Bank, UN; International 'Water' Institutions like World Water Council, Global Water Partnership; corporates, some governments; and some NGOs. This has been facilitated by two trends in the 90's-1) The growing acceptance of privatisation of public services as a way of dealing with inefficiency, poor delivery and fund shortage. 2) Institutional backing of World Bank (WB) and IMF for water privatisation. Within the governments in the region, given the growing scarcity and increasing demand for water, there are two mindsets. 1) To increase 'production' and bring in more water available in nature to the 'usable' category. 2) To then build water reservoirs and infrastructure to store water that is going "waste" into the environment. Hence water is seen as subject to laws of supply and demand. Such an approach then is extended well with the more blatant market approach propagated by institutions like WB and ADB. The argument here is that effective resource manage-ment requires that water is given an economic value. Hence water rights should be defined and water trading allowed. The underlying premise is that if markets are given a free play, private sector allowed in, the state only plays a facilitating role; the market will ensure that supply side meets the demand. Within this, Public-Private Partnership (PPP) is held as a model for improved services, better efficiency and better investment.

Given that water is fast becoming a scarce resource, there is also a growing trend to merchandise it for profit. In its most blatant forms, giant corporations are rapidly acquiring control of water through the ownership of dams, waterways, water infrastructures, municipal corporations, development of new technologies such as water desalination and purification, among others. There have also been attempts to give water, both an economic and social content. Significant here is the Integrated Water Resource Management (IWRM) approach which tries to combine the social, environmental and economic approach to water. This IRWM has its intellectual roots in the United Nations Conference on Environment and Development (UNCED) that was held in Mar del Plata in 1977. Important to the emerging discourse of IWRM has been the Dublin Principles which espoused interdependencies within natural systems, as well economic and social systems. However, IWRM has been critiqued for defining the unit of management as the river basin. It is argued that this is based solely on hydrological characteristics and takes no consideration of social, cultural, political or economic characteristics that shape water governance. Dissenting voices question the universal applicability of IWRM with leading water experts calling for a renewed analysis of the relevance of some of its core assumptions.

3.Alternative approach/ water as social good and a basic human right: Proponents of this approach include social activists, academics, environmentalists and NGOs who vary widely but share a common stance that water is a basic human right, a common pool resource and cannot be reduced to a tradable commodity. These groups have been criticising the hierarchical approach and privatisation of water that ignores people and community based approaches to water. They argue that water and human rights are interlinked at several levels. Water is quintessential for life, livelihood and survival; the provision for safe drinking water combined with hygienic sanitation facilities is a precondition for health and successful fight against poverty, hunger, child deaths and gender inequality. This also plays a significant role in protection of the rights of the displaced people and their cultures are affected by mega projects and dams; environmental and ecological concerns (Singh Richa, 2008).

Typologies of conflicts over water

Different typologies contribute to an improved understanding of water conflicts. These typologies serve

21

different purposes and use different categories. In the following, typologies that distinguish conflicts according to their level, their basis, their scale, and the actors involved and the impact of conflicts are presented.

Level of conflict

Conflicts can be distinguished according to the level at which they occur: whether at the local, national or transboundary level. The field of 'water and conflict' relates to a broad array of settings – it could be the (unlikely) scenario of a war over water between countries, competition over water resources at a regional level, or conflict over access to irrigation within a community.

At the transboundary level, examples from the Middle East are frequently discussed. The Jordan basin is among those most frequently referred to (e.g. Haddadin and Shamir, 2003). The arid climate and frequent droughts compounded with inefficiencies in water use, increasing demand through industrialisation and population growth put stress on water resources (Fröhlich, 2012: 147). This is intertwined with the political situation as reflected in disparities in water allocation. Water consumption by Israelis and Palestinians reflect stark inequalities. While estimates vary, they suggest that Israelis consume about three times as much water per person per day (250 litres) as Palestinians (84 litres) (Ibid: 150).

The Euphrates-Tigris basin shared between Turkey, Iraq and Syria is another basin very often referred to in studies on water conflicts. Turkey as the upper riparian claims the right to use water for electricity generation and irrigation. The conflict revolves primarily around the Southeast-Anatolia-Project (GAP GüneydoguAnadoluProjesi) consisting of 22 dams and 19 power plants and the associated water use (Fröhlich, 2012: 155). The role of ISIL adds to the complexity of the conflict, as the insurgents have seized dams in Iraq putting them in control of cutting water supplies and causing flooding (Pacific Institute, 2015).

Yet another 'hot' basin is the Nile. The Nile Basin Initiative (NBI) is a regional platform for water management, multi stakeholder dialogue, and joint planning in the Nile Basin. It is led by 10 riparian countries, namely Burundi, DR Congo, Egypt, Ethiopia, Kenya, Rwanda, South Sudan, Sudan, Tanzania, and Uganda. Eritrea participates as an observer. The NBI is supported by the World Bank, the EU and many other organisations. It has gone through phases of confidence building and institutional strengthening, but challenges remain (NBI, 2015). Most recently, the development of the Grand Renaissance Dam on the Blue Nile in Ethiopia has brewed new tensions, in particular with Egypt (Veilleux, 2013).

These examples reflect a trend in the literature on water conflicts: There is a tendency to focus on the most volatile basins, which makes it difficult to draw general conclusions (Wolf, 2003: 3). It is true that competition and conflict over water have an important transboundary dimension. There are 276 transboundary basins in the world, and more than 2000 transboundary aquifers have been identified (UN-Water, 2013). More than 45 percent of the earth' surface lies in transboundary drainage basins, and 40 percent of the world's population live in transboundary basins (Manno, 2010). In many instances, transboundary water resources are necessary to secure access to water. Egypt, for example, relies almost entirely on exogenous water resources (Libiszewski, 1999: 120). From a legal perspective, it is important to distinguish the transboundary dimension of conflicts over water. As discussed above, additional questions arise in terms of the application of human rights law in a transboundary context.

However, to some extent, the focus on the question whether there might be actual wars between states over water distracts from other conflicts over water – that are often on a smaller scale, often at the local level, and often non-violent. Even transboundary conflicts often have an internal or local dimension with conflicting interests in the use of the share of water resources available within the state. Such local conflicts between different user groups, ethnic groups, different parts of a country, or other competing interests require greater emphasis. Seeking to address this gap, the 'Competing for Water Research Programme' developed inventories of water conflicts and cooperation in selected districts in Asia, Africa and Latin America (Ravnborg et al., 2012). At the local level, rather than having a discrete number of transboundary basins, the settings where conflicts can take place are virtually unlimited, hence the necessity of selecting a number of districts for the purposes of the programme.

Scale of conflict

Wolf et al. focus on conflicts and cooperation in transboundary basins in their typology for identifying basins at risk of dispute (BAR scale). They apply a scale from conflict to cooperation from the most conflictive at -7 (war) to the most cooperative at +7 (the voluntary merging of countries) using political, diplomatic and economic hostile actions, verbal hostilities, verbal support, different types of agreements and the signing of treaties to define the various scales in between (Wolf et al., 2003: 5).

The 'Competing for Water Research Programme' developed a scale for local water conflicts inspired by the BAR scale. It ranges from -7 (organised collective violence) to +7 (merging access rights) with various events of conflict and cooperation on this scale such as different forms of violence, demonstrations, violations of access rights, verbal disputes, joint activities, verbal agreements, joint organisation fora and joint decision-making authority (Ravnborg et al., 2012: 341). Overall, the study found that events are equally distributed between conflict and cooperation over water, but that violent conflict is rare (Ravnborg et al., 2012: 356).

Basis of conflict

A Water Conflict Chronology developed by the Pacific Institute categorises conflicts according to the basis of conflict and the role water plays in the conflict using the following categories:

➢ "Control of Water Resources (state and non-state actors): where water supplies or access to water is at the root of tensions.

➢ Military Tool (state actors): where water resources, or water systems themselves, are used by a nation or state as a weapon during a military action.

➢ Political Tool (state and non-state actors): where water resources, or water systems themselves, are used by a nation, state, or non-state actor for a political goal.

➢ Terrorism (non-state actors): where water resources, or water systems, are either targets or tools of violence or coercion by non-state actors.

➢ Military Target (state actors): where water resource systems are targets of military actions by nations or states.

➢ Development Disputes (state and non-state actors): where water resources or water systems are a major source of contention and dispute in the context of economic and social development" (Pacific Institute, 2015). The database currently includes close to 350 entries of water-related conflicts. Some of these categories relate to conflicts over water, whereas others show that water can also be used in a tactical way in a conflict, for instance depriving the opponents of access to water or contaminating their water supply (Pacific Institute, 2015; see also USAID 2014: 5).

Recent examples of conflicts from the Middle East include Israeli sanctions on Gaza that caused water shortages, a conflict in Iran over the diversion of water used by farmers, and tensions in Jordan over water supply exacerbated by Syrian refugees (Pacific Institute, 2015).

Actors involved in the conflict

Houdret suggests an actor-centred typology of water conflicts that focuses on the interests certain groups have in water use (Houdret, 2008: 11 ET seqq). Such a typology points to

➢ Conflicts between different geographical areas, such as conflicts between urban and rural areas as growing urban centres rely increasingly on water resources from farther away (Molle and Berkoff, 2006).

➢ Conflicts between different sectors of water use, for instance between tourism relying on golf courses and resorts on the one hand and agricultural users on the other hand; or between industrial users who may extract large amounts of water or contaminate water that other users rely on for domestic or agricultural use.

➢ Conflicts between different users within the same sector such as agricultural users that rely on the same source or irrigation system. This may involve large-scale agricultural use (often aimed at export and sometimes linked to large-scale land acquisitions and water grabbing) and small-scale farmers whose livelihoods rely on access to water (Mehta, Veldwisch and Franco, 2012); or allocation within urban areas where rationing in times of drought may affect different areas in a city to a varying extent;

➢ Conflicts between different population groups for instance between indigenous peoples and others; or between long-time residents in a country and refugees (European Union 2015).

Political tensions and costs of noncooperation

So if there is little violence between nations over their shared waters, what is the problem? Is water actually a security concern at all? In fact, there are a number of issues where water causes or exacerbates tensions, and it is worth understanding these processes to know both how complications arise and how they are eventually resolved. Non-cooperation costs result primarily in inefficient water management, leading to decreasing water quantity, quality, and environmental health. But political tensions can also be impacted, leading to years or even decades of efficient, cooperative futures lost.

Tensions and Time Lags : Causes for Concern

The first complicating factor is the time lag between when nations first start to impinge on each other's water planning and when agreements are finally reached. A general pattern has emerged for international basins overtime. Riparians of an international basin implement water development projects unilaterally—first on water within their own territory, in attempts to avoid the political intricacies of the shared resource. At some point, one of the riparians, generally the regional power, will implement a project that impacts at least one of its neighbours. This might be to continue to meet existing uses in the face of decreasing relative water availability as, for example, Egypt's plans for a high dam on the Nile (Waterbury J. 2002) or India's diversions of the Ganges to protect the port of Calcutta (Biswas A K1996)] or to meet new needs reflecting new agricultural policy, such as Turkey's SAP (Turkish acronym for Southeast Anatolia Project) project on the Euphrates and Tigris. In the absence of relations or institutions conducive to conflict resolution, the project can become a flash point, heightening tensions and regional instability, and requiring years or, more commonly, decades to resolve—the Indus treaty took 10 years of negotiations, the Ganges 30, and the Jordan 40—and, all the while, water quality and quantity degrades to such a dismal low where the health of dependent populations and ecosystems are damaged or destroyed (Kibaroglu A. 2002).

The timing of water flow is also important; thus, the operation of dams is also contested. For example, upstream users might release water from reservoirs in the winter for hydropower production, whereas downstream users might need it for irrigation in the summer. In addition, water quantity and water flow patterns are crucial to maintaining fresh water ecosystems that depend on seasonal flooding. Freshwater ecosystems perform a variety of ecological and economical functions and often play an important role in sustaining livelihoods, especially in developing countries. As awareness of environmental issues and the economic value of ecosystems increases, claims for the environment's water requirements are growing. For example, in the Okavango basin, Botswana's claims for water to sustain the Okavango Delta and its lucrative eco tourism industry have contributed to a dispute with upstream Namibia, which wants to use the water passing through the Caprivi Strip on its way to the delta for irrigation (Nakayama M, ed. 2003).

Excessive amounts of nutrients or suspended solids can result from unsustainable agricultural practices, eventually leading to erosion. Nutrients and suspended solids pose a threat to freshwater ecosystem and their use by downstream riparians, as they can cause eutrophication and siltation, respectively, which, in turn, can lead to loss of fishing grounds or arable land. Suspended solids can also cause the siltation of reservoirs and harbors; for example, Rotter dam's harbour had to be dredged frequently to remove contaminated sludge deposited by the Rhine River. The cost was enormous and consequently led to conflict over compensation and responsibility among the river's users. Although negotiations led to a peaceful solution in this case, without such a framework for dispute resolution, siltation problems can lead to upstream/downstream disputes such as those in the Lempa River basin in Central America (Lopez A.2004).

Overcoming the costs of non-cooperation: from rights to needs to interests

Most of the international negotiations surveyed are hamstrung for so long primarily because of entrenched and

28

contradictory opening positions. Generally, parties base their initial positions in terms of rights—the sense that a riparian is entitled to a certain allocation based on hydrography or chronology of use. Upstream riparians often invoke some variation of the Harmon doctrine, claiming that water rights originate where the water falls. India claimed absolute sovereignty in the early phases of negotiations over the Indus Waters Treaty, as did France in the Lac Lanoux case and Palestine over the West Bank aquifer. Downstream riparians often claim absolute river integrity, claiming rights to an undisturbed system or, if on an exotic stream, historic rights on the basis of their history of use. Spain insisted on absolute sovereignty regarding the Lac Lanoux project, whereas Egypt claimed historic rights against first Sudan, and later Ethiopia, on the Nile (Waterbury J. 1979).

In almost all of the disputes that have been resolved, however, particularly on arid or exotic streams, the paradigms used for negotiations have not been rights based at all—neither on relative hydrography nor specifically on chronology of use, but rather needs based. Needs are defined by irrigable land, population, or the requirements of a specific project. See below for examples of needs-based criteria.

Examples of needs-based criteria

Treaty	Criteria for allocations
Egypt/Sudan (1929, 1959, Nile)	Acquired rights from existing uses, plus even division of any additional water resulting from development projects
Johnston Accord (1956, Jordan)	Amount of irrigable land within the watershed in each country

India/Pakistan (1960, Indus)	Historic and planned use (for Pakistan) plus geographic allocations (western versus eastern rivers)
South Africa (southwest Africa)/Portugal (Angola) (1969, Kunene)	Allocations for human and animal needs as well as initial irrigation
Israel-Palestinian Interim Agreement (1995, shared aquifers)	Population patterns and irrigation needs

From rights and needs to interests: baskets of benefits

One productive approach to the development of transboundary waters has been to move past rights and needs entirely and to examine the benefits in the basin from a regional approach. This has regularly required the riparians to go beyond looking at water as a commodity to be divided—a zero-sum rights based approach—and to develop an approach that equitably allocates not the water but the benefits derived therefrom—a positive sum integrative approach. The boundary waters agreement between the United States and Canada, for example, allocates water according to equal benefits, usually defined by hydropower generation. This result in the seemingly odd arrangement that power may be exported out of basin for gain, but the water itself may not. In the 1964 treaty on the Columbia, an arrangement was worked out whereby the United States paid Canada for the benefits of flood control, and Canada was granted rights to divert water between the Columbia and Kootenai rivers for hydropower. Likewise, the 1975 Mekong accord defines equality of right not as equal shares of water but as equal rights to use water on the basis of each riparian's economic and social needs. The relative nature of beneficial uses is exhibited in a 1950 agreement on the Niagara, flowing between the United States and Canada,

30

which provides a greater flow over the famous falls during "show times" of summer daylight hours, when tourist dollars are worth more per cubic meter than the alternate use in hydropower generation (Muckleston K. 2003).

In many water-related treaties, water issues are dealt with alone, separate from any other political or resource issues between countries—water qua water. By separating the two realms of "high" (political) and "low" (resource economical) politics or by ignoring other resources that might be included in an agreement, some have argued, the process is either likely to fail, as in the case of the 1956 Johnston Accord on the Jordan, or more often to achieve a sub optimum development arrangement, as is currently the case on the Indus agreement, signed in 1960. Increasingly, however, linkages are being made between water and politics as well as between water and other resources. These multi resource linkages may offer more opportunities for the generation of creative solutions, allowing for greater economic efficiency through a basket of benefits (SadoffCW,Gray D. 2002).

Lessons learned

The most critical security lessons learned from the global experience in water security are as follows:

1. Water crossing international boundaries can cause tensions between nations that share the basin. Although the tension is not likely to lead to warfare, early coordination between riparian's can help ameliorate the issue. Furthermore, water is a useful inducement to dialogue and collaboration, even in settings of intense political tension.

2. Successful agreements move generally from thinking in terms of rights to needs and finally to interests, allowing for an equitable distribution of benefits. Whereas focusing on allocating water mires negotiators in a zero-sum game, thinking in terms of benefits allows riparians to move

beyond the river, (and even beyond water) with new possibilities for the basket of benefits to be enhanced. Once international institutions are in place, they are tremendously resilient over time, even between otherwise hostile riparian nations, and even when there is conflict over other issues.

3. More likely than violent conflict occurring is a gradual decrease in water quantity or quality, or both, which overtime can affect the internal stability of a nation or region, and act as an irritant between ethnic groups, water sectors, or states/provinces. The resulting instability may have effects in the international arena.

4. The greatest threat of the global water crisis to human security comes from the fact that millions of people lack access to sufficient quantities of water at sufficient quality for their well-being (Wolf T Aaron 2007).

The threats of conflict

Conflicts over transboundary water can threaten international peace and security. Many international basins will face a strong increase in demand for water as a result of demographic pressures, industrialisation and urbanisation. Simultaneously, in many cases supply will recede, due to both earlier mismanagement and the impacts of climate change (Falkenmark and Jägerskog 2010). Climate change might decrease water supply in many basins through changes in precipitation and greater evaporation. Other basins may witness increases in floods and droughts, or shifts in the seasonality of rain or snowfall. And even as climate pressures may alter the amount and timing of water availability, climate stresses may also increase the demand for water, e.g. for irrigation and cooling. These changes have security implications at both the national and the international level.

First, insufficient or irregular access to water can imperil agricultural production and rural livelihoods, threaten municipal drinking water and sanitation, compromise electric power generation, and jeopardise public health, posing manifold security risks at the sub national level. Some affected states may find it difficult to share the costs of climate change in a way that is agreed by societal groups. Water scarcity may therefore reduce the perceived legitimacy of the government. Pastoralists in the Horn of Africa – who usually carry arms – may need to find new feeding grounds for their livestock, and impoverished farmers in Afghanistan may migrate to Kabul because their fields have been desiccated. Such scenarios are likely to (further) undermine social and political stability and enhance the risk of violent conflict. These risks are mirrored in the potential consequences of sea-level rises for farmers and people living in coastal communities in littoral zones and river deltas such as in Southern Bangladesh. These examples of water insecurity and conflicting interests at the sub-national level can also have transboundary impacts if impoverished migrants or refugees fleeing natural catastrophes seek to cross borders, or if the resulting grievances draw in foreigners, e.g. via shared ethnic ties. In this way, water insecurity and climate change may put additional pressure on individuals, institutions and states that are already vulnerable.

Second, conflicting interests over the use of often-scarce water resources can also directly contribute to interstate tensions. Such conflicts may arise around the construction of dams on Transboundary Rivers. Recent examples that have captured headlines include the Grand Ethiopian Renaissance Dam in Ethiopia, the Xayaburi Dam in Laos, and the Rogun Dam in Tajikistan, all of which have raised tensions between riparian states. The countries pursuing such projects argue that the new dams will enable them to generate renewable hydropower, enhance flood security, and increase water storage to buffer against varying availability. However, downstream countries frequently fear these same structures could be used to control or reduce the water flowing to them, placing their own water needs at risk.

Wherever nations share common water supplies, their ability to meet their water needs will be interdependent. Yet fewer than half of the world's transboundary basins are subject to any formal agreement outlining how the resources are to be divided and managed (Giordano et al. 2013). There are even fewer water bodies with institutionalised cooperation: only 116 out of 276 transboundary basins have ever had a river basin organisation (RBO) (Schmeier 2013). Yet most experts agree that an RBO is a key institutional formation for cooperation, policy coordination, risk management, and conflict resolution. Such institutions have been identified as more important than any physical 'water stress' indicators for peacefully coping with rapid changes in a given basin (Wolf et al. 2003). This being said, the mere existence of a treaty is not enough to prevent conflict because such agreements often lack robust conflict management mechanisms; this is the case, for example, with the existing agreements in the Tigris- Euphrates basin (Lorenz and Erickson 2013). Even hitherto successful institutions may be at risk. The Indus Waters Treaty, for example, suffers from insufficient governance in so far as it contains no rules on how to adapt to the changes that climate change may bring about and in so far as there is no integrated water management that could provide the necessary long-term solutions to rapidly growing scarcity (Swain, 2013).

Beyond the weakness of institutional mechanisms and the question of what issues treaty terms do or do not cover – water quality, variability, conflict resolution, etc. – lays the issue of what parties are involved in the agreements. In both the Indus and the Tigris-Euphrates, the existing agreements do not include all riparians. This is particularly problematic in the case of the Tigris-Euphrates, where no tri-lateral accord brings together Iraq, Syria, and Turkey. Geographical incompleteness might undermine agreements' potential resilience and riparian states' ability to advance collective management in the face of climate change. Rising water demands and climate change-induced variability and uncertainty thus threaten the survival of existing water-sharing agreements while simultaneously making better, collective management more urgent.

The extent to which each country securitises water – i.e., transforms water into a key aspect of its national security whose protection justifies the use of extraordinary means – will depend on national perceptions of how the country will be impacted by climate change, both in absolute terms and relative to its (potential) rivals. Deteriorations in position – whether actual or perceived – may in many cases increase political stress and help fuel conflict (climate diplomacy 2014).

Water Cooperation

Cooperation is an essential characteristic of international relations, as it plays a key role in maintaining the cordial nature of relations among states. It can be defined as a procedure by which two or more parties or states work together to accomplish mutual goals that could not be achieved by one state unilaterally. On a similar note, the term water cooperation implies an establishment of coordination among two or more parties or states over the distribution, utilization, and management of their shared water resources.

Water cooperation has gained significant attention in recent years because several countries are approaching water scarcity and because several disputes have emerged among states in recent history over the distribution of their common transboundary water resources, which have needed to be resolved through the establishment of cooperative measures.

Several states rely on freshwater for their agricultural subsistence and energy production.

When states own transboundary freshwater resources, they claim their ownership over it as a means of expressing their sovereign right over that water resource. If a common watercourse passes through two or more states and they are geographically the upper and lower riparian states, then this creates a problematic situation when the upper riparian state utilizes more than its share of water by diverting a significant quantity toward its own land for agricultural or any other purposes, subsequently resulting in a shortage of water in the basin of that water resource for the lower riparian state. Such exploitation is now prohibited by international law. However, in the event of violation or incomplete compliance of international law by the upper riparian state, the lower riparian state feels the need to resort to dialogue or some other cooperative measures to convey its concerns to the upper riparian state. Hence, this establishes a need for cooperation among riparian states. In this regard, international law also includes special provisions for maintaining efficient mechanisms of cooperation among riparian states. Through these cooperative measures, riparian states can avoid causing harm to one another by utilizing their shared transboundary water resource (Qureshi 2017).

The need for cooperation

Freshwater bodies that connect two or more countries, either above or below surface, cover about 45 percent of the world´s land mass. There are 276 international river basins, of which 60 percent do not have any framework in place to manage these shared resources cooperatively. This could be a cause for concern, as water resource issues have heightened tensions throughout history. Collectively, there have been 37 incidents of conflict over water since 1948.

Besides being a catalyst for peace and security, water cooperation is important for development. About 70 percent of the world's freshwater that is withdrawn goes to agriculture. Of the water withdrawn for industrial activity, about 80 percent is for energy generation. As countries grow economically, this nexus between water, food, and energy places more stress on water resources. World population growth is expected to occur most heavily in areas that rely largely on other regions for food production. The result is inter-regional dependency in which countries to have share either virtual or real water.

While economic and population growth demand more water, climate change has placed enormous strain on supplies of freshwater in many parts of the world. An interesting example is the glaciers in the Himalayas feed rivers that provide drinking water to over half of the world's population. Warming has accelerated glacial melt, and projections for glacial decline expect these rivers to become more seasonal. Increased flooding followed by a seasonal lack of freshwater will implicate countries across borders and make cooperation vital to maintain water resource levels. In other places around the world, variability in the frequency of rainfall and changes in mean temperatures will pose challenge.

Despite the potential for conflict, common needs for shared waters allow countries to come together in search of shared benefits from managing resources. More than 200 water treaties have been negotiated over the last 50 years. As more pressure builds on the world's water resources, previous experience cooperating towards water sustainability serves as useful guidance for future agreements (Adeel, 2015).

Moving towards cooperative water management

Although there are many links between water and conflict, and competing interests are inherent to water management, most disputes are resolved peacefully and cooperatively, even if the negotiation process is lengthy.

Cooperative water management mechanisms—probably the most advanced approach—can anticipate conflict and solve smouldering disputes, provided that all stakeholders are included in the decision-making process and given the means (information, trained staff, and financial support) to act as equal partners. Cooperative management mechanisms can reduce conflict potential by:

- Providing a forum for joint negotiations, thus ensuring that all existing and potentially conflicting interests are taken into account during decision-making;
- Considering different perspectives and interests to reveal new management options and offer win-win solutions;
- Building trust and confidence through collaboration and joint fact-finding; and
- Making decisions that are much more likely to be accepted by all stakeholders, even if consensus cannot be reached (Kramer 2004).

At international level, river basin commissions with representatives from all riparian states have been successfully involved in joint riparian water resources management. Especially in transboundary basins, achieving cooperation has been a drawn-out and costly process. Recognizing this, the World Bank agreed to facilitate the Nile Basin Initiative negotiation process for 20 years.

Capacity building—to generate and analyze data, develop sustainable water management plans, use conflict resolution techniques, or encourage stakeholder participation—should target water management institutions, local non-governmental organizations, water users' associations, or religious groups. At international level, strengthening less powerful riparian's negotiating skills can help prevent conflict. At local level, strengthening the capacity of excluded, marginalized, or weaker groups to articulate and negotiate their interests helps involve them in cooperative water management. The every river has its people project in the Okavango River basin, for instance, aims to increase participation by communities and other local stakeholders in decision-making and basin management through educational and training activities.

Cooperative water management is a challenging issue that requires time and commitment. Extensive stakeholder participation might not always be feasible; in some cases, it may not even be advisable. On any scale of water management, if the level of dispute is too high and the disparities are too great, conflicting parties are not likely to reach consensus and might even refuse to participate in cooperative management activities. In such cases, confidence and consensus-building measures, such as joint training or joint fact-finding, will support cooperative decision-making.

Water management is, by definition, conflict management. For all the twenty-first century wizardry dynamic modelling, remote sensing, geographic information systems, desalination, biotechnology, or demand management and the new-found concern with globalization and privatization, the crux of water disputes is still about little more than opening a diversion gate or garbage floating downstream. Yet anyone attempting to manage water-related conflicts must keep in mind that rather than being simply another environmental input, water is regularly treated as a security issue, a gift of nature, or a focal point for local society. Disputes, therefore, are more than "simply" fights over a quantity of a resource; they are arguments over conflicting attitudes, meanings, and contexts.

Obviously, there are no guarantees that the future will look like the past; the worlds of water and conflict are undergoing slow but steady changes. An unprecedented number of people lack access to a safe, stable supply of water. As exploitation of the world's water supplies increases, quality is becoming a more serious problem than quantity, and water use is shifting to less traditional sources like deep fossil aquifers, wastewater reclamation, and interbasin transfers. Conflict, too, is becoming less traditional, driven increasingly by internal or local pressures or, more subtly, by poverty and instability. These changes suggest that tomorrow's water disputes may look very different from todays.

On the other hand, water is a productive pathway for confidence building, cooperation, and arguably conflict prevention, even in particularly contentious basins. In some cases, water offers one of the few paths for dialogue to navigate an otherwise heated bilateral conflict. In politically unsettled regions, water is often essential to regional development negotiations that serve as de facto conflict-prevention strategies. Environmental cooperation especially cooperation in water resources management has been identified as a potential catalyst for peacemaking (Wolf, 2005).

International legal framework for water cooperation

International law plays an important role as a legal framework for the settlement of transboundary water disputes. Accordingly, international agreements often form part of cooperative endeavours, but they do not constitute a prerequisite for them.

In 1971, the International Law Commission (ILC) began drafting a convention on the principles of transboundary water cooperation on the basis of the 1966 Helsinki Rules. Then in 1997, the Convention on the Law of the Non-navigational Uses of International Watercourses was adopted by the UN General Assembly. To this day, the convention has however not been ratified by sufficient states to enter into force. The convention has thus had no legally binding effects so far. But it contains recognized principles with a broad ambit. Germany supports this initiative in as much as it has ratified it and expects that it will enter into force soon.

Moreover, there are numerous conventions and international declarations that deal with transboundary water cooperation. In the last 50 years, over 200 agreements have been signed on the shared use of international surface waters. Together with rulings by the International Court of Justice, they form a basis for the definition of obligations and principles that are considered, and applied, as international customary law.

The principle of equitable and reasonable utilization and participation (article 5 of the UN convention) means that all riparian states have a right to enjoy the benefits of the use of international water resources. When defining agreements on resource use amongst the riparian states, several factors always have to be taken into consideration and weighed up against each other, for example, needs, present use and envisaged purpose (Transboundary, 2006).

The obligation not to cause significant harm (article 7 of the UN convention) derives from the principle of restricted territorial sovereignty and stipulates that a state may only use an international watercourse in a way that causes no significant harm to another riparian state. The principle can pertain to water quantity and quality alike. If harm is caused (which must, however, be significant), the question of compensation shall be discussed.

The principle of cooperation (articles 8, 9, and 11 of the UN convention) relates to the procedural dealings amongst the riparian states and essentially comprises two distinct obligations. On the one hand, it obliges the parties to exchange data on the condition of the water resource regularly, on the other; parties are obliged to provide prior notification of planned activities affecting the condition of the water resource.

Finally, the obligation to seek peaceful settlement of disputes is stipulated in the charter of the United Nations (article 33) and underlies article 33 of the UN convention.

41

This article obliges disputing states to seek a solution by negotiation, enquiry, mediation, conciliation, arbitration, judicial settlement, or other peaceful means of their own choice.

This international legal framework contains general principles that can serve as a guideline for specific cooperative endeavours in the area of transboundary water cooperation, but they need to be applied in the form of substantive provisions in every particular case. This holds, for example, for the principles of doing no harm and of equitable and reasonable utilization of international inland waters. It is largely incumbent on the parties involved to decide whether harm has been caused and whether the principle of equitable and reasonable utilization has been met in a given instance. Thus, the binding character of these principles is confined to committing the parties to seek to reach agreement on the interpretation they regard as binding.

Existing international conventions and agreements include only few aspects on transboundary groundwater, which is why the UN International Law Commission (ILC) is currently drawing up a convention on the use of transboundary groundwater resources.

In 2004, the International Law Association formulated the Berlin Rules, which complement the UN convention on the law of the Non-navigational Uses of International Watercourses and develop its ideas further (Transboundary, 2006).

Active water cooperation

Active water cooperation means commitment of riparian countries to most of the following activities, or more, where such commitment is translated into action programmes implemented with agreed time frames or on an on-going basis

- Joint management of the water body with decision making authority on water allocation and resource management submitted to a river basin organization
- Joint investment programme and joint decision making on allocation of financial resources pertaining to projects to accrue benefits from the river or lake
- Joint management of flood control
- Coordination of water quality and reduction of pollutants to harmonise quality between countries
- Joint programme of action for environmental protection of water body with deadlines which are implemented
- Consultation between riparian countries on construction of dams or reservoirs with data exchange accepted by all countries or joint construction and management of dams
- Joint management of water flows in all their aspects.

Active water cooperation does not mean mere signing of a treaty for allocation of water or for data exchange or for establishing a river basin organisation unless there is verifiable joint management of water resources as delineated above.

For instance, the following do not meet the criteria of active water cooperation

➢ Indus Water Commission between India, Pakistan, since it is only about allocation of rivers without any joint management elements

➢ Aral Sea Basin Commission (International Commission for Water Coordination of Central Asia) which is only a treaty to establish a river basin organisation but without any operational joint management or decision making with regards to environmental protection, dam, quality coordination or any other significant aspects

➢ Nile Basin Initiative (in parts) as it functions as per the above criteria between White Nile basin countries but not between Blue Nile basin countries.

War means military confrontation or armed hostilities of any kind or direct or indirect involvement in cross border terrorism or a risk of any such events that could result in significant loss of human life in the short or medium term, irrespective of temporary calm.

Reason means any reason whatsoever which may or may not be related to water and may include land, ideology, and rivalry for supremacy, among others.

Any two countries engaged in active water cooperation do not go to war for any reason whatsoever. Out of 148 countries sharing water resources, 37 do not engage in active water cooperation. Any two or more of these 37 countries face a risk of war in future.

Evolution of water cooperation

Cooperation on transboundary water resources has evolved ever since international water law took its strongest roots after World War II. Important negotiations in the 1950s and 1960s, such as agreements made on the Mekong, Indus, and Senegal rivers, helped gain experience and lessons were learned on how to make cooperation successful. While some of these were bilateral agreements, parties like the Tennessee Valley Authority, the World Bank, and United Nations were called upon to bring expertise and help in reaching a deal.

Since then, more international framework and knowledge sharing has taken place, and negotiations have moved more from being bilateral to multilateral. 1992 marked a crucial point in the increased raise of awareness for water cooperation in the world when the UNECE Water Convention was adopted. Five years later, the UN General Assembly adopted the Convention on the Law of the Non-Navigational Uses of International Watercourses. Both conventions complement each other as global frameworks based on principles of cooperation, no harm, and equitable usage of water resources. However, the UNECE Water Convention uses mandatory principles and supports them with its own institutional mechanism.

Institutionalization of river basin development has been seen throughout the evolution of cooperation on water, and several studies have been done about the formation of "water regimes." Alexander Wendt, who has written about social theory of international politics, wrote, "this process of institutionalization is one in which actors internalize new understandings of self and other and, furthermore, move towards increasingly shared commitments to the norms of the regime." Agreements in Africa often form such institutions to develop areas cooperatively, such as the 1999 Nile Basin Initiative and 2002 Senegal River Charter. In the latter, a 4-Year Water and Environmental Management Project was funded by GEF, which has played an important role in funding other projects within the framework of the Water Convention.

In February 2011, the push for water cooperation advocacy gained huge momentum. The UN General Assembly decided to proclaim 2013 as the International Year of Water Cooperation (IYWC) to promote action at all levels and achieve water related development goals through cooperation. Tajikistan, which has been a key initiator for action on water cooperation, held a Preparatory Conference in 2011 that developed recommendations for the Rio+20 Summit in June 2012, where a thematic session specifically for Water Cooperation was held. The 2012 International Conference on Transboundary River Basin Management in Thailand also showed the shift to action on knowledge as the event marked the first of a series of biennial conferences for the Mekong River Commission.

The 2013 IYWC's first event was the International Annual UN-Water Conference in Zaragoza. It built upon previous progress made in water cooperation with case studies, dialogue, and presentations around global experiences with water treaties or conventions. Tajikistan hosted the High Level International Conference on Water Cooperation in August 2013 (Dushanbe). This event in many ways was a tipping point for progress. Dialogue with the Open Working Group began and has continued since then, keeping water cooperation in mind for the post-2015 Sustainable Development Goals. Throughout the year, synergies with other initiatives helped give the UN a stronger voice for joint advocacy.

In 2014, despite the IYWC having passed, there were several events that kept water cooperation at the forefront of topics. As a way to build capacity on the subject, UNESCO reached an agreement with Sweden to open an International Centre for Water Cooperation. The centre will undertake independent research regarding transboundary water issues and provide advisory services (adeel, 2015).

Monitoring transboundary cooperation

Cooperation around transboundary water resources (or the lack there of) is the most widely and systematically reported modality of all types. There is a wealth of information establishing baselines for transboundary cooperation and a few of these use their respective baselines to assess progress. A number of monitoring and reporting initiatives on basin and regional scales and global assessment efforts help paint this rich landscape further.

The UN Watercourses Convention was ratified in 2014, paving the road to establishment of a secretariat and subsequent formulation of the various mechanisms needed for its implementation, which are yet to take place. It can be safely speculated that these mechanisms will include an assessment and monitoring scheme in due course.

On a global scale, systematic and comprehensive efforts include Systematic Index of International Water Resources Treaties, Declarations, Acts and Cases, by Basin (FAO 1978a, FAO 1978b); Atlas of International Freshwater Agreements (UNEP, FAO, and OSU, 2002), and various reports, articles, and compilations. In addition, there are programmers, initiatives and databases with global scope which focus on, or relate to, monitoring, analyzing, and reporting on the legal arrangements, including treaties, conventions, and laws. Some of these are UNESCO's PCCP Programmed, Oregon State University's International Freshwater Treaties Database and Transboundary Freshwater Disputes Database, International Centre for Water Cooperation in Stockholm, FAO's WaterLex, and UN-Water's related initiatives.

UNESCO's World Water Assessment Programme (WWAP), although not designed for transboundary waters, has provided data, indicators, examples, and assessments useful to understanding transboundary waters, when the Programme's mandate was global assessments between 2000 and 2013 (World Water Development Reports 1 through 4, 2003, 2006, 2009, 2012).

Monitoring and reporting initiatives at the regional level are diverse and uneven. On one end of the spectrum is Europe's systematized and coherent reporting effort (First and Second Assessments of Transboundary Rivers, Lakes and Groundwater's, UNECE 2007 and 2011) carried out within the implementation of the Convention on the Protection and Use of Transboundary Watercourses and International Lakes (UNECE, 1992), which has recently been opened to the non-UNECE states (February, 2013 www.unece.org/env/water).

Other broad programs include an ongoing, multi-agency effort, Transboundary Waters Assessment Programme (TWAP), implemented under Global Environment Facility (GEF) International Waters Programme (www.geftwap.org). This indicator-based program aims to provide a baseline assessment to identify and evaluate changes in transboundary systems caused by human activities and natural processes, and the consequences that these have on dependent human populations. The data and indicators generated through this transboundary assessment are organized and presented in a common data portal for policy-makers, donors, and other users for such purposes as exploring the status of, and monitoring the trends in transboundary water systems, in response to national, regional and international management efforts, and for setting funding priorities Monitoring and reporting for transboundary waters in regions other than Europe is neither systematic nor periodic. With the exception of the basins where an entity has been established, such as a river basin organization or secretariat to a river treaty, varying levels of reporting abound on the cooperative programs and projects while regional-level assessments and reporting are intermittent and are typically driven or funded by bilateral assistance and development partners (World Bank, 2014).

Lastly, it must be stated that defining transboundary cooperation is no easy task. Much research and a great variety of indicators emanating from the research are available for the interested reader, painting a very complex and broad picture. There is also discussion if all forms of cooperation are good and any conflict is bad (e.g. Zeitoun and Mirumachi, 2008) with examples indicating the opposite can be true, especially when a conflicting interaction leads to or catalyzes the initiation of meaningful cooperative process.

Water and institutions

The international community has long grappled with effective institutional arrangements for managing shared water resources. From the international to the local, grappling with the institutional implications of shared waters has taken many forms, from international declarations to guiding principles to treaties and local management.

Institutional Development : Contributions from the International Community

Acknowledging the benefits of cooperative water

management, the international community has long advocated institutional development in the world's international waterways and has focused considerable attention in the twentieth century on developing and refining principles of shared management. In 1911, the Institute of International Law published the Madrid Declaration on the International Regulation regarding the Use of International Watercourses for Purposes other than Navigation. The Madrid Declaration outlined certain basic principles of shared water management, recommending that co riparian states establish permanent joint commissions and discouraging unilateral basin alterations and harmful modifications of international rivers. Expanding on these guidelines, the International Law Association developed the Helsinki Rules of 1966 on the Uses of Waters of International Rivers. Since then, international freshwater law has matured through the work of these two organizations as well as the United Nations and other governmental and non-governmental bodies.

The past decade, however, has witnessed a perhaps unprecedented number of declarations as well as organizational and legal developments to further international community's objective of promoting coopera-tive river basin management. The decade began with the International Conference on Water and the Environment in the lead-up to the 1992 UN Conference on Environment and Development (UNCED) in Rio. Subsequently, actions taken by the international community have included the pronouncement of non binding conventions and declarations, the creation of global water institutions, and the codification of international water principles. Although clearly more work is required, these initiatives have not only raised awareness of the myriad issues related to international water resource management, but also have led to the creation of frameworks in which the issues can be addressed.

Conventions, declarations, and organizational Developments

The 1992 UNCED served as a forum for world policy makers to discuss problems of the environment and development. As such, management of the world's water resources was only one of several topics addressed. Water was, however, the primary focus of the International Conference on Water and the Environment (ICWE), a preparatory conference held in advance of the Rio Earth Summit. The ICWE participants, representing governmental and non-governmental organizations, developed a set of policy recommendations outlined in the Conference's Dublin Statement on Water and Sustainable Development, which the drafters entrusted to the world leaders gathering in Rio for translation into a plan of action. Although covering a range of water resource management issues, the Dublin Statement specifically highlights the growing importance of international transboundary water management and encourages greater attention to the creation and implementation of integrated water management institutions endorsed by all affected basin states. Moreover, the drafters outlined certain essential functions of international water institutions including "reconciling and harmonizing the interests of riparian countries, monitoring water quantity and quality, development of concerted action programmes, exchange of information, and enforcing agreements" (international conference 1992).

One result of the Rio Conference has been an expansion of international freshwater resource institutions and programs. The World Water Council, a self described "think tank" for world water resource issues, for example, was created in 1996 in response to recommendations from the Rio Conference. Since its inception, the World Water Council has hosted three World Water Forums—gatherings of government, nongovernment, and private agency representatives to discuss and collectively determine a vision for the management of water resources over the next-quarter century. These forums have led to the creation of the World Water Vision, a forward-looking declaration of philosophical and institutional water management needs, as well as the creation of coordinating and implementing agencies such as the World Commission on Water for the 21st Century and the Global Water Partnership. The Second World Water Forum also served as the venue for a ministerial conference in which the leaders of participating countries signed a declaration concerning water security in the twenty-first century. The recent World Summit on Sustainable Development (WWSD) has helped to sustain the momentum of these recent global water initiatives. In the Johannesburg Declaration on Sustainable Development, delegates at the WWSD reaffirmed a commitment to the principles contained in Agenda 21 and called upon the United Nations to review, evaluate, and promote further implementation of this global action plan (United Nation 2002).

Institutional lessons for the international community

A review of international water relations and institutional development over the past 50 years provides important insights into water conflict and the role of institutions. The historical record of water conflict and cooperation suggests that international watercourses can cause tensions between co riparian states, but acute violence is the exception rather than the rule. A much more likely scenario is that a gradual decline in water quantity or quality, or both, affects the internal stability of a nation or region, which may in turn impact the international arena. Early coordination among riparian states, however, can serve to ameliorate these sources of friction. Thus, in combination with its existing efforts, the international community might consider focusing more attention on the specific institutional needs of individual basin communities by assisting riparian states in the development of cooperative management networks that take into account the following key factors:

1. Adaptable management structure. Effective institutional management structures incorporate a certain level of flexibility, allowing for public input, changing basin priorities, and adding new information and monitoring technologies. The adaptability of management structures must also extend to nonsignatory riparians by incorporating provisions addressing their needs, rights, and potential accession.

2. Clear and flexible criteria for water allocations and water quality management. Allocations, which are at the heart of most water disputes, are a function of water quantity and quality, as well as political fiat. Thus, effective institutions must identify clear allocation schedules and water quality standards that simultaneously provide for extreme hydrological events; new understanding of basin dynamics, including groundwater reserves; and changing societal values. Additionally, riparian states may consider prioritizing uses throughout the basin. Establishing catchment-wide water precedents may not only help to avert inter riparian conflicts over water use, but also protects the environmental health of the basin as a whole.

3. Concrete mechanisms to enforce treaty provisions. Once a treaty is signed, successful implementation is dependent not only on the actual terms of the agreement but also on an ability of the parties to enforce those terms. Appointing oversight bodies with decision making and enforcement authority is one important step toward maintaining cooperative management institutions.

4. Detailed conflict resolution mechanisms. Many basins continue to experience dispute even after a treaty is negotiated and signed. Thus, incorporating clear mechanisms for resolving conflicts is a pre requisite for effective, long-term basin management (Wolf 2007).

Conclusion

Transboundary water governance presents significant challenges and opportunities for foreign policy makers to prevent conflict and harness opportunities for greater regional cooperation. Both will become even more important as water quality deteriorates and demographic and socio-economic development increases the demand for freshwater resources. This trend is further aggravated by climate change contributing to supply shortfalls, salinisation, saltwater intrusion, floods, and extreme weather-related disasters. Environmental changes are likely to sharpen existing and trigger new social and political conflicts over water, in particular in regions that lack robust institutions for cooperation. As this report shows, various conflicts in the Sahel region are related to conflict over water and interstate tensions over water loom in the Nile basin, the Middle East, and South and Central Asia. Environmental change may even put hitherto successful institutions such as the Indus Waters Treaty at risk because they do not provide the necessary instruments for adapting to growing scarcity.

Yet environmental changes may also nudge governments and other stakeholders towards closer cooperation. They will make better, collective management of transboundary waters more urgent to safeguard sufficient availability of water, but also to ensure that the measures undertaken by governments in the interest of water security do not undermine it elsewhere. The role of dams is particularly crucial in this respect. Dams are important for clean energy, irrigation and flood control, and they have served as focal points for sharing benefits, from South America via West Africa to South Asia. Yet when undertaken unilaterally and/or without regard to their environmental consequences for fishing, agriculture, sediment transport, and water availability downstream, they simultaneously constitute the most dangerous flashpoints of conflict over water. The benefits of collaborative management of transboundary waters therefore cannot only be counted in the direct economic gains, but also in the benefits of conflicts avoided.

Most often, international attention and resultant financing, is focused on a basin only after a crisis or flashpoint. Such has been the case on the Indus, Jordan, Nile and Tigris Euphrates basins. It is worth noting that in the exceptions to this pattern, the Mekong and La Plata commissions provide for example, an institutional framework for joint management and dispute resolution was established well in advance of any likely conflict. It is also worth noting that the Mekong committee's impressive record of continuing its work throughout intense political disputes between the riparian countries, as well as the fact that data conflicts, common and contentious in all of the other basins presented, have not been a factor in the Mekong. In fact, the experience of the commission such as those of the Amazon, La Plata or Mekong may suggest that when international institutions are established well in advance of water-stress they help preclude such dangerous flashpoints. As noted earlier, other basins have equally resilient institutions, which have survived even when relations on other issues were strained.

Early intervention is also beneficial to the process of conflict resolution, helping to shift the mode of dispute from costly, impasse oriented dynamics to less costly, problem solving dynamics. In the heat of some flashpoints, such as the Nile, the Indus and the Jordan, as armed conflict seemed imminent, tremendous energy was spent just getting the parties to talk to each other. Hostilities were so pointed that negotiations inevitably began confrontationally, usually resulting in a distributive approach being the only one viable.

In contrast, discussions in the Mekong committee, the multilateral working group in the Middle East and on the

Danube, have all moved beyond the causes of immediate disputes on to actual, practical projects which may be implemented in an integrative framework. Of course, to be able to entice early cooperation, the incentives have to be made sufficiently clear to the riparian's. In all of the cases mentioned above, not only was there strong third party involvement in encouraging the parties to come together, extensive funding was made available on the part of the international community to help finance projects which would come from the process.

The purpose of this document is to inform and guide practitioners of water development, human rights and peace building to more effectively promote water as a force for unity and life, rather than division and violence. Part I provided data about water security and inequities on a global scale; described concrete conflicts and their causes; and presented principles, paradigms and protocols for water cooperation. Part II framed water development within a peace building paradigm, presented tools and techniques, and suggested appropriate actions in several typical conflict scenarios. The Appendices at the end of this report summarize various approaches to risk assessment, point to valuable online resources, and provide the key references used in the preparation of this text. To some, the document may seem overly abstract. To others, it is too full of practical details. To still others, the balance may seem just about right. Our hope, in any case, is that this document opens a broad window on the often turbulent world of water and provides a focused framework for practitioners seeking to prevent and mitigate violent confrontations around water - the most vital of natural resources.

This report is a work in progress and, hopefully, one that will stimulate further inquiry. It may serve as an invitation to plunge more deeply into specific core issues, such as transboundary conflicts or human rights, or a call to follow a number of current issues that were not fully explored, such as those around gender and water. It may also lend itself as a basis for organizational training courses. The possibilities are many. Overall, CRS believes this effort to be a unique contribution to the expanding literature focused on water and conflict. The document also complements recent works, such as Conflict Resolution and Negotiation Skills for Integrated Water Resources Management. A next step within CRS will be to test the utility of this work in the field and to determine if it can provide effective guidance for practitioners.

Water already contributes to conflicts among nations, and future conflicts over water are increasingly likely. Nations fight over access to water resources in some regions of the world and use water and water supply system as instruments of war, while growing populations and developments are increasing the competition for limited water supplies, and many countries depend on source of supply that are under the control of other nations.

Human's needs for water are growing. Many countries of the Middle East and elsewhere already use water at a rate faster than natural processes can replenish it, leading to falling ground water levels, reliance on expensive desalination project, and imports of water across borders. Oddball scheme that would have been laughed at a few decades ago are now being implemented or seriously considered, including the importation of water in tankers, pipeline thousands of kilometers long, or the diversion of icebergs from the Polar Regions.

Global climatic changes will increase the demand for water for human and industrial uses, change irrigation requirements and alter in unpredictable ways the availability and quality of fresh water resources. Countries or regions that use a significant fraction or their total available supply are vulnerable to slight changes in flow or water quality. Countries or regions with considerable dependence on irrigation water or hydroelectricity are vulnerable to changes in flow and the vagaries of a changing climate.

The Middle East and the Persian Gulf exhibit much vulnerabilities to water related conflict, as do certain countries of Africa, Europe and Southern and central Asia. Given the high level of political conflict already evident in some of these areas and the inability of nations in these regions to reach agreement on water sharing, future water related dispute appear inevitable. Conflict over the Nile, the Jordan, the Euphrates, the river of central Asia and the Ganges/Brahmaputra river system appear increasingly likely because of growing competition for limited water resources or because of dispute over the ownerships and the right to use the resource. Dispute may also arise because of the contamination of shared water by upstream parties on the Colorado, the Rhine, and the Mekong; because of the compilations of managing multiple interest in a river, such as with the Danube, the Mekong, the Niger, and the Zambezi; or because of the difficulty of rationally sharing hydroelectric generation on international river such as the Zambezi and the Parana.

Water related disputes are more likely to lead to political confrontations and negotiations than to violent conflict. But recent disturbing examples of water related conflicts, the apparent willingness to use water supply systems as targets and tool of water and growing disparities among nations between water availability and demand make it urgent that we work to reduce the probability and consequences of water related conflict. Hydrologist and water resources specialist must begin to collect and more widely disseminate data on the supply and use of shared water resources, and on the ways of reducing inefficient uses of water. International legal experts must better understand the link among natural resources, needs, national sovereignty, and water rights. And academic and military scholars need to better understand the threats of conflict arising from a wide range of resource and environmental problems and to hone the tools for preventing those conflicts.

Water scarcity is becoming a more prevalent phenomenon everyday for an increasing number of people throughout the world. With mounting population growth rates, climate change, rising demand for freshwater and inefficient water management policies, the pressing problem of water scarcity will only become more urgent in the future. Mismanagement of transboundary water resources is one of the many causes of water shortage in countries around the world and one of the gravest threats to security, development, productivity and human livelihoods today. The promotion of cooperation for transboundary water resource management is essential going forward in order to achieve poverty reduction, economic development and reduce the chaos and devastation and conflict that can result from increased competition for scarce resources. By focusing on the shared benefits of cooperation regarding the utilization of transboundary water resources, fostering more open discussion and negotiation and placing transboundary water resource management high on the international agenda, the global community has the ability to combat water scarcity and its potentially catastrophic effects as well as promoting general cooperation among competing states. Ultimately, there is no other option; water scarcity is a reality that demands cooperative solution that will be peaceful and lasting.

By establishing a program of preventive diplomacy focused on water, the UN could coordinate its extensive but diffuse expertise. Such a program would assess basins at risk and bolster the early-warning process for regions with conflict potential. The program would also enhance institutional capacity between nations (by reconciling national legal frameworks over water issues, for example) and craft a "one-stop shop" with tools to develop programs that encourage transboundary cooperation. Through a Global Fund for Water—with special emphasis on understanding the Southern perspective and integrating conflict prevention units—the UN could improve water management and facilitation skills, reduce duplicate efforts, and use water to build confidence and prevent conflict.

Reference:
- Adeel Zafar, 2015 "Water Cooperation" United Nations University.
- Arase, D. (2010). Non-Traditional Security in China-ASEAN Cooperation. Asian Survey, 50(4), 808-833.
- Biswas A K, Hashimoto T, edsv.1996. Asian International Waters: From Ganges-Brahmaputra to Mekong. Oxford: Oxford Univ. Press.
- Climate diplomacy, report 2014, the rise of hydro-diplomacy, strengthening foreign policy for transboundary waters.
- Earle, anton; anders, Jägerskog and JoakimÖjendal (eds.) 2010, transboundary water management: principles and practice. london: earthscan, 157-171.
- Elliott, L. (2003). ASEAN and environmental cooperation: norms, interests and identity. The Pacific Review, 16(1), 29-52, 47.
- European union 2015, Conflict and cooperation over water The role of the EU in ensuring the realisation of human rights.
- Falkenmark, Malin and Anders Jägerskog 2010: sustainability of transnational water agreements in the face of socio-economic and environmental change.
- Fröhlich, C. (2012), Water: Reason for Conflict or Catalyst for Peace? The Case of the Middle East, L'Europe en formation n° 365, 139-161.

- Fernquest, J. (2012, 25.10.12). Rice Exports: Fall from1st to 3rd. Bangkok post Retrieved from http://www.bangkokpost.com/learning/learningfrom-news/318215/rice-exports-falls-from-1st-to-3rd, retrieved 05.01.13.
- Gehrig Jason with Mark M. Rogers Edited by Dennis Warner, Chris Sere met, and Tom Bamat).
- Gleick Peter H.1998. World's Water: The Biennial Report on Fresh Water Resources. Washington D.C.: Covels, California, Island Press.
- Gleick, P. H. (1993). Water and Conflict: Fresh Water Resources and International Security. International Security, 18(1), 79-112.
- Goh, E. (2006). China in the Mekong River Basin: The Regional Security Implications of Resource Development on the Lancang Jiang. In Caballero-Anthony, R. Emmers& A. Acharya (Eds.), Non-Traditonal Security in Asia. Hamshire and Burlington: Ashgate.
- Gorbachev M. 1987. "Reality and guarantees for a secure world", Moscow News, No.39, p. 3287.
- Graeger, N. (1996). Environmental Security? Journal of Peace Research, 33(1), 109-116.
- Haefner Andrea, 2013, Non-Traditional Security: The Case of Environmental Challenges in the Mekong Subregion.
- Haque M.Shamsul. 2002. "Non-Traditional Security and the Environment in North east Asia", Work in Progress, Vol.16, No.3, summer. P.24.
- Houdret, A. (2008), Scarce Water, Plenty of Conflicts?, Local Water Conflicts and the Role of Development Cooperation, Policy Brief, Duisburg, Institute for Development and Peace.
- International Conference, Water Environment, 1992. Development issues for the 21st century. The Dublin Statement and Rep.Conf.,Dublin, Irel.,26–31Jan. Geneva: World Meteorol. Organ.

- Joffe J. 1992. "Entangled forever", in C. W. Kegley Jr. and E.R. Wittkoff, eds., The Future of American Foreign Policy. New York: St. Martin's Press, P.35.
- Kaushik k. Aditya, "Regulating Water Security in Border Regions: The Case of India and Pakistan" August 1st, 2017.
- Kibaroglu A. 2002. Building a Regime for the Waters of the Euphrates-Tigris River Basin. Hague, Neth.: Kluwer Law Int.
- Kramer Annika, 2004, Water and Conflict, Washington, DC: Adelphi Research, Center for International Forestry Research, and Woodrow Wilson International Center for Scholars, 2004.
- Kramer, A.E. 2011. Warming Revives Dream of Sea Route in Russian Artic. New York Times.
- Kreamer K. David, (2012), The Past, Present, and Future of Water Conflict and International Security Universities Council on Water resources Journal of Contemporary Water research & education issue 149, pages 88-96.
- Libiszewski, S. (1999), International Conflicts over Freshwater Resources, in: Suliman, Mohamed (ed.), Ecology, Politics and Violent Conflict, 115-138.
- Lopez A.2004.Environmental conflict sand regional cooperation in the Lempa River basin: the role of Central America's Plan Trifinio. EDSP Work. Pap. 2. Environ. Dev. Sustain. Peace Initiat., Berlin.
- Lorenz, Frederick and Edward J. Erickson 2013: strategic water. iraq and security planning in the euphrates- percent tigris basin water. Virginia: Marine Corps University press.
- Lowi, M. R. (1999). Water and Conflict in the Middle East and South Asia: Are Environmental Issues and Security Issues Linked? Journal of Environment and Development, 8(4), 376-396.

- Manno, J. (2010), Water Issues, International Encyclopedia of Peace, Oxford University Press, Oxford.
- Mehta, L.; Veldwisch, G. J. and Franco, J. (2012), Introduction to the Special Issue: Water grabbing? Focus on the (re)appropriation of finite waterresources, Water Alternatives Vol. 5(2), 193-207.
- Molle, F. and Berkoff, J. (2006), Cities versus Agriculture: Revisiting Intersectoral Water Transfers, Potential Gains and Conflicts, International Water Management Institute, Colombo.
- Muckleston K. 2003. International Management in the Columbia River System. Paris: UNESCO IHP Tech. Doc. Hydrol., PCCP Ser. 12.
- Nakayama M, ed. 2003. International Waters in Southern Africa. Tokyo: UN Univ. Press.
- Ohlsson, Leif. (2000). Livelihood conflicts: Linking poverty and environment as causes of conflict. Stockholm: Swedish International Development Agency, Department of Natural Resources and the Environment.
- Pacific Institute (2015), Water Conflict Chronology, available at:http://www2.worldwater.org/chronology.html
- Phillips, D., Daoudy, M., McCaffrey, S., Ojendal, J.&Turton, A. (2006). Transboundary Water Co-operation as a Tool for Conflict Prevention and Broader Benefit Sharing. Global Development Studies No. 4. Ministry of Foreign Affairs Sweden.
- Qureshi *Dr. Waseem Ahmad, 2017, "The Indus Basin: Water Cooperation, International Law and the Indus Waters Treaty".
- Ravnborg, Helle Munk et al. (2012), Challenges of local water govemance: the extent, nature and intensity of local water-related conflict and cooperation, Water Policy, Vol. 14, 336-357.
- Rifkin J. 1991. Biospheric Politics: A New Consciousness for a New Century. New York: Crown. p.2.

- Sadoff CW, Gray D. 2002. beyond the river: the benefits of cooperation on international rivers. Water Policy 4(5):389–404.
- Sarvat N. Hanif, 2013 "Acess to water catalyst for cooperation, peace building".
- Schmeier, Susanne 2013: governing international watercourses. River basin organizations and the sustainable governance of internationally shared rivers and lakes. New York: Routledge.
- Schneider, K. (2011). Fierce competition over water threatens China's economic progress and global food, energy prices. Yale Global.
- Singh Richa.2008. "Trans-boundary Water Politics and Conflicts in South Asia: Towards 'Water for Peace" New Delhi-110016.
- Strategic Foresight Group, 2013, Water Cooperation for a Secure World Focus on the Middle East.
- Swain, Ashok 2013: sharing Indus River for development and peace. brussels: presentation at international council for human rights, 20 march 2013.
- Transboundary Water Cooperation, July 2006, A BMZ Position Paper.
- United Nations. 2002. Report of the World Summit on Sustainable Development.Doc.A/CONF.199/20,SalesNo.E.03.II.A.1. NewYork:UN.http://www.un.org/jsummit/html/document s/summit docs/131302 wssd report reissued.pdf.
- UNW-DPAC, 2013a. Water Cooperation in Action: approaches, tools and processes http://www.un.org/ waterforlifedecade/water_cooperation_2013/pdf/water_co operation_in_action_approaches_tools_processes.pdf
- U.S. Department of State. 1997. "Environmental Diplomacy: The Environment and U.S. Foreign Policy", U.S. Department of State, Washington, D.C.
- Veilleux, Jennifer C. (2013), Water: Cooperation or Conflict?, The Human Security Dimensions of Dam

Development: The Grand Ethiopian Renaissance Dam, Global Dialogue, Vol. 15(2).

- Waterbury J. 1979. Hydropolitics of the Nile Valley. New York: Syracuse Univ. Press.
- Waterbury J. 2002. The Nile Basin: National Determinants of Collective Action. New Haven/London: Yale Univ. Press.
- Wolf, Aaron T. (1999, June). Water and human security (AVISO 3). Victoria, Canada: The Global Environmental Change and Human Security Project.
- Wolf T Aaron; Yoffe, Shira B. and Giordano, M. (2003), International Waters: Indicators for Identifying Basins at Risk, Unesco,Paris.
- Wolf T. Aaron, 2003, "Transboundary Water Conflicts and Cooperation".
- Wolf T. Aaron, Kramer Annika, Alexander Carius, and Geoffrey D. Dabelko, Managing Water Conflict and Cooperation, The Worldwatch Institute, 2005.
- Wolf T. Aaron, 2007, "Shared Waters: Conflict and Cooperation" Annual Review of Environment and Resources Volume 32, 2007.

Chapter-II

Water Sharing between India and Pakistan: Indus Water Treaty

Indus River Basin

The Indus river basin is one of the largest basins in Asia covering an area of 1,165,000 km2 (Swain, 2004). The river flows through four countries in South Asia including, China in north- east, India in east, Afghanistan in north-west and Khyber Pakhtunkhwa and majority of plains of the Punjab and Sindh in Pakistan (Rehman et al., 2005). The Indus river basin comprise of Indus river, its two western tributaries the Kabul and Kurram rivers and five eastern tributaries the Jhelum, Ravi, Beas, Sutlej and Chenab rivers. Indus and Sutlej originate from Lake Manasarovar in Tibet. Chenab River originates from Himachal Pradesh in India and flows through Kashmir valley and into Pakistan. Ravi also originates from Himachal Pradesh but directly flows into Punjab and then Pakistan. Beas originates and flows entirely in India. Jhelum originates in the Kashmir valley of India and flows to Pakistan (Zhawari, 2004, 2009). Kabul River rises in Afghanistan and flows through the Peshawar valley to join the Indus at Attock. These five main left bank tributaries have an aggregate length of more than 2,800 miles and Kabul River and Kurram River together cover more than 700 miles (Allouche, 2005).

The basin is the home to three world's mightiest mountain ranges (Karakoram, Himalayan and Hindukush). The basin originates at 17,000 feet above sea level in Tibetan plateau. The river passes through Jammu and Kashmir, enters into north area of Pakistan and finally merge into Arabian Sea. Most of its flows around 69% originate from India, compared to 12% for Tibet and Afghanistan and 19% for Pakistan (Khosla, 1958). The drainage area which extends into India is 45,000 square miles and contribute to an average annual inflow (including all rivers) of 175 million acre feet (Qureshi et al., 2011). The snow melting in the Himalayan- Hindukush regions and precipitations in mountains are the major components of the annual flow of these rivers. Climate is not uniform over Indus basin region. It varies from arid to semi arid to temperate sub-humid in the plains of Sindh and Punjab provinces. Annual precipitations range maximum 2000 mm on mountain slopes and between 100 to 500 mm in the lowlands. Abundant flow is during the monsoon season (July- September), which contributes 51% of annual flow

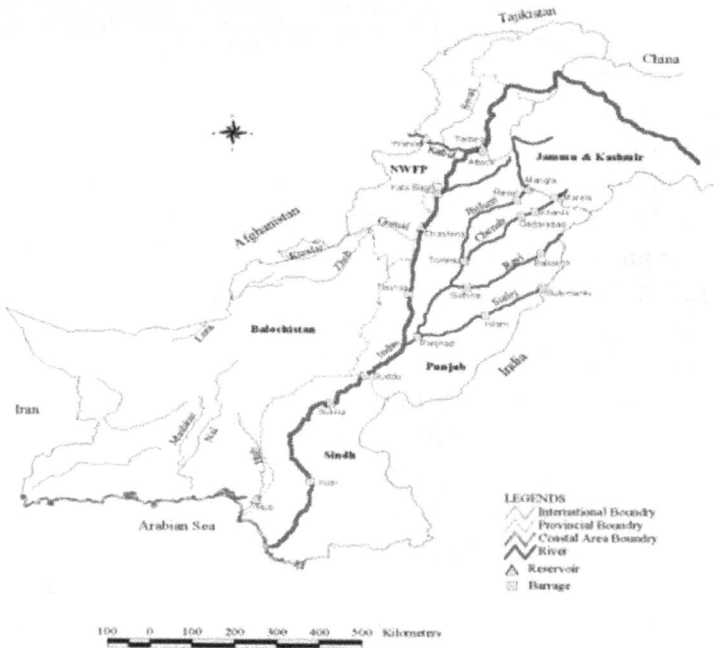

Indus Basin
Source: (Sridhar, S., http://www.bharat-rakshak.com/SRR/Volume13/sridhar.html)

Indus River system and its importance for India and Pakistan

Indus river basin drains the highland of four riparian countries, Pakistan, India, Afghanistan and China. The rough terrains surrounding the river in China and Afghanistan have so far minimized these states' ability to develop the river within their border but China and Afghanistan are asserting their rights to a reasonable and equitable share of the Indus tributaries flowing through their territory (Salman, 2008). Afghanistan has started to build a dam on Kabul River for hydropower generation but mainly India and Pakistan are dependent on the Indus river system. Out of about 193 million total populations, 72 percent of Pakistan and 23 percent of Indian live in Indus basin system (Laghari, et. al. 2011).

Table 1: Riparian States in the Indus River Basin

Basin name	Area in sq. km	Countries	Area of country in basin(sq. km)	Country percent area
Indus	1,138,800	Pakistan	597,700	52.48
		India	381,600	33.51
		China	76,200	6.69
		Afghanistan	72,100	6.33
		Chinese control, claimed by India	9,600	0.84
		Indian control, claimed by China	1,600	0.14
		Nepal	10	0.00

Source: (ASIA: International River Basin register (updated August 2002)

http://www.transboundarywaters.orst.edu/publications/regist er/tables/IRB_asia.html

The Indus River system is a major source of water for Pakistan and north-western part of India (Swain, 2009). For relatively arid north- western province of India, which has become the country breadbasket, the Indus River provides the economic foundation (Zahwari, 2009).

For Pakistan, Indus River is the main source for domestic, industrial and agricultural water. Agriculture is vital for Pakistan's welfare and its role is like a backbone in national economy. This sector employed 43% of Pakistan's labour force and contributed about 25% of Pakistan GDP. In spite of the above fact, Pakistan agriculture is mostly dependent on irrigation network because of little rainfall, low quality ground water etc. Of the total irrigated area of Indus River, 74 % is located in Pakistan (Laghari, et. al. 2011) that provides over 60% of the water utilized for irrigation purposes through the world's best and largest irrigational network (Miner et al., 2009). The irrigational network comprises of 3 reservoirs (Tarbela, Chashma on Indus River and Mangla on Jhelum River), 19 large river barrage and 45 independent irrigational canal commands, some 1.6 million km water courses and 144 large dams (Kamal, 2008). The irrigational network almost spread out more than one third part of country. About 78% of Pakistan's cultivated area is under irrigation and it ranks second in the world after Egypt (Ahmed et al., 2007).

Background

The canals and barrages built under the British rule to serve Indo-Pak continent were under partition in 1947. As a result of partition, these canal networks are divided into East Punjab that is in India and West Punjab in Pakistan. For India, the real problem arose when out of 26 million acres of land annually irrigated by Indus and its tributaries, 21 million acres became part of Pakistan (Allouche, 2005). But, the headworks of the entire network remained in India.

During the division of Punjab into East and West regions, Punjab partition committee was established to settle down the dispute related to division of assets between East and West Punjab provinces. In 1947 both east and west Punjab agreed that water shall be divided equally.

Pakistan and India disputes over Indus water erupted soon after eight months of independence, when India cut off the water coming across the border into Pakistan in 1948. East Punjab cut off the supplies of every single canal that crossed the border and declared its decision not to restore the flow of these canals, unless west Punjab recognized that it had no rights to the water and resumed the flows only after Pakistan made a payment to India. This situation was extremely stressful for west Punjab farmers dependent upon them (Uprety et al., 2010).

In May1948, Shimla agreement was signed but, Pakistan rejected it in early 1950s arguing that it has been forced upon them. From the early 1950s the situation had reached a deadlock and there was no communication over water between both countries for a long period of time (Allouche, 2005).

Composition of the Indus water treaty

The Indus Water Treaty consists of three parts; the preamble, twelve articles and annexure A to H. The principal subjects covered in the treaty's annexure are: the exchange of notes between the governments of India and Pakistan, India's agricultural use of certain tributaries of the Ravi, India's agricultural use of the upper reaches of the western rivers, Indian generation of hydroelectric power and the storage of water from the western rivers, a procedure to solve disputes and differences through a commission, a neutral court of arbitration, and allocation to Pakistan of some water from eastern rivers during the period of transition.

Table 2: Articles and 8 appendices of Indus Water Treaty, which are titled as:

Contents of the Treaty	
Article I	Definitions
Article II	Provisions regarding Eastern Rivers
Article III	Provisions regarding Western Rivers
Article IV	Provisions regarding Easter Rivers and Western Rivers
Article V	Financial Provisions
Article VI	Exchange of Data
Article VII	Future Cooperation
Article VIII	Permanent Indus Commission
Article IX	Settlement of Differences and Disputes
Article X	Emergency Provisions
Article XI	General Provisions
Article XII	Final Provisions
Annexure A	Exchange of Notes between Government of India and Government of Pakistan
Annexure B	Agricultural Use by Pakistan from certain tributaries of the Ravi
Annexure C	Agricultural Use by India from the Western Rivers
Annexure D	Generation of Hydroelectric Power by India on the Western Rivers
Annexure E	Storage of Waters by India on Western Rivers
Annexure F	Neutral Expert
Annexure G	Court of Arbitration
Annexure H	Transitional Arrangements

Principles of water sharing

Before the IWT, Pakistan emphasized historical uses while India as an upper riparian claimed absolute rights on the Indus Basin system. The treaty tried to find a solution that was not driven by legal principles, but instead by principles of water engineering and economics. There were conflicting principles put on the table, India invoking the principle of equitable utilization, the favourite of International Law Association, while Pakistan stressing "no appreciable harm" the favourite of International Law Commission. The Treaty instead of dividing the water of rivers, divided the six rivers comprising the Indus Water system between India and Pakistan, which gave them independent control and regulation of supplies within their own territories. However each country was allowed certain uses in the rivers allocated to other, subject to certain qualifications contained in separate annexure in Treaty. Under the Treaty:

❖ All the waters of the Eastern Rivers shall be available for the unrestricted use of India (Article 2). Pakistan was permitted by way of exception to take water for domestic use, non-consumptive use and certain limited agricultural use.

❖ Pakistan shall receive "unrestricted use of all water of Western Rivers" which India is under obligation to flow,(Article 3(1)) and shall not permit any interference with these water except for the domestic, non-consumptive, agriculture, generation of hydroelectric power and storage works(Akhtar,2010).

Salient features of Indus Water Treaty

Distribution of the Eastern and the Western Rivers

i. All the waters of the eastern rivers (Ravi, Sutlej and Beas) shall be available for unrestricted use of India. Pakistan shall be under an obligation to let flow and shall not permit any interference with water of the Sutlej Main and the Ravi Main in the reaches where these rivers flow in Pakistan and have not yet finally crossed into Pakistan. Pakistan however can only use it for non-consumptive and domestic purposes.

ii. All the waters, while flowing in Pakistan, of any tributary which in its natural course joins the Sutlej main or the Ravi Main after these rivers have finally crossed into Pakistan shall be available for the unrestricted use of Pakistan.

iii. Pakistan shall receive unrestricted use of all the waters of the western rivers (Indus, Jhelum and Chenab). India shall be under an obligation to let flow all the waters of the Western rivers, and shall not permit any interference with these waters.

General provisions

i. The use of the natural channels of the rivers for the discharge of flood or other excess waters shall be free and not subject to limitation by neither party, nor any party shall have claim against the other in respect of any damage caused by such use.

ii. Each party declared its intention to prevent, as far as practical, undue pollution of the waters and agreed to ensure that, before any sewage or industrial waste is allowed to flow into the rivers, it would be treated, where necessary, in such manners as not to materially affect those uses.

iii. India was given entitlement not only to continue irrigate areas of 0.26 million ha from western rivers which were so irrigated as on the effective date, but was also entitled to irrigate another area of 0.28 million ha from the western rivers thereby making total provision of 0.54 million ha (68% of which was from the River Jhelum and 23% from the Chenab).

iv. The agreement precluded building of storages by India on the rivers allocated to Pakistan. However, if India wants to generate hydroelectric power it can only build run-of-the-river hydroelectric projects (unlike a dam or a reservoir), which do not create storages. In Article III of the Treaty allows and Annexure D and E explain that how India can use the waters of western rivers for hydroelectric projects.

v. Pakistan agreed to make arrangements through replacement works for transfer of water from western rivers to eastern rivers for irrigation of command areas, headwaters of which were allocated to India (Manzoor 2015).

Indus Water Treaty (IWT)

The President of International Bank of Reconstruction and Development, Mr. Eugene Black offered his good office to settle the water dispute. After close to eight years of negotiation the IWT came into existence. The IWT was concluded by India and Pakistan with the World Bank's mediation on 19th of September 1960 (Swain, 2009). IWT based on the allocation of Indus and its tributaries. According to IWT the three Eastern Rivers (Ravi, Beas and Sutlej) allocated to India and three Western Rivers (Indus, Jhelum and Chenab) allocated to Pakistan. India has unrestricted use of the Eastern Rivers and Pakistan has a right for the exclusive use of Western Rivers. India can use the water of Western Rivers for hydropower generations, to meet the domestic, Industrial and irrigation requirements of Jammu-Kashmir and also develop these tributaries for flood protection, floating of timbers and fishing (Zahawari, 2009). It clearly mentioned in IWT that, Pakistan has to construct infrastructure to meet the Eastern Rivers needs from the Western Rivers and India has to pay fixed amount of money to Pakistan to build infrastructures. Both parties have to regularly exchange flow data.

A Permanent Indus Commission (PIC) was established to supervise implementation of the IWT. Implementation of

IWT with the involvement of PIC is one of the successful agreements for resolving trans-boundary water issues. PIC worked very well for maintaining the soul of treaty. The commissioners are obliged to meet once a year, altering their meetings places between the two countries. During their meetings, they plan and organize their tours, exchange data and information regarding the current and future developments. If either of the countries have questions, regarding the projects and maintenance work, the problems can be referred to PIC. If PIC is unable to resolve the issues, then the question becomes a difference and could be referred to a Neutral expert, either appointed by two members of commission or by a third party (World Bank's) (Uprety et al., 2010). If the neutral expert failed to solve the difference then it should be treated as disputes and then International Court of Arbitration (ICA) could be established to resolve the disputes (Swain, 2009).

Indus Water Commission

In accordance with Article VIII of the Treaty, both India and Pakistan each created one post of Indus Water Commissioner which together constitutes Permanent Indus Water Commission. The Commissioner of each country acts on behalf of his government for all the matters of the Treaty and servers as regular channel of communication unless either of the government decides to take any Commission meets regularly at least once in a year, or when requested by either of the Commissioner alternately in each of the countries and can inspect assisted by up to two advisors, works on Indus basin of both the countries. The major functions of the Commission include:

- To establish and maintain cooperative arrangements for implementation of the treaty, to promote cooperation between the parties in the development of the water of rivers particularly on specified aspects.

- Furnish yearly other desired reports to both the governments by fixed date.
- To shares, on a regular basis, extensive and comprehensive data on the water flows in each river, and water withdrawn from each reservoirs etc.
- To inform each other with relevant data of "'engineering project" if either of the two countries plans to construct any of such projects on any of the rivers this causes interference in the water flow.
- To undertake once in every five years a general tour of inspections of the rivers for ascertaining the facts connected with the various developments and works on the rivers.
- To undertake promptly, at the request of the either Commissioner a tour of inspections of such works or sites on the river as may be considered necessary by him for ascertaining the facts connected with those works or sites.
- Make efforts to settle the difference between the parties promptly in accordance with the relevant provisions of the treaty.

Water crisis in the Indus Basin

Pakistan is one of the world's most arid countries with an average rainfall of less than 240 mm (Briscoe et al., 2005). Indus water is the only source of water for domestic agriculture and industrial needs. Agriculture is like the backbone in Pakistan's economy. Indus flow plays a major contribution in maintaining and developing Pakistan's economy as it provides over 60% of the water utilized for irrigation purposes (Miner et al., 2009). Continuation in population growth with high demand of food, water and energy increasing strains on limited water resources. Now a day Pakistan faces a very severe water crisis. One third of the country population is living under water stress condition. An estimated report of November 2008 shows that out of 165 million population of Pakistan, 25% are below poverty level, 98 million rely on agriculture, 50 million do not have access to safe drinking water and 74 million have no sanitation. The gap between demand and supply is widening. In 2004, water shortfall was 11 MAF which is expected to ascend to 31 MAF in 2013. Water availability has been declining at an alarming rate from 5000 cubic meter per capita in 1951 to about 1100 cubic meter currently and it has been projected to less than 700 cubic meter by 2025 (World Bank, 2006). Pakistan's total water demand in 2025 is projected to 338 bcm suggesting a gap of 100 bcm (Toufiq, et al., 2004).

Compared to Pakistan, India is a semi arid country. Over 70 percent Indians live in rural areas and agriculture is the primary source of their livelihood. About 200 million people are directly employed by agriculture (Government of India Ministry of Agriculture 2005). Population is growing rapidly after China, India is the second largest country having population of 1,241 million (2011 world population datasheet). Rising population with high demand of water put more pressure on limited resources. India's per capita water availability has declined from 5000 cubic meters in 1950 to 1800 cubic meters in 2005 (Akhtar, 2010) and it has been assumed that per capita water availability will fall below 1000 cubic meters by 2050. Growing demand of food and energy pushed India to concentrate for water conservation and power generation projects. Many analysts argue that GDP growth of 7 percent per year requires a 10 percent increase in annual supply. India's booming economy needs energy to grow particularly in Jammu and Kashmir that has many potential hydroelectric sites despite the fact that, Jammu and Kashmir faces energy crisis. Despite the potential of 30,000MW of power, 25 percent of our population has no access to electricity and 75 percent is getting episodic electricity (Parvaiz, 2011).

High demands of water to meet the challenges of rapid

increase in population, increased urbanization and industrialization creating a competing environment for a limiting water resource. Limited water availability with high demand also creates some sort of intrastate tensions in Pakistan and India. Both countries desperately need water for booming their economy and trying hard to get access as much as they can. Although, the Indus water treaty has been successful in managing the war between Pakistan and India two and half times and worked very well for more than 50 years. But, there are series of disagreement going on between both these riparian countries.

Baglihar Hydroelectric Dam

Baglihar Dam was one of the most controversial issues. India planned to build Baglihar dam on the Chenab River 60 miles up streams from the Pakistani border. Under the IWT India has a right to build upstream non storage facilities but it must not alter or influence the flow of the river. Pakistan had a number of objections over the construction of this dam.

Criteria (a) states that the work shall not be capable of raising the water level artificially above the full poundage level specified in design. Pakistan claimed that dam design is excessive and provided ability to India for raising artificial water level above the full poundage level (Bhatti, 2011 and Uprety et al., 2010). Criteria (b) requires that the maximum poundage in the operating pool not to exceed twice the poundage required for firm power and Pakistan claimed that the poundage in operating tool mentioned by India is excessive. So it should be reduced (Bhatti, 2011 and Uprety et al., 2010). Criteria (c) state that if the conditions for gated spillway are necessary, the bottom level of gates in normal closed position shall be located at the highest level consistent with sound and economical design. Bone of contention on this point was Pakistan's claim that the design was not based on reality and correct estimates of flood discharge. Pakistan claimed that spillway was not necessary. Either un-gated or surface gated spillway could be provided with the bottom of the gates with the highest level (Bhatti, 2011 and Uprety et al., 2010). Criteria (d) requires that intake for the turbine shall be located at the highest level coherent with sufficient and economical construction and operation of the plant as run off river plant. Pakistan had an objection that the location of intake power is not at the highest level as mandated in IWT (Bhatti, 2011 and Uprety et al., 2010).

Although, both countries tried hard to settle the issue by themselves but bilateral negotiation did not bear any productive result. So, first time in the history of IWT, on January 15, 2005, Pakistan asked for World Bank to appoint a neutral expert to resolve the differences over Baghliar dam. After five months of the original request, Raymond Lafitte, Professor of Swiss Institute of Technology in Lausanne was appointed as a neutral expert to address the differences regarding Baglihar Project (Mohammad 2011).

In February, 2007, Lafitte delivered his final decision to both parties and also one copy of decision to World Bank. In his report he partly addressed some objections of Pakistan like, reduced the poundage capacity, increased 3m height of power intake and acknowledged India's right to construct gated spillway. Both countries agreed to follow the final decision of the neutral expert (Ibid). But, the dispute again got activated when India filled the dam during the dry season in 2008 that seriously disturbed the livelihood and agriculture production of Pakistan. Pakistani media and local people blamed that India stole water having deprived Pakistan of its rights. The filing of Baglihar dam above Marala reduced the flow as low as 20000 cusec, whereas India obliged to maintain the minimum inflow at the level of 55,000 cusec (Bhatti, 2011). Pakistan lost about 2 MAF of water from August, 25, 2008 to September, 4, 2008 and it adversely affected Pakistan's wheat crop (Kugelman, 2009). President of Pakistan even raised the issue in his speech to the UN General Assembly (Swain, 2009). Pakistan strongly protested and claimed that India is violating the IWT. But this time, Pakistan decided to solve the issue by negotiation. Indian commission admitted that reduction was because of unavailability of any mechanism to pass the flow at the low level. He explained that this happened because we were expecting heavy rainfall during these days. Pakistan's Indus commissioner in an interview told that although "Pakistan felt that parameter and procedure mentioned in IWT were not followed during the initial filling of the dam. We have resolved the differences on the initial filling of the dam in a spirit of cooperation and good will and India gave us the insurance that it will be careful in future" (Parasi, 2010).

Wullar Barrage/ Tulbul Navigation Project

Wullar Barrage or Tulbul Navigation Project being constructed by India on Jhelum River just below Wullarlake located 25 kilometres north of Srinagar at 5180 feet above sea level (Noorani, 1995). The project has been started by government of Indian state of Jammu and Kashmir. The dispute emerged in 1985 when Pakistan learnt through the notification of tender notice in newspaper. Pakistan calls it a Wullar Barrage constructed by India for storage purposes and India refers it as a Tulbul Navigation project for transportation of fruits and timbers (Misra, 2007).

Pakistan strongly opposed the construction of this project. Pakistan claimed that construction of such a project on that site had a potential to unfavourably affect the triple canal project in Pakistan namely, Upper Chenab Canal, Upper Jhelum Canal and lower Bari Doab Canal. Pakistan believed that construction of this barrage would provide India with the means to control over River Jhelum that could facilitate India to stop water flow during winter (Bhatti, 2011).

The Mangla Dam on Jhelum River, which is a main source of irrigation and electricity for Punjab, would be adversely affected. Moreover, Pakistan has an apprehension that India could close the gate of barrage during war so, enhancing the ability of Indian troops to come in Pakistan. Pakistan remembered in the connection of 1965 war, when Indian army had failed to cross the Bambanwali Ravi Bedian Link Canal because of its full flow.

Indian government argues that, the purpose of Tulbul project is only to improve the navigations in Jhelum River during lean month in order to connect Srinagar with Baramula (Misra, 2007). Indian claimed that 90 percent of this project would be beneficial to Pakistan, as it would increase the power generation capacity of Mangla. The project would regulate the supply of Mangla dam as well as increase the efficiency of irrigation network in Pakistan Punjab. India argues that the Tulbul Project would be effective in reducing the flow of water during the flood seasons and suggest that Pakistan should bear the share of construction (Uprety, 2010). Pakistan assert that the Wullar Barrage capacity is more than 300,000 acre feet and according to IWT, India is only allowed to construct storage work on western tributaries, if it does not exceed 100000 acre feet and the design has been approved by Pakistan. Pakistan referred this issue to the Indus Water Commission in 1986, but the Commission failed to resolve it. Pakistan then decided to take the case to a International Court of Arbitration (ICA), but India postponed the construction. About ten rounds of talk have already been done but only with little progress. Pakistan gave an option to stop the construction of Kishanganga Project on Neelum River, which would affect the Neelum-Jhelum Project constructed by Pakistan.

Kishanganga Hydroelectric Project (KHEP)

Now the current controversy is related to Kishanganga Hydroelectric Project (KHEP) that entangled two countries in conflict. This is the 330 MW Hydropower project in India about 160 km upstream of Muzaffarabad. The KHEP involves the 100 km diversion of Kishanganga River (called the Neelum River in Pakistan) to a tributary named BunarMadumatiNullah of Jhelum near Bunkot, through a 22 km tunnel. The water will rejoin the Jhelum through Wullar Lake near the town of Bandipur in Baramula district. Neelum is the greatest tributary of Jhelum River and runs about 150 km in Pakistan controlled Kashmir before it joins the Jhelum River near Muzafarabad. Because of this diversion, instead of Muzafarabad it will rejoin Jhelum in Indian controlled Kashmir. This diversion will change the direction of river about 204 km before it joins the Jhelum River near Muzafarabad, the site where Pakistan Neelum-Jhelum hydel Project is situated (Akhtar, 2010).

Objectives of India on Kishanganga project

The Indian objectives over the construction of Kishanganga hydropower projects are:

- To augment power output of Uri Hydel Power Project (480 MW) by additional regulating water.
- To augment supplies in the Wullar Lake for use during the lean period.
- To utilize the hydroelectric potential of J&K for the states of Punjab, Haryana, Himachal Pradesh, Chandigarh, Rajasthan and Delhi (Admin, 2009).

Table 3: Salient Features of Kishanganga Dam

Type of dam	Concrete gravity dam
Length	268 m
Height	75.5 m
Live storage	1,40,700 acres
Total storage	1,78,200 acres
Dead storage	46.25 m3
Maximum discharge	70,500 cusecs

Capability of reservoir	220 m3
Capacity	330 MW
Number of gates	4
Type of spillway	Gated type
Length of spillway	60 m
Crest level	2422 m

Source: (Admin, 2009)

Pakistan's apprehensions

Pakistan first received a report about India's plan of this project in 1988, while India officially confirmed it in 1994. Pakistan claims that India is violating the IWT by diverting the water and water drawn from a given tributary must be return to the same river. According to IWT, upstream must release as much water as downstream have the capacity to store it and the diversion will also affect the ecosystems, it submerged the Pakistan controlled Kashmir and entire Neelum valley. It will affect 133, 000 hectors of irrigation in the Neelum valley. Pakistan also claims that 11 percent of water flow in summer and 27 percent flow in winter would reduce due to Kishanganga project. The Hydropower generation capacity of 969 MW Neelum-Jhelum Project which Pakistan is constructing on Jhelum River would reduce by 11 percent. The Kishanganga dam could reduce Pakistan's total water availability from an estimated 154 MAF per year and may affect a significant portion of the Mangla dam storage capacity besides declining the pressure required to generate electricity in Neelum-Jhelum Power Project. Pakistan also claims that the feasibility study of Neelum-Jhelum project has acquired right in favor of Pakistan (Admin, 2009).

India's apprehensions

India argues that the diversion will not affect the flow of water because the quantum of water will be the same as it

82

before. The diversion of river is not matter instead of meeting in Pakistan controlled Kashmir it would meet in Kashmir. India also rejected Pakistan's objection of favoring feasibility study by quoted the Indus Water Treaty according to that the project authorized first would give top priority (Admin, 2009).

In May 2004, India promised to freeze all its work on the site and hold a meeting with Pakistan to remove its objections. Pakistan raised six objections of which one related to the power generation scheme, two to the diversion of water and three related to the design of dam. The issue was discussed in five meetings from November 2004 to November 2005 but it did not bear any prolific results. In 2006, India submitted the revised plan of the project, brought down the storage capacity by reducing the height of dam from 75.48m to 35.48 m. Pakistan rejected the revised plan having objection over the diversion of the water. Because, it will adversely affect the Neelum-Jhelum Project capacity, that Pakistan has a plan to complete in 2015 one year before the completion of KHEP.

According to the press report Pakistan Indus Water Commission SayedJamat Ali Shah said that New Delhi is not cooperating with us. Indian Government is not providing any project information before According to Indus Water Treaty the states have to share information on any new project before six month of starting. "India never stole or blocked Pakistan's share of waters and has assured Pakistan that New Delhi would implement Indus Water Treaty in letter and spirit", Indus Water Commissioner of India G. Auranganathan said. (Shaukat, 2010) .

Chairman Indus Water Treaty Council Hafiz Zahoor-ul-Hassan Dahr has stated that like the 131 round talk between Pakistan and India under Indus Water Treaty not bore any fruit and the latest series of dialogue would meet the same result (The Nation, 2010). India is still willing and in favor of bilateral talk but Pakistan decided to take this issue to World Bank. So, Pakistan sent a legal notice to India on 20 May 2010 on Kishanganag hydropower project (Sify news, 2010).

Because of the technical and legal objections, first time in the history of IWT, Pakistan took this issue to ICA. Pakistan nominated Jan Paulsson, head of Norwegian international law firm, and Bruno Simma, of the International Court of Justice, as its arbitrators in the Court of Arbitration. India nominated Peter Tomka, Vice-President of the International Court of Justice at Geneva and Lucius Caflisch, a Swiss international law expert who is a professor at the Graduate Institute of International Studies to represent it in the dispute. Although the two countries have rejected each other's nominees for the Court of Arbitration, they decided to set up a panel comprising a chairman, a legal member and an engineer to select the umpires, by drawing lots. In response to the Pakistan appeal, ICA on 25 September 2011 has barred India from going ahead to work on controversial KHEP on Neelum River (Raza, 2011).

Limitations in IWT

Agreements on water have the prime importance in water allocation. It brings the national and international community to the same table for the joint management of their common resource. Signing agreements over water sharing might be easy but the real problem is to keep alive the agreements in letter and spirit. Agreements over share water resource not only motivate the riparian states to work together but also can be a source to promote peace and cooperation among states on other mutual issues. But the validity of agreements depends on the mutual interest of all the stakeholders, strength of their relationship, level of interdependency and cooperation. States with a good political relationship and mutual interest tend to co-operate more efficiently than adversarial states. Agreements with good characteristics need to be workable for a long period of time. Only then they can positively contribute in peace and cooperation within a basin by addressing the future water needs of the riparian countries (Swain, 2007).

The 1960, Indus water agreement (IWT) signed for water allocation of Indus River between Pakistan and India. IWT worked very well for more than 60 years. During this time period both states have a difference on many issues but they settle the dispute by themselves. PIC tried hard to work in letter and spirit for the implementation of IWT. But one of the main drawbacks is the amputation surgery of the Indus basin into two. According to IWRM the whole basin should be treated as a single unit so that states can cooperate in more effective ways for the sustainable management of river and land resources. But, this division reduced the level of cooperation among states. Although both states are highly interdependent on each other for the construction of infrastructure and pollution control but in this agreement the level of joint basin management seems to be missing.

Another drawback is missing the perception of all stakeholders, their needs and future demands. Jammu and Kashmir is one of the states of India. At the time of treaty the population of Jammu and Kashmir was 3.5 million which now has increased three times. Increasing population demands more water and energy for boosting their economy. While, according to IWT Jammu and Kashmir can use only 10% of hydroelectric potential and 40% of cultivable land. Due to this restrictive use, people in Jammu and Kashmir are facing high energy crisis. IWT signed in 1960, with the simple division of Indus basin without considering the future need. According to IWT, annually 135 MAF water were allocated to Pakistan. Compare to that time Pakistan population now has grown three times. Population growth results in declining per capita water availability. Now, Pakistan is under water scarce situation and the situation becomes worst in future if the current circumstances go as such.

Parsing the Indus Water Treaty

In retrospect, the Indus Waters Treaty only became possible after an encompassing principle was discovered agreeable to India and Pakistan. Indeed, it was soon apparent that the bureaucrats and technical experts negotiating the Treaty were not capable of resolving the political differences underlying the dispute. In essence, the World Bank scheme only carried forward the logic of partition by extending the logic of partition, and sequestering the physical and natural assets of the two countries. It is a matter of great significance that the IWT was reached between a civilian and a military leader. General Ayub Khan, it would be recollected, had seized power in 1958 from the weak and squabbling civilian governments in Karachi. The pivotal role of the military thereafter in Pakistan's decision-making apparatus is well-documented while, in India, civilian control over the decision-making is an equally well-established principle. In this milieu, the continuance of the Indus Waters Treaty over the last six decades indicates that the Pakistan military believes that its advantages outweigh its disadvantages.

Viewed from the Indian perspective, gaining access to the three Eastern Rivers permitted the construction of the Bhakra Dam and the Rajasthan Canal, crucial for developing (East) Punjab and Rajasthan. However, the IWT has its critics in India who argue that India needlessly surrendered 80 percent of the Indus waters by agreeing to reserve the three western rivers for the exclusive use of Pakistan. As the upper riparian state, India had a preemptive right to these waters. In consequence, the remaining 20 percent of the Indus river waters has proven inadequate to meet the needs of the growing population in India that subsists on these waters, like the agriculturists in the Kashmir Valley. Besides, pressure is growing on the demand for water in the Indus basin for potable and industrial purposes. It should be appreciated that Pakistan had entered into a military alliance with the United States in 1954, and had, later, become part of the CENTO and SEATO alliances. Its proximity to the United States and its NATO allies gave Pakistan a clear advantage in these World Bank dominated negotiations vis-a-vis India that reposed faith in a non-aligned foreign policy conceived by Nehru.

India's official disenchantment with the terms of the IWT reflected later in its rejection of a multibillion dollar proposal made by President Carter in 1978 to support "an eastern version of the 1960 Indus water accord, Ganges-Brahmaputra agreement that would have led to massive financial investments in flood control, hydroelectric power and irrigation to spur development in the subcontinent's poor and densely populated northeastern corner." The World Bank was willing to finance this project and undertake the complex negotiations with Nepal and Bangladesh to operationalise it. But, India did not evince any interest in this proposal as its water specialists were "opposed to the idea of an international regime for the eastern waters, echoing their long-standing view that India had lost out to Pakistan in water-sharing arrangements under the Indus Water Treaty"(Chari 2004).

Principles of cooperation

The Treaty lays down principles of cooperation in Article 6&7 which relate to exchange of data and future cooperation. This is intended to ensure optimum development of the rivers and cooperation and collaboration between the two countries. The data regarding the daily flow in and utilization of the water of the rivers is to be exchanged regularly. This includes,

• Daily gauge and discharge data relating to flow of the rivers at all observation sites.

• Daily extraction for or releases from reservoirs.

- Daily withdrawals at the heads of all canals operated by government or any other agency, including link canals.
- Daily escapages from all canals, including link canals.
- Daily deliveries from link canals.
- This data is to be transmitted on monthly basis by each party to the other (Akhtar, 2010).

Advantages of Treaty

- The Indus Water Treaty was signed by India and Pakistan in 1960 had some advantages for example,
- With this treaty both countries became able to operate water supplies of rivers of their own shares.
- The treaty made the system more reliable under seasonal variations.
- This treaty provided opportunity to both countries for use of water.
- This treaty also reduced the tension between the two countries.
- Due to this treaty a permanent Indus Commission was set up to adjudicate any dispute in future (Begum Toheeda, 2011).

Demerits of the Treaty

- Besides the advantages there were some drawbacks of the Indus Water Treaty, which are:
- From Pakistan's perspective, allocation of only 75% of water as against 90% of irrigated land violated the principle of "appreciable harm". From India point of view, allocation of 75% of water to Pakistan violated the principle of "equitable utilization".
- Pakistan had to forego the entire perpetual flow of fresh waters of eastern rivers (24 MAF), which it historically used to receive for irrigation.
- Due to loss of regular flow in eastern rivers, silting has occurred in the channels and subsequent floods cause greater destruction in Pakistan, in addition to other environmental effects.

- The traditional flood irrigation, the most ancient way of using rivers waters, on Sutlej, Beas and to some extent on Ravi disappeared. As a result, no cultivation was possible in the flood plains of these rivers, thus rendering a large extent of area barren.
- Storages are not substitutes of perpetual flow water as the storages have limited life. Pakistan is already feeling the effect of silting up of its major reservoirs (Ahmed, 2012).

Divergent and conflicting views on IWT

There are different opinions regarding the IWT. There is a dominant view that holds that the IWT has been a successful conflict solving mechanism—internationally as well as among some people in India and Pakistan. However, often what is not highlighted is the discontentment with the treaty. One of the major problems with the IWT has been that it has led to regional disparity and discontent. In the state of Jammu and Kashmir (J&K), the IWT is widely perceived to be discriminatory. According to ArjimandTalib, the IWT was geared more towards safeguarding India's interest in Punjab and the Bhakra-Nangal project, and totally ignored the needs of Kashmiris. Rather than looking at the whole basin, restriction placed on India's use of the western rivers made it virtually impossible for J&K to derive any benfits of irrigation, hydroelectric power, and navigation, from the waters of the Jhelum and Chenab rivers which flow through it. Many people point out that it is ironic that the state, despite being rich in its hydel resources, faces acute shortage of hydro-electric power, particularly during winter months. It is a reality that J&K accounts for only 0.9 per cent of the hydel power generated in the country. As Biswajeet Saikia states, the IWT made Punjab prosperous by using the three river waters for agriculture and power, but put Jammu and Kashmir behind. On 3 April 2002, the Jammu and Kashmir Legislative Assembly, cutting across party affiliations, denounced the treaty, calling for its review.

Similarly in Pakistan, dispute has simmered between Sindh and Punjab. Matters came to a head in the 1980s, when the military government of General Zia-ul-Haq announced the inception of the Kalabagh dam on the Indus, the third large-scale storage and hydroelectric reservoir, after Mangla and Tarbela. The Kalabagh dam issue became immediately controversial, and led to large scale protests in Sindh, where it was seen as a further attempt by the Punjab-led military government at encroaching upon the lower riparian water entitlements. Water allocation remains a critical factor in inter-provincial politics in Pakistan. The treaty also totally neglects environmental concerns and issues of displacement. Others, like Ramaswamy Iyer lambast the surgical division, but argue that this was the best and most practical solution given the circumstances of Partition and the difficult relationship between the two newly formed countries. However, as is becoming evident, the IWT is facing far more problems now over dams and water issues than in the past, leading some to call for new visions and possibilities to be explored regarding the IWT.

Violations of Indus Water Treaty by India from Pakistan perspective

Controversial Hydro projects: For almost two decades (1960s1970s), the Indus Water Treaty was followed by either side in its true form and spirit. Starting from the decade of 1980s, India started creating problems for Pakistan on the water sector on one or the other pretext. Since signing the treaty, India has violated it many times. Pakistan had been accommodating these for quite some time. Pakistan protested and even asked for the arbitration from the World Bank, but no worthwhile results could be achieved, (Khan, 2011). The major Indian projects that have become controversial from time to time and involved issues around the compliance of Indus Water Treaty include Salal, Wullar Barrage/Tulbul Navigation project, Baglihar, Kishanganga, DulHasti, Uri II and NimooBazgo and many more.

1. Salal Hydroelectric Project

This hydroelectric project is situated on River Chenab in India occupied Kashmir. Salal was the first Indian project that became controversial between Pakistan and India. The construction of the dam was decided in 1970. India provided information about the project in 1974, Pakistan objected to the design and storage capacity of dam. In 1976, both countries entered into a series of talks to resolve the issue. Pakistan contended that the dam would enable India either to interrupt the flow of the water or to flood to western Punjab. There were two rounds of intensive talks in 1976, India provided details of the project and showed flexibility by agreeing to alter the design of the dam to remove Pakistan's objection. On April14, 1978 India and Pakistan entered into a treaty on the Salal hydroelectric project and this was the first major dispute which was successfully resolved bilaterally under this treaty (Siddiqui, 2010).

2. Wullar Barrage Project

The Wullar Barrage, which Indian refers to as Tulbul Navigation project, was the second Indian project that became controversial and still remains unresolved. The proposed barrage is located on the Jhelum in Kashmir. India wants to build the barrage on the mouth of Wullar Lake which is the largest fresh water lake in occupied Kashmir. India did not provide information on the project in time and started construction on the project in 1984, Pakistan learnt about the project in 1985 and raised objection and requested India to stop work on it (Akhtar, 2010).

Under the provisions of Indus Water Treaty 1960, the water of three western rivers Indus, Jhelum and Chenab have been allocated to Pakistan for unrestricted use except for certain uses by India in the areas located in Kashmir and India is not allowed to build any storage on the Main Jhelum River. The matter was accordingly taken up by the Permanent Indus Commission for resolution under Article IX

91

(1) of the treaty. However, in spite of several meetings, the Commission failed to resolve the issue and the construction work which India had already started continued up to September 1987, when finally it got suspended. On the request of the India, bilateral negotiation started at the Secretary level. Up to 2008 as many as thirteen rounds of talks had been held but no result was so far found. The current factual position is that although the work at the site remains suspended, India still intends to restart the work. The issue is part of the composite dialogue between Pakistan and India (Siddiqui, 2010).

3. Baglihar Hydroelectric Project

Baglihar was the third Indian project that became controversial and the first one that went to the Neutral expert for determination on technical questions raised by Pakistan. This project has been in operation since October 2008. It is located on Chenab River in district Doda. The project has two stages and both are of 450MW capacity. Pakistan raised six objections to the design of the dam and argued that the project was not in conformity with the Indus Water Treaty. Pakistani experts also feared that India could also weaken Pakistan's defence by stopping the Chenab flow through the project's spill-ways as two canals emanate from Head Marala and Sialkot, which irrigate central Punjab and are also constructed for defence point of view, could be dried as and when New Delhi desires. Thus, Pakistan has decided to construct Msngla-Head Marala Link Canal to ensure water in the two canals that originate from Head Marala (Akhtar, 2010).

In March 2009, Pakistani Minister for water and power informed the Parliament that Pakistan has demanded of India either to compensate for the losses or provide water equal to 0.2 million acre feet. Pakistan took up this case with India and Indus Water Commissioner. Pakistan made an urgent visit to India in this connection; India accepted the Pakistani claim of drop in Chenab flow during August and September. The two meetings were held by Indus Water Commissioner, Pakistan with its counterpart in India, but the meetings remained inconclusive. India as usual stuck to its traditional obduracy and inflexibility which is causing loss to Pakistan. Pakistan however, determined that India must accept the violation by it and address it in future (Siddiqui, 2010).

4. Kishanganga Hydroelectric Project

After Baglihar, India and Pakistan have got locked in a dispute over the configuration of Kishanganga hydroelectric project and the matter is now going to Court of Arbitration for settlement. The 300-MW, Kishanganga Hydroelectric Project is located about 160km upstream of Muzaffarabad. Pakistan first received reports about Indian intentions to develop the Kishanganga project in 1988 but India officially confirmed it in June 1994 when it provided information regarding the storage work. Initially Pakistan raised three objections to the project. In May 2004, amid reservations voiced by Pakistan on the construction of Kishanganga Hydroelectric Project, India promised to freeze all work at the site for six months and hold a meeting with Pakistan for removing its objections. India told the meeting that it was working on the foundation of the dam and the powerhouse. Pakistan protested and said that construction work should not have begun before removing its objections. The issue was discussed in five meetings of the Commission held from November 2004 to November 2005 but differences over the project remained; further India did not supply the data regarding the project. In May 2005, Pakistan raised six objections of which three related to design of the dam, two of the diversion of water and one to the power generation scheme. Pakistan also accepted an Indian proposal to set 15 July as deadline for resolving the Kishangana project issue (Akhtar, 2010). As reported in the international press, Indian cabinet has approved to go ahead with 330MW Kishanganga project in Indian held Kashmir, in violation of Indus Water Treaty. It intends to complete the project by the year 2016, one year ahead of Pakistan project of diversion of Neelum River to Jhelum River. The Indian project would divert the River Neelum to Wullar Lake upstream of the Pakistan project and would leave very little water for Pakistan's project, so Pakistan has gone to the International Court of Arbitration for resolution of the issue (Siddique, 2010).

5. DulHasti Hydroelectric Plant

The two-stage DulHasti hydropower project with an installed capacity of 390 MW is located on the main Chenab in district Doda. Pakistan believed it was just not a hydroelectric station but a full-fledged dam aimed at storing water for irrigation needs as seen in the case of Baglihar dam.

This project was originated in 1983 by the Indian Prime Minister Indira Gandhi at a cost of Rs 34 billion. This project envisages the construction of 180.5m long and 59.5 high concrete gravity dam upstream of Baglihar hydroelectric project on river Chenab. The construction of this dam was started in 1991. Compared to Salal and Baglihar Projects, the effect of this project on Pakistan is not grave since the stoppage of water can be of the order of 1-2 days only. However, it is imperative to discourage India from providing under-sluices type gated spillways in the body of the dam (Ahmed, 2012).

6. Uri-Ii Hydel Power Project

This hydel power project is located on the Jhelum in Baramulla district of Indian Kashmir. The project is planned immediacy downstream of Uri-I and will pick up its tail water to make use of the gross head of about 130m available in the course of the river between Uri-I tailrace outlet. In October 2002, Pakistan asked India to supply information about Uri-II project. In July 2004, Pakistan again asked India to provide the said information, in March 2005, Pakistan repeated the request and India finally provided some information about the plant. In April 2006, Pakistan sent its observations to India. India did not inform Pakistan and started unilateral construction on the project, in June, 2007, India rejected Pakistan's demand for stopping work on the Uri-II project while Pakistan threatened to seek World Bank intervention if India did not stop construction work (Sharma, 2007). India remained insistent and did not stop work. Some adjustments have been made on Uri-II and the construction work has reached its final stage and is set for completion at the end of 2011.

7. Nimoo Bazgo Hydro Project

Nimoo Bazgo Hydel project 45 MW is a run of the river scheme. It is located on the main Indus in Ladakh district. The construction work of dam is in full swing. On March 29, 2010 in a meeting of the Indus Commissioner India handed over construction plans and maps of the project to Pakistan. Pakistan expressed reservations on this project and showed its fear that the Indian projects might obstruct smooth supply of water to Pakistan. Pakistan has raised six objections to NimooBazgo. At the July 2010 meeting of the Indus Commissioners, India expressed its inability to discuss construction of NimoBazgo hydropower project saying it was not part of the ongoing negotiations. Pakistan has also not been allowed yet to visit site of this project (Akhtar, 2010).

Bursar Dam

This dam is considered as the biggest project built by India on two major rivers Jhelum and Chenab flowing through the state of Kashmir into Pakistan. This dam would be constructed near Hanzal village in Doda District on the Marusudar River, the main right bank tributary of the river Chenab. According to the sources, it will store 2.2 MAP and generate 1020 MW of electricity and will be completed within 6-7 years at a cost of Rs. 43.78 billion. The construction of this dam would be a serious violation of the Indus Water Treaty as it stores the 2.2 MAP which is much beyond permissible limits. (Ahmed, 2012). The height of this dam will be 829 ft, while in comparison, the Tarbela dam height is 485ft, Mangla dam height is 453 ft. actually this dam will be a storage facility, which will regulate the flow of water to all downstream projects like DulHasti project, Baglihar dam and Salal dam.

This proposed dam violates the Indus Water treaty as well as international environmental convention. It will cause water scarcity in Pakistan, and it would also contribute towards melting of Himalayan glaciers. More than 4900 acres of thick forest would be submerged and the whole population of Hanzal village would be displaced.

According to some experts, the project is located in Kishtwar High Altitude National Park (about 2 million acre feet) which is an environmentally protected area. Spreading over an area of 400km, the park contains 15 mammals' species including the musk dear and Himalayan black and brown bear and some rare birds for which an environmental impact assessment study is necessary(Ahmed,2012). Pakistan's Commissioner for Indus Waters has repeatedly asked his Indian counterpart to provide details of the proposed water storage and hydropower projects, including Bursar dam, but India has taken the stand that it was aware of its legal obligations and it would inform Pakistan about the project details and relevant data six months before construction activities as required under the Treaty (Ahmed, 2012).

The Court of arbitration decision about Kishanganga Hydro project, victory or defeat

The Court of Arbitration had granted a stay order against the construction of the Kishanganga dam structure on 25 September, 2011, both Pakistan and India initially claimed victory after the announcement of the Court of

Arbitration's interim order. The court has granted the stay order against construction of the dam structure but has allowed India to continue work on allied facilities, like the tunnel required to construct the dam. That India may not construct any permanent structures on or above the river bed is explicitly stipulated in the order:

"Except for the sub surface foundations of the dam, India shall not proceed with the construction of any permanent works on or above the Kishanganga / Neelum riverbed at the Gurez site that may inhibit the restoration of the full flow of that river to its natural channel" (Bhutta, 2011).

While Indian Government and media highlighted that one clause and gave full coverage, extrapolating that saves the permanent structures and they allowed going ahead with the construction. On other side Pakistan claimed that the decision was in its favour because that order bars India from continuing work on the dam construction. The former Indus Water Commissioner of Pakistan Syed Jammat Ali Shah said that the real issue was to stop the India from the construction of the dam, which the court has ordered.

Kishanganga dam: threat to Pakistan

Kishanganga dam is perceived also a big threat to Pakistan because with the construction of the dam, India would divert water from the Kishanganga River which is known as Neelum river when enters into Azad Kashmir. India constructed a 23-kilometer long tunnel which produces 330 MWs or power. The water will subsequently be discharged into the Wullar Lake and ultimately flow through Jhelum River to Muzaffarabad. If this project completed, the dam would result in a 21% drop in Neelum River's inflow, thereby reducing the prospective energy generation from Pakistan's Neelum-Jhelum hydroelectric project by 10%. According to Pakistan's officials, India has completed 15% of the construction work on Kishanganga but according to some other resources, India has completed 43% of the work (Bhutta, 2011).

India's Justification Using Water of Western Rivers

India has been betraying the international community for its foul play on western rivers, quoting two excuses. First; Pakistan is unable to preserve its water by constructing dams and water storages in its territory, resulting into a large quantity of water flowing down to Arabian Sea, therefore India is securing the water while the second reason is that these dams and storages are for the utilization of the people of Kashmir, either to produce electricity and irrigation. But these both arguments of India are baseless and without logic. India is planning to permanently deprive Pakistan of its share of water, thus converting the agricultural Pakistan into desert and barren Pakistan, the current requirements of electricity in Kashmir is 5000 MWs and only a limited portion of the land could be irrigated by the water of rivers because mostly land of Kashmir is arid. So it is clear that the purpose is shifting of the water of these rivers to Indian Territory through a program. Actually, India is working on these projects to produce over 43,000 MWs of electricity, which is more than the need of the Kashmir. Then this electricity would be used for the heavy industrialization of India. While on other side it is true that we have not been able to build sufficient water reservoirs to preserve the surplus water especially during the rainy season for many reasons, nevertheless, this does not give India with enough cause to encroach over the Pakistani share of water (Khan, 2011).

The perceived threat to Pakistan

During the last few years, the issue of water between India and Pakistan has gained much importance. The violation of the Indus Water Treaty (1960) by construction of dams on western rivers, which are given to Pakistan by this treaty, Pakistan has to describe India as their eternal enemy and accuse India of trying to suffocate the Pakistan economy. Pakistani leaders blamed India for acting under an international conspiracy led by America, Israel and India against Pakistan. Over the years, India has planned construction of round about 100 large and small hydroelectric projects and reservoirs on the Indus, Chenab and Jhelum.

In early 2008, an editorial in the Urdu newspaper Roznama Ausaf accused India of planning a "WATER BOMB" strategy to strangle Pakistan economically and India wants to achieve through a water bomb, what it could not achieve through the three wars waged over the past six decades. India is planning 50 dams to raid the water of rivers flowing into Pakistan. The IBWC warned: "If this is not foiled, Pakistan will face the worst famine and economic disaster" (Ahmed, 2009).

One month after the inauguration of first phase of the Baglihar project by Indian Prime Minister Manmohan Singh, Jammat Ali Shah, Pakistan's Indus Water Commissioner and liaison between the countries within the frame work of the treaty, warned that India plans to make Pakistan barren by 2014 by stopping its water. Within a week of the dam's inauguration, Major General Athar Abbas, a spokesman for the Pakistan Army expressed concern over the Baglihar, describing it as a "defence security concern". He stated that a number of canals, drains and artificial distributaries used for irrigation purposes are crucial during times of war. The strategic importance of the Indian water projects in Kashmir is so significant that officials from the Pakistan Army headquarters attended a government meeting on the issue in February 2009 to discuss the impact of the said dams on Pakistan's water and defence interests...the Armed Forces became alarmed when they learned the projects could wreak havoc... if the same dams were to collapse or malfunction (Ahmed, 2009). Gen.Zulfiqar Ali, former chairman of Pakistan's Water and Power Development Authority expressed that by building dams on rivers in Kashmir, India wants to make Pakistan a Somalia by stopping its water and India has achieved military, economic and political supremacy vis-à-vis Pakistan (Ahmed, 2009).

A number of Pakistani experts and commentators warned that the water issue may incite nuclear war between the two countries. The convener of the All Parties Hurriyat Conference, Syed YousafNaseem stated that Pakistan is facing a water crisis and that the Indian efforts to affect cuts in its water share from the rivers flowing into Pakistan could compel Pakistan to use unconventional weapons against India and the Kashmir issue is cardinal to Pakistan-India relations. Unless this issue is resolved, the Damocles' sword of a nuclear clash will remain hanging over the region. Kashmir is very important for Pakistan and a delay in the resolution of this issue will jeopardize the peace of the region.

The famous editor Majeed Nizami accused India of blocking water from River Chenab and further proclaimed that India wants to destroy Pakistan, saying: "Our crops are not getting water, if the situation continues, Pakistan will become Somalia and Sudan (Ahmed, 2009).

Pakistan also fears that the cumulative live storage of these projects would have adverse impact both in terms of causing floods and running the Chenab and the Jhelum dry in the time when Pakistan needs the water more. The sheer number of the dams/schemes that India is building on three Western rivers is massive, generating fears in Pakistan about their adverse implications for flow of water to Pakistan. India is to build 135 big or small dams, 24 on the Indus, 77 on the Jhelum and 34 on the Chenab. Pakistan is apprehensive that even with strict compliance with the provisions of the Treaty in each case, India might taking all the projects together acquire a measure of control over the water of the Western rivers and might potentially be able to inflict harm on Pakistan (Ramaswamy, 2010).

IWT: Internal Problems

Besides these dam projects, there are several internal and regional issues that strain the Indus Waters Treaty. The most important is the view of the people in Jammu and Kashmir who see the Treaty as exploiting their rights by both India and Pakistan and their call for its annulment as an economic liability. People of the northern areas in Pakistan are also opposed to dam projects in Pakistan like the Mangla dam.

Second, hostile anti-Pakistan segments in India view the Indus Waters Treaty as giving undue concessions to Pakistan, which Prime Minister Nehru signed to 'purchase peace'. Since it did not bring peace to Kashmir, they want to revisit the concessions given to Pakistan under the Treaty.

Third, Pakistan also has serious problems regarding the sharing of Indus waters among its four provinces. This is evident with entrenched controversy being present in the country on every planned dam. The shortage of water has deep political, economic and social effects. For example, farmers in Sindh point their fingers at Punjabi landlords, and accuse them of 'stealing their share' of the Indus's water.

Finally, there are environmental and ecological changes which call for consideration. Because of climate change, the Himalayan glaciers are melting at an alarming rate. For water resources, this means an increase in water initially due to flooding. Within the next 50 years, however, experts believe there will be a 30 to 40 percent drop in glacial melt because the glaciers will have receded. A strategy to create more storage capacity for water is the only option available, but one has to remember that glacial melt is not only water but also silt that will reduce the capacity of the reservoirs. This aspect has not been considered at the political level or at least has not gained prominence.

Essentially the following two features have shaped Pakistan-India water politics

- The underlying concern of both states is the political aspects that water entails. This aspect is believed to be the catalyst behind the hydro politics in which both countries are engaged. Thus, the discussion on water issues has always been there in almost every dialogue between India and Pakistan, and now it figures in the high level talks that reflects the dominance of water issues.

- Most of the time, Pakistan being the lower riparian follows up on these issues on sharing of waters more vigorously. It has objected to almost all the projects planned by India on the western rivers calling them a violation of the Indus Water Treaty. Nonetheless, India does not accept this view and takes defensive positions (Wasi 2009).

Strategy for effective implementation of water sharing treaties

Water has become a growing source of tension in many parts of the world between nations striving for growth. As population of India, Bangladesh and Pakistan rapidly expanding, water is critical to both the nations. Pakistan contains the world's largest contiguous irrigation system, water experts say. The rivers that traverse Punjab, Pakistan's most populous province and the heart of its agriculture industry are the country's lifeline, and the dispute over their use goes to the heart of its fears about its larger, stronger neighbour. For India, the hydro projects are vital to harnessing Himalayan water to fill in the serious energy shortfalls that crimp its economy. About 40 percent of India's population is off the power grid, and lack of electricity has hampered industry. Water experts concur, but say Pakistan does have a legitimate cause for concern. The real issue is timing. If India chooses to fill its dams at a crucial time for Pakistan, it has the potential to ruin a crop (Polgreen and Tavernise 2010). It is estimated that if India builds all its planned projects, it could have the capacity of holding up about a month's worth of river flow during Pakistan's critical dry season, enough to wreck an entire planting season. Here in Bandipore, where engineers and laborers work long shifts to build the powerhouse and tunnel for the long-awaited dam, the work is not merely a matter of electricity. National pride is at stake, they said. "This dam is a matter of our national prestige," one of the engineers on the project said. "It is our right to build this dam, and our future depends on it"(Ibid).

The cooperation between India and Pakistan is essential, in order to meet the water demands of both the countries. The IWT did not seek to develop the full potential of the Indus system in terms of storage, flood cushioning and hydropower through integrated basin development and management. Pakistan, too, cannot develop the full potential of the three Western rivers allocated to it without cooperation with India. Even drainage problems in the lower regimes of the rivers and canal networks could be better overcome through collaborative arrangements. Hostility between the two countries has precluded India from developing the Eastern Rivers, even within the ambit of the Treaty, in view of objections by Pakistan. The Tulbul barrage on the Wulur Lake is a case in point. This envisages a low structure at the point where the Jhelum exit the Lake, to impound the flood waters of the river at no more than bank level and regulate its releases through the lean season. The scheme has faced a virtual veto. This, despite the fact that it would moderate silt flows into Pakistan and marginally improves the efficiency of the Mangla dam(Sachan&Haq 2015).

According to The New York Times the Kishanganga dam project in Kashmir is a crucial part of India's plans to feed its rapidly growing but power-starved economy. Hopefully, Indo-Pakistan relations will improve sooner rather than later. When that happens – and even in anticipation of that day – it is necessary to think ahead and conceptualize building on the 1960 Treaty. One can envisage storages on the upper Indus, Jhelum and Chenab, over and above what is presently permitted, that could benefit both countries. These could enhance conservation, flood moderation, lean season regulation, and the generation of additional energy and improve the management of the upper catchments.

The idea may appear remote at the present time. But the very exercise of looking ahead would reveal the opportunity costs of non-cooperation and belligerence. Both northwest India and Pakistan are water stressed and energy short, and the potential of the Indus river system has not been exhausted. Despite receiving many accolades for being the example of cooperation between adversarial states, India and Pakistan's peaceful management of their Indus River remains largely unexamined (Priscoli 1996). It is posited that an institution needs not only flexibility to respond to change, conflict resolution mechanisms and an efficient and equitable allocation of water, but it also should oversee the multipurpose use of water and permit the involvement of local users to facilitate collaboration (Bernauer 1997). It provides a framework for future research, calling for an examination of such things as the types of property rights, issues covered, legal framework, financial transfers, monitoring and openness of the institution. Thus, it can be concluded that the nature of cooperation between India and Pakistan over their Indus River system is behaviour altering and that both states have accepted losses as they cooperated. Some strategies for effective implementation of treaties for ensuring sustainable National development have been proposed like integrated water management, market efficiency improvement, equity and equality etc (Sachan & Haq 2015).

Lack of trust and cooperation

Effective transboundary cooperation over shared water resources is closely related to the establishment of institutional organizations. Sufficient institutional capacities within an enabling environment are necessary for promoting good cooperation in order to manage the international river basins. Cooperation over shared water resource maintains regional stability by promoting peace and improving economic efficiency. Cooperation will enable better management of ecosystem, providing benefits to the river and underpinning all other benefits that can be derived. Cooperation over shared water resource can ease tension and provide gains in the form of savings that can be achieved (Sadof, et al., 2002).

Sustainable international rivers development depends on the cooperative management strategies. The IWRM concept of building cooperation at political, institutional and technical level within an enabling environment is the complimentary element for sustainable river basin management. Transboundary cooperation depends on the political, geographic and cultural circumstances. The countries having a bad history of political relations are less cooperative than others. Even in the presence of bilateral agreements, such countries are more reserve to cooperate unconditionally because of trust deficits. The establishment of an internationally acceptable legal principle to share the common rivers may itself not bring a solution. Complex water disputes can only be solved by co-operations and compromises (Swain, 2007).

IWT 1960 agreement is a successful bilateral agreement that obliged both states to cooperate on water management issues under the supervision of PIC. The commission is trying hard to monitor and implement the IWT. A both states are striving to utilize limited resources with full potential by constructing hydropower projects and storage reservoirs.

105

Pakistan claimed that India is not providing fair information on time as obliged in IWT to share information on any project before six month to start. Pakistan as a lower riparian has a fear of flood and drought by the construction of Indian's projects on western rivers and have a perception that India would be able to harm Pakistan during war time. These unilateral actions performed by upstream bear a fear of water scarcity to lower riparian.

Although, India is denying Pakistan's objections but this distrust environment is a result of lack of joint river basin management institutions, poor political relations and lack of cooperation. Due to poor historical political relations and lack of information exchange, a trust deficit environment has been developed between both states, that has become a major obstacle to achieve potential cooperation. This lack of trust and cooperation has led to several negative social, environmental and economic impacts, creating regional instabilities by affecting the livelihood of local people in Pakistan.

High politics

International rivers are more prone to conflict because of the involvement of more than one state interest. Poor state relations and lack of trust makes the water issue more politicized. States focused on other issues like national security instead of considering the overall cooperative management of shared water resources. The involvement of political bodies in policy making and implementation put the water in less priority.

Indus river system also has the same effect. Because of the hostile relationship between Pakistan and India the element of effective joint cooperation seems to be missing. Kashmir issue and pressure of fundamentalist group of people from both sides are the major obstacles in resolving water related issues jointly. Moreover, as Indus seems to be a more political case; lack of accountability and transparency is highly observable in Indus water issue. Water governing authorities from India fear to give relevant information before time. All these situations are the hindrances in joint management of Indus River Basin.

Revision of treaty

Many analysts from Pakistan claim that IWT is not in favour of Pakistan and experts from Kashmir have opinion that IWT is limiting their right to use water. The 1960 agreement of IWT does not fulfill the requirement of IWRM. IWRM is holistic and has a participatory approach; focuses on the integration of all the sectors in decision making and implementation by considering the perspective of all stakeholders for sustainable management. This element of all stakeholder participation seems to be missing in 1960 agreement. The other major limitation of IWT is missing the considerations of future water demands. Treaty was signed when water was in abundance and now due to high population growth and climate change both countries are facing water scarcity. Some experts also argue that IWT is not supporting the concept of IWRM because of the partition of Indus into two parts. According to IWRM, the whole basin should be taken as a single unit and it is essential to consider its social, economic and environmental interest for sustainable management. The partition of Indus basin into two has divided the interest of the users and also affected the environment and ecosystem of Indus basin.

IWT worked very well for more than forty five years, till now both countries are striving to implement the treaty with soul and spirit. The current circumstances reveal that IWT does not seem to work efficiently in future. Both countries have high water need for boosting their economy and to meet the future demands. To prevent the future disasters of acute water shortage, there is a dire need to revise the treaty according to the present and future demand of all the states while keeping in mind the environmental sustainability and equity.

Although, IWT obliged both countries to be interdependent before taking any action on Indus River but the level of cooperation is very low. The unilateral actions of India like construction of dams for hydropower generation and navigation projects extremely affecting the livelihood of Pakistan. As Indus is the life blood for Pakistan, is facing a high water scarcity situation and the conditions will become worst in near future. Now, there is a need for both countries to come forward and reconsider the IWT in a comprehensive way by involving the participation of all major stakeholders and considering their interests, needs and future demands.

Sustainable river basin management needs an effective role of river basin organizations. Organizations for managing share water resources could work efficiently, if they are independent to make decisions and willing to cooperate fairly.   Under the revised treaty, a joint river basin organization should be established for sustainable and efficient utilization of Indus water resource. The organization should be independent and free to make decisions without any political pressure. There should not be any political interference in decision making and management of river resources. Working efficiency of joint river basin organization can become stronger by the participation and joint work of technical staff from riparian countries in analyzing the situation and decision making process.

As in case of Columbia River, the 1964 Colombia River treaty between USA and Canada has provided significant benefits through the coordinated river basin management to both countries. To analyze the future flood and power situation both countries are cooperating on joint river basin management. There is no interference from political sides, only technical staffs are responsible to analyze the future needs and management requirements. After analyzing the whole situation the member of technical staff is free to take decision that is beneficial for both countries (U.S Army Corps of Engineers, 2009). There is a need to organize such type of joint Indus River basin organization for the sustainable management of limited Indus water resource. Establishment of joint river basin organization could be a catalyst to build trust among these two hostile riparian and will also enhance the benefit of sharing. Sharing the benefits of cooperative water management is an integral part of the successful treaty design and implementation. In revised treaty, whole basin should be considered as a single unit and all states should oblige to cooperate fairly.

Cooperation at political, institutional and technical level is vital to manage share water resources effectively. Effective cooperation between states on shared resource not only improves the better management, it also enhances the regional stability by reducing the tensions at international levels. Establishment of joint river basin organization will be helpful in promoting cooperation by improving the level of transparency and accountability.

Indo Pak relations and the future of IWT

India is third after US and China in dam building and has constructed 4365 dams. Also India is considering to build 62 more hydroelectric dams on Pakistani rivers, which will enable India to close down the two Pakistani rivers Jhelum and Chenab hence turning Pakistan barren by 2014. India is also accused of Water theft by using Pakistan's share of water through tunnels. In the meantime India is also negotiating a dam on river Kabul with Afghanistan for setting up Kama hydro-electric project which will utilize 0.5 MAF of Pakistani water (Khanzada, 2008). Pakistan is of the view that India is withholding the waters and terms it as a violation of the Indus Waters Treaty, while the Indians always come up with the answer that Pakistan's assumption that India is withholding its water is wrong and says that it is the flow of water that has decreased in the respective rivers causing lesser flow of water to Pakistan due to the global climate change, which Pakistan calls as water theft by India.

Haroon Ur Rashid, a Pakistani columnist thinks a possible tension between the two nations was feared to erupt on water sharing of the Indus Water. Pakistan's policy towards Kashmir is deeply influenced by the water factor and it does not seem possible in the long run for Pakistan to change its policy on Kashmir. This blame game is coming along for the last 63 years and has yet brought no significant progress to any side, especially affecting Pakistan. What is needed now is an urgent resumption of dialogues between the two countries, the dialogues should be aimed particularly at the water dispute and both countries should try to resolve the conflict peacefully as water is the most important necessity on earth.

The water dispute is indeed fuelling the Islamic extremists who consider India as their prime enemy and have issued warnings to India of dire consequences in case India does not follow IWT. Danish Mustafa, a water specialist and geography professor at King's College in London, in his recent interview to the BBC said, "Pakistan exists because of the Indus, the recent horrific floods in Pakistan happened largely because of the poor management and the diversion of Indus waters because it does not have room to expand or flow, the way it used to flow". He further comments that,"Although dams have their usefulness, river managers in Pakistan should recognise the importance of wetlands to modulate the overflow of flood water".

Pakistan will have to think a treaty much stronger than the IWT with India so as it could effectively and efficiently work out its plans for future dams. But again Pakistan faces several problems both at home and abroad to carry out any such projects. At home, the Central Government of Pakistan must also take all the smaller provinces in confidence and should address their concerns without any further delay. And India, being an emerging economic power, needs to work on hydro-electric projects but must also listen to Pakistan so as there is no way leading to conflicts as both the countries can, in no way bear the burden of war because of the impoverished conditions of the poor people (Anna 2002).

But the question that lies in the minds of many is whether the two nuclear states will ever go to war because of the water disputes. Researchers predict that water conflicts may lead to war, but so far both states have shown flexibility and at the moment they indeed need to go beyond the IWT and sign a new agreement benefitting both of them. A war is very unlikely to break out in the near future if India reacts more generously as so far India has been blamed most occasions for all the steps taken to stop or decrease the flow of water to Pakistan, because the source of all the rivers lies in India territory (Ibid).

It would be extremely unfair to hold India responsible for the water conflict as this nation has kept upholding the treaty for more than fifty years, but however, constant hostility between the two states is overcoming any good work done on behalf of India. The objection of Pakistan on decreased water flow is not only because of water theft but it could be caused by the increase in population of India. New strategies are direly in need of implementation between the countries to come out of the water crisis mainly because of environmental degradation, global warming, and increasing population. It is the time now that both countries set aside all the hostilities and think for the betterment of the poor masses (Anna 2002).

Critical review of the treaty

It has been stated elsewhere that bombs and shells cannot make as much damage to the lands of Pakistan as can potentially be done through blockage of water by India. Therefore, one of the biggest advantages of the treaty was that it prevented an imminent war between the two basin states. Researchers at Oregon State University have found that the world's 263 transboundary rivers generate more cooperation than conflict. Over the past half century, 400 treaties have been signed on the use of rivers. Of the thirty seven incidents that involved violence, 30 occurred in dry and bitterly contested region formed by Israel and its neighbors.The treaty is therefore said to provide a good foundation for resolving water dispute between the two riparians being subject to the provisions of the treaty are adhered to in true letter and spirit. As a result of the treaty, each country became independent of using, planning and developing waters of the rivers allocated to it as per its own wish, will, demand, supply and interests without interference of either country, which reduced chances of disputes and tensions. Resultantly, substantial storage reservoirs, inter-river link canals and barrages based on diversion infrastructure was developed owing to which canal diversions in Pakistan increased from 83 BCM to 129 BCM. That facilitated to make the irrigation system more demand oriented while it was earlier based on run of the river diversions contrary to the hydrological features of the basin having almost 80 percent of waters available only during monsoon months of July to September.

Nevertheless, disadvantages of the treaty cannot be overlooked. The treaty in fact resulted in distribution of rivers rather than distribution of their waters. On overall basis, Pakistan lost its historic legitimate share of waters of Indus basin (Waseem, 2007). India secured full rights for use of the waters of the three eastern rivers allocated to it and compelled downstream users to abandon traditional sailaba (flood) irrigation due to disappearance of seasonal flood waters which used to permit cultivation on considerable part of the area. It also severely damaged ecology of the eastern rivers some of which present a scene of either wastewater stream or river bridges constructed on sand dunes. The infrastructure developed also required additional heavy burden of financial resources for repair and maintenance and supplementing the silted up reservoirs. Social, environmental and economic implications of storage reservoirs developed inter-provincial controversies which not only compelled to abandon, or defer, several development projects but also threatened to rip the very fabric of the country. Kalabagh dam is still the issue of inter provincial hot debate and commencement of construction of Bhasha dam is yet to be realized, whereas existing dams are silting up at an alarming rate of 0.25 BCM per annum.

The Indus Water Treaty was signed in an era when groundwater development hardly started in the subcontinent. The Treaty, therefore, does not envisage any article or clause regarding usage or development of groundwater resources. Now when groundwater development has boosted up and become a substantial supplemental source of irrigation water, India is geographically in much better position for harnessing groundwater as well. The eastern rivers, which India has fully secured, were the primary sources of groundwater recharge in the peripheries of doabas. In the absence of the recharge sources and owing to rapid growth of tube wells, groundwater mining is occurring at an alarming rate in Pakistan in the lower reaches of eastern rivers. Natural slope of eastern river doabas is also from Indian side towards Pakistan's territory. India has promoted rapid development of tubewells and their operation at highly subsidized electric tariff. That is certainly affecting the yield potential of downstream highly transmissive aquifer on western Punjab in Pakistan.

The treaty also does not take into account the climate change implications and the ecological changes that would occur half a century later, which may reduce runoff from its mountainous glaciers. As such the Treaty requires

113

reconsidering the regimes of excess and scarcity of water (Dawn February 20, 2010). The Treaty gives very flimsy touch to the today's hot issue of pollution, the direct victim of which are always downstream inhabitants. The text of the relevant clause (Article 5 Clause 10) endeavors to conserve quality, without appropriate monitoring and surveillance provisions, required for the intended uses. As the surface water based water supply schemes are developing, downstream riparian would have serious health consequences because of deteriorated water quality at the upstream due to agricultural, industrial and population growth. Mr. Abbassi, a Pakistani Water Expert, is of the view that a satellite-based, real-time telemetry system in Indian Kashmir, installed at a minimum of 100 locations for monitoring water quality and quantity would help remove mistrust on data exchange (The Express Tribune, January 12, 2012).

Furthermore, Kashmir is an earthquake prone area where dam safety is of immense importance. Whereas India's dam success rate is not so good and 7 out of 67 have collapsed so far. Dam collapse always has catastrophic impacts on downstream settlements, but Indus Water Treaty does not envisage any clause for compensations to the victims. Another lacuna of the Treaty is that no country is bound to exchange any data when any project is at the planning stage and data sharing is carried out only six months before the commencement of construction. By the time the aggrieved country, after completing all the prerequisites of the Treaty, refers to the Neutral Expert and/or Court of Arbitration, the construction work continue and reach the advanced stage before the final verdict is declared, and ultimately gives leverage to the country having already completed substantial part the project. Making self serving explanations of the treaty, India has either completed or near to completion of several projects on western rivers.

Those dams, inter alia, would substantially enhance evaporation and seepage losses as well. Economists are therefore of the view that the construction of large number of dams on the western rivers would enable India to maneuver or block water supplies especially in low flow periods. Resultantly, the delaying or missing of irrigation would have severe harmful impacts on our agriculture which constitutes more than 21% of GDP and is key contributor to our food security, international trade and for providing raw material to textile and sugar industries. Consequently Pakistan's food security and economy will both be at stake (Khan, 2008).

Conclusion

Water as a sign of life is essential to maintain the daily life routine. Water as a limited resource is under stress due to the high population density, climate change, urbanization and poor management. Competing demand on a limited resource contribute in arising acute water conflicts and disputes among the users whose livelihood mainly depend on it. In case of the international rivers the situations become more complicated. The rivers cross political boundaries, sometimes difficult to manage because of the poor political relationship.

Indus River is shared between four riparian countries. Pakistan and India are the two major countries dependent on Indus water flow. The 1960 agreement of Indus Water Treaty was signed between Pakistan and India for sharing the Indus water resource. This agreement was based on the amputation surgery of Indus River that gave the right of three eastern tributaries (Ravi, Beas and Sutlej) of Indus to India and western tributaries (Jhelum, Chenab, Indus) to Pakistan. Now, because of the high population density, climate change and high water demand both countries are facing water stress situation and trying hard to get as much water as they can. Construction of dams, hydropower units and navigational project is a need to meet the future challenges of water and energy crisis. Building of such infrastructure without considering the value and norms of other creates conflict among both countries. The reason behind this conflict is the lack of cooperation because of the poor political relationship and distrust among both countries. In case of international river basin cooperation and coordination is necessary for the regional stability and sustainability (Mohammad, 2011).

Sustainable river basin management is necessary for the prosperity and regional stability and it depends on the political will, cooperation, coordination and compromise. Application of IWRM approach at basin level is best for sustainable Indus river management. In the presence of high political will and commitment, the IWRM framework of enabling environment, institutional arrangement and managing instrument are the best tool for the successful application of IWRM at basin level. It is not always possible to apply all the elements of general IWRM framework at once. So, a step by step proceeding is vital for effective application of IWRM (GWP, 2009). In case of Indus River, it can be easier as compared to other international rivers, because of the already existing international water agreement and organization. Now, there is just a need to revise the 1960 agreement by considering the future needs and perception of all stakeholders. An independent joint river basin organization should be established that make policy and decision without any political pressure by inviting and considering the perception of all major stakeholders for sustainable management.

The Indus Water Treaty is coming under stress due to both growing water scarcity in India and Pakistan ecological threat to the Indus basin rivers system. The treaty was signed as a permanent solution to the water sharing problem between the two countries when water was in abundance in the Indus system. The Indus Water Treaty provides opportunity for future cooperation on water issue but unfortunately, since the signing of the treaty, no project has been undertaken under the provisions of "future cooperation". Due to climatic changes and water insecurity in the basin has heightened resulting in politicization of the water issue between the two countries. The growing water stress has coincided with India's ambitious plan to construct a great number of large hydropower plants, especially on the Chenab and Jhelum rivers. The fact that India has not been forthcoming in sharing information and engineering details regarding these projects as required in the Treaty has aroused Pakistan's apprehension. The projects of hydroelectric power made by India are not merely of run of the river structures as allowed under the treaty but their number and structures allow India to acquire manipulative control that could be used to hamper water flows into Pakistan. The worst scenario for Pakistan is the Indian ability to stop water in lean period and release it in wet season. Further the Indian projects have adverse transboundary impacts both environmental and in terms of power generation as is evident in the case of Neelum-Jhelum project. All these things created a vacuum of mistrust between India and Pakistan and water issue got much importance, now it got top position in bilateral meetings between the two countries. There is a larger political dimension to the whole problem of the rivers water distribution between Pakistan and India. To Pakistan the Kashmir issue is irrevocably linked to the Indus Water Treaty as the headwaters of all the rivers of Pakistan and meant for Pakistan flow through Kashmir and India happens to be the upper riparian state. The fear exists that India could manipulate the water to starve Pakistan so water issues are now a core issue in Indo-Pak relations.

The utilisation of water remained the bone of contention between the two countries and has widened the trust gap. In recent years, the differences over utilisation of water became so grave that the Indus Water Treaty was in the clutches of controversy between the two, especially over share and quantity of water and differences about certain projects. Tulbul, Baglihar and Kishanganga, Dulhasti, Bursar, Nemo-Bazgo projects have posed serious challenges to India, Pakistan and to the Indus Water Treaty itself. These projects have also intensified the possibility for future conflicts at various levels.

Given the present circumstances and discussions over utilisation of water, it seems that the treaty has limited the ability of both countries to manage and utilise water resources in an efficient manner. It appears that finding solutions in terms of water utilisation beyond the treaty is the best and viable option for both the countries. Hence, it can be suggested that both the countries will have to take steps are to resolve the issue of water management and utilization to maintain peace and harmony of the region.

References:

- Admin, 2009. Kishan Ganga Hydro Power Project and its Effects OnNeelum Jhelum Hydel Project: views to news press 26 october 2009.
- Ahmed, Tufail(2009, July31) Water disputes between India and Pakistan, Henary Jackson Society.
- Ahmad, Azhar(2012), Indus Waters Treaty A dispassionate analysis, Monthly Digest, 209(1), 1-14.
- Akhtar, Shaheen(2010), Emerging challenges to Indus Water Treaty, FOCUS, XXVIII(3),15-25.
- Annan Kofi, World Water Day 2002 "Indus Waters Treaty and Resolution of Water Conflicts Between Two Nuclear Nations (Pakistan and India)".
- Begum Toheeda, Nosheen, "Indus Water Treaty & Emerging Water Issues" Abasyn Journal of Social Sciences. Vol.4 No.2.

- Bernauer T. (1997). Managing international rivers. In: Global governance: Drawing insights from the environmental experience, O. R. Young, (eds.), Massachusetts Institute of Technology Press, Cambridge, pp. 155–197.
- Bhatti, J. A., 2011. Indo-Pakistan Water Dispute. Available at: http://www.waterpakistan.com/indo-pakistan-water-dispute/#respond.
- Bhuttazafar(2011), Kishanganga dam: is partial stay order a comprehensive victory for Pakistan? TRIBUNE.
- Chari PR, 2004, Indus Waters Treaty-II Optimizing the Potential, IPCS Discussion Paper.
- Dawn (2010). The daily Dawn 20th February, 2010. An article by Ahmad Bilal Sufi.
- Gulhatiniranjan D (1973), The Indus Water Treaty, An Exercise in International Mediation, Bombay, Allied Publishers.
- Global Water Partnership (GWP), 2009. A Handbook For Integrated Water Resources Management In Basins. Published by Global Water Partnership (GWP) and International Network of Basin Organization (INBO).
- Khan, raja Mohammad (2011March9), Implications of US warning for a water War, The Frontier Post.
- Khan, S.M. (2008). Economics of Indus Basin Treaty, www.cssforum.com.pk.
- Kugelman, M., and Robert, M. H., 2009. Running on Epmty Pakistan's water crisis. Woodrow Wilson International Center for Scholars, Washington, D.C.
- Mohammad Hafiz Ammad,2011, Water Sharing in the Indus River Basin: Application of Integrated Water Resources Management
- Manzoor Dr., Ahmad Malik, Dr. Muhammad AslamTahir and Engr. Ahmad ZeeshanBhatti ,2015, Pak-India Transboundary Cooperation on Shared Water Resources – Past and Present Perspective.

- Misra,A., 2007. An Audit of India Pakistan Peace Process. Australian Journal of International Affairs, Vol. 61, No.4, Pp506-528.
- Noorani, A. G., 1995. 'CBMs for the Siachen Glacier, Sir Creek and Wullar Barrage', Crisis Prevention, Confidence Building and Reconciliation in South Asia (St. Martin's Press, New York).
- Parasi, G., 2010. India, Pakistan resolveBaglihar Dam Issue. The Hindu News. Available at: http://www.thehindu.com/news/article443923.ece.
- Polgreen, L. and Tavernise, S. (2010, July 20). Water dispute increases India- Pakistan tension, The New York Times.
- Priscoli, J.D. (1996). Conflict resolution, collaboration and management in international water resource issues, Alternative Dispute Resolution Series, Working Paper no. 6. US Army Corps of Engineers, p. 3.
- Ramaswamy Iyer (2010), Water through Pakistan eyes.
- Raza, S.I., 2010. India told to stop work on Kishanganga dam. Dawn News Sep.25, 2011. Available at: http://www.dawn.com/2011/09/25/india-told-to-stop-work-on-kishangangadam.html.
- Sachan Bandana, Haq Prof. Nisarul, 2015, "Importance Of Water Sharing Treaties Between India, Pakistan And Bangladesh" Jan. 2015. Vol. 4, No.9.
- SattarAbdul(2007), Pakistan's Foreign Policy(1947-2005), Karachi, Oxford University Press.
- Sharma, Rajeev (2007), Uri Project, Pakistan threatens to approach WB, Tribune.
- Shaukat, S., 2010. India plays the Water Card. Available at:http://newsgroups.derkeiler.com/Archive/Sci/sci.military.naval/2010-04/msg00358.html.
- SiddiquiH. Iqtidar(2010), Hydro politics and water wars in South Asia, Lahore, Vanguard Books.
- Sify News, 2010. Pak Serveslegal notice to India over Kishanganga dam construction issue.

- Singh Richa, "Trans-boundary Water Politics and Conflicts in South Asia: Towards 'Water for Peace", New Delhi-110016.
- Sridhar seema(2008), Kashmir and Water: conflict and cooperation inshahidimtiaz Advanced Contemporary Affairs(Ed), Lahore: Advanced Publishers, pp 263-269.
- Swain, A., 2009. The Indus II and Siachen Peace Park: Pushing the India-Pakistan Peace Process forward. Uppsala center for sustainable development, Department of peace and conflict research, University of Uppsala, Sweden.
- Tabassum, shaista(2001), The role of CBM in resolving non-military issues between India and Pakistan: A case study of the Indus Water Treaty,InAhmerMoonis(Ed), The challenge of confidence-building measures in South Asia, New Delhi, Haranand Publications,p.396.
- Tariq, Muhammad sardar(2009), The Indus Water Treaty and Emerging water management issues in Pakistan, Problems and Politics of water sharing in Pakistan, Islamabad, Policy Research Institute, pp 87-90.
- Tariq Sardar Muhammad, 2014, "Managing the Indus Waters: Alternative Strategies" Institute of peace and Conflict Studies.
- The Express Tribune, January 12th, 2012. An article published.
- Uprety, K., and Salman, S.M.A., 2010. Legal Aspect of Sharing and Management of Transboundary Waters Insouth Asia Preventing Conflicts and Promoting Cooperation. Hydrological Sciences Journal.
- WasiNausheen, sep.2009, "Harnessing the Indus Waters perspectives from Pakistan", IPCS Issue brief 128.
- Waseem, A. (2007). Irrigation Engineering II. Pinto, Jeffrey K. (2009). Project Management - Achieving Competitive Advantage (Custom Edition). Upper Saddle River, New Jersey: Pearson. ISBN 978-0-558-20289-7 (Dulhasti HE Project).

Chapter-III

Conflict on water between India and Pakistan

Introduction

The twentieth century British poet WH Auden, once said, "Thousands have lived without love, not one without water." His words are especially relevant in the context of South Asia, which is home to more than a fifth of the world's population and where the economies are largely dependent upon agriculture.

Unfortunately, South Asian countries, particularly India and Pakistan, have both faced challenges in water management and proper river basin management. The consequence of this has been a severe water crisis, which has a bearing on both ground and surface water. A cursory glance at the data on fresh water availability per person, per year reveals this vulnerability. South Asia's renewable freshwater resources are about 1,200 cubic meters per capita. In comparison, a large number of countries have between 2,500 – 15,000 cubic meters per capita. Some like Canada and Norway have over 70,000 cubic meters per capita (World Bank 2017).

The difficulties in managing surface water are especially complex in South Asia. River basins are the ultimate source of all water used in households, agriculture and industry (like hydropower companies), as well as the receptors of most wastewater. The system of rivers in the Indus basin comprises 2,000 miles of the river Indus and its five tributaries from the East - Jhelum, Chenab, Ravi, Beas and Sutlej, with an aggregate length of often transgress international borders. Since actions upstream can lead to disruption of the natural flow of rivers, water pollution, diversion of the waters with the occasional threat of even blocking the flow of water, water sharing can often lead to political tensions and acrimony, as has happened in the case of India and Pakistan. The lower riparian countries become especially vulnerable. Effective river basin management therefore necessitates that water users take into account the relationships, interaction and impact that their actions have on others, especially those downstream (Vaid&Maini 2012).

The India Pakistan water dispute started immediately after India gained independence from the British in 1947, and the subcontinent was partitioned to form the two countries. The dispute is serious not just because it concerns water, but also because of the ongoing political rivalry.

The Indus Water Treaty, which was signed in 1960, has remained intact for more than 50 years even during periods of unrest. Under the treaty, India gained control over the Sutlej, Ravi, and Beas rivers, while Pakistan received control over Chenab, Indus, and Jhelum. However, since the Pakistan-controlled rivers first flow through India, in the background of mutual hostility and suspicion between the two countries, Pakistan has the tendency to believe that the water scarcity that they experience is somehow attributable to India (as opined by RamaswamyIyer, the former Secretary for Water Resources in India).

According to the Asian Development Bank report, Pakistan is one of the most water stressed countries in the entire world. According to projections, India will become water stressed by 2025. Pakistan is likely to be classified as water-scarce soon, and India is set to become water-scarce by the year 2050.

Pakistan draws a lot of water from its existing reserves, thus putting the country in great danger of water shortages in the future. According to the Asian Development Bank, the water storage capacity of Pakistan amounts only to a 30 day supply, significantly lower than the 1000 days that is recommended for countries that have a similar climate. Correspondingly, the water storage capacity of India is 120 days.

The Indus Water Treaty, at the time, was the best option that both countries could get after a long negotiation of eight years. It was not the best treaty, but it was the only one that was acceptable by both. As time passed, increasing water pressure has put new demands on both countries. In order to address the current situation, the treaty needs to be amended, but this does not seem likely because of recurring conflicts and ongoing bilateral tensions.

In 1947, when the subcontinent was partitioned, India and Pakistan were born to become rivals. Several other conflicts have also had an impact on the water relationship between the two countries.

One of the reasons why Pakistan suffers greatly with respect to water is because of its weak lower riparian status. Also, the country does not have a good supply-side management structure. This results in wastage of almost 35 percent of its water resources. An imbalance in water distribution across Pakistan is also another reason for some areas getting less water than required.

The ongoing water stress contributes to the turbulence and conflict between India and Pakistan, but it is not likely to cause a full-blown water war. Both countries are taking steps to adapt and survive with the help of desalination plants and drip-in irrigation.

For a long lasting solution to the water problem, the Indus water Commissioners must learn to trust each other. Rather than an asset to water as a source of conflict, both countries must start looking at it as a source of cooperation. Though it may not immediately solve any problems, the change in narrative will definitely have an impact in thinking for the future.

Indo-Pak water dispute: The origins

India and Pakistan have been at odds since the partition of British India in 1947. After nine years of negotiations, the

Indus Waters Treaty (IWT) was finally signed on September 19, 1960, with the cooperation of the World Bank. Future prospects persuaded the two countries to agree to a partition of the Indus Basin waters. Both countries were expected to exploit their respective water shares with the help of an Indus Basin Development Fund to be administered by the World Bank.

Pakistan referred the Wular Barrage case to the Indus Waters Commission in 1986, which, in 1987, recorded its failure to resolve it. However, in February 1992, Pakistan added another condition that India should not construct the Kishanganga (390 MW) hydropower- generating unit. India refused to accept this condition. According to Pakistan, the Kishanganga project on River Neelam affected its own Neelam-Jhelum power- generating project, located in its Punjab province. The issue of Wular Barrage was one of the disputes on the agenda highlighted for the Indo-Pak talks, both at the Lahore meeting in February 1999, and at the Agra Summit of July, 2001 (International Union for Conservation of Nature and Natural Resources, 2010).

Under dispute since 1992, the Baglihar Dam on the Chenab River is nearing completion in 2009. The river runs from India directly through Jammu and Kashmir and then into Pakistan. However, Pakistan has opposed the hydroelectric plant's construction, arguing that its design violates the Indus Water Treaty because of its potential to store or divert waters destined for Pakistan.

The dispute over the proposed Kishanganga dam (330 MW) also remains unresolved. Under the plan, India seeks to build a hydroelectric plant on the Jhelum River in the Jammu and Kashmir region. As with the Baglihar and Tulbul project, Pakistan claims the project violates the Indus Water Treaty because of its down- stream effects. Pakistani officials and environmentalists also argue that this project may "submerge vast tracts of land in the Gurez area and displace local residents". Though India has agreed to review the portions of the project to which Pakistan objects and both sides have gone through several rounds of negotiations, no resolution has been found. As of March 2009, the Pakistan Commission of Indus Water notified India that it would request a World Bank neutral arbitrator to resolve the conflict. Pakistan, meanwhile, is planning construction of the Neelhum-Jhelum Dam along the same river. Like India's project, this endeavour would involve building a hydroelectric plant on Pakistan's side of the Jammu and Kashmir border.

Pakistan has lodged a complaint in the court of arbitration that Indian bid to build Kishanganga dam was violation of World Bank brokered Indus Waters Treaty of 1960. The spokesman further clarified that Pakistan had sought from India an undertaking for construction in the light of international law which the latter had rejected. The International Court of Arbitration (ICA) has issued an interim order, restraining India from going ahead with the controversial hydro power project over river Kishanganga in Gurez area of Jammu Kashmir. Under the ICA order, India will not construct a permanent structure over River Neelum / Kishanganga, as per statement issued by a Presidential spokesman. India will not go ahead with building a structure that may affect the flow of water downstream, the spokesman clarified.

The Indo-Pak dispute on the Indus basin has drawn immense attention in South Asia and across the world, largely due to the nature of the tense political relationship between the two countries. This attention has grown more intense in recent years, in the aftermath of the Mumbai attacks on 26 November 2008, which had kindled fears of a nuclear war. Analysts began exploring, not only the sources of the tension between the two nuclear states but also areas which had the potential for increased cooperation and thereby would reduce the possibility of a war at any point in the future. Water is one such area, especially the Indus basin.

The system of rivers in the Indus basin comprises 2,000 miles of the river Indus and its five tributaries from the East — Jhelum, Chenab, Ravi, Beas and Sutlej, with an aggregate length of 2,800 miles (Arora 2007). Most of the upper reaches of the Indus basin lie in India. All these rivers combine in Mithankot in Pakistan and flow into the Arabian Sea near Karachi.

The Indus system of rivers has been used for irrigation ever since civilization took root in the area. The water disputes too date back to the pre-partition era, when there were significant inter-state differences between Punjab, Sind, Bahawalpur and Bikaner (Ibid). After Pakistan was created in 1947, this inter-state dispute amongst the four states became an international water dispute between the two newly formed nation states. The issues around water sharing were now between West Punjab of Pakistan and East Punjab of India. Lands on the West (which are today part of Pakistan) are fertile and the British, wanting to take advantage of the fact, developed the Indus Basin irrigation system. On the other hand, the land in Haryana and the East Punjab (which is today part of India) was not considered particularly fertile. At the time of Partition, Sir Cyril Radcliffe, who was entrusted with the task of boundary demarcation, drew a line across the Indus, dividing not just the land, but the waters and the integrated Indus canal system. Thus, at Independence, the newly formed states had the onerous responsibility of finding a proper mechanism to share and jointly manage the irrigation system for the future (Verghese, 2011).

Over the years, India built its irrigation system which could serve the needs of Himachal Pradesh, Punjab, Haryana and Rajasthan. On the other side, the fact that the source of the rivers of the Indus basin were in India resulted in fear of droughts and famine in Pakistan. In fact, until the signing of the Indus Water Treaty (IWT) in Karachi on 19 September 1960, significant disagreements persisted between the two countries. To quote a defining example, although the Inter-Dominion Conference was held in May 1948, and an agreement between the two countries was signed, wherein India assured Pakistan of not withdrawing water delivery, without allowing time for Pakistan to develop alternate sources, Pakistan communicated its dissatisfaction with the ground situation. On 16 June 1949, Pakistan sent a note to India which called for a conference to resolve the "equitable apportionment of all common water" and suggested giving the World Court jurisdiction on the application of either party. But India categorically objected to third party involvement and instead suggested that judges from each side be allowed to narrow the disputes first (Arora 2007, 63).

In August 1951, Eugene Black, President of the World Bank, invited prime ministers of both the countries to Washington and they finally agreed on an outline of essential principles and arrived at a common understanding that neither side will reduce the river water supplies for existing uses (Ibid:64).

The World Bank then came out with its own proposal which suggested division of the western tributaries to Pakistan, and the eastern tributaries to India, besides a proposal of continued deliveries to Pakistan during transition period of ten years. India accepted the proposal while Pakistan gave its qualified acceptance on March 25, 1954. Later when the World Bank arranged an international Indus Basin Development Fund and raised $893 million, the Indus Water Treaty was finally signed by both the countries on 19 September 1960. The World Bank effectively brokered a settlement on the dispute arising out of water sharing of Indus River and it continues to play a significant role whenever the two countries are unable to resolve issues bilaterally in this area.

Conflict Definition

Indus water basin comprises of six rivers Indus, Jhelum, Chenab, Sutlej, Beas and Ravi. The Indus River originates from Tibet, flowing through India, Pakistan and Afghanistan carrying glacial waters and eventually emptying into the Arabian Sea. Pakistan accounts for 60 percent of the catchment area of the Indus basin, India about 20 percent, Tibet about 15 percent and Afghanistan about 5 percent. These rivers flow through the Indian Territory and then into Pakistan, thus making India the upper riparian country and Pakistan, the lower riparian country. The transboundary waters of the Indus and its tributaries are shared by India and Pakistan regulated by the Indus water treaty (IWT) that was signed in 1960. According to the treaty India has exclusive rights to Ravi, Beas, Sutlej, and Pakistan has rights to Indus, Jhelum, and Chenab.

Since the 1960s India and Pakistan have fought three wars and the Indus Water Treaty has prevented water to be used as a tool in the conflict. Thus, the IWT is usually cited as one of the world's most successful water sharing undertaking. Currently, rapid economic development through the construction of irrigation infrastructure, population growth and pollution of watershed has hampered distribution of water supply thus, escalating tensions between the two nations. Overexploitation of water resources coupled with climate change impacts such as melting of glaciers and irregular monsoons, has posed a serious environmental security challenge. Any sort of water stress is an existential crisis and as the Indus water basin affects over a billion people, there is a fear that these recent developments can trigger a conflict between the two nations. The Indus basin is also seen as a key strategic interest as its headwaters originate from Kashmir which is a region of dispute between the two countries. In light of current events of terrorist

129

activities that has affected India and allegedly perpetrated from across the border, Indian Prime Minister NarendraModi said "Blood and water cannot flow at the same time". It appears from his statements that water could be used as a diplomatic weapon in the future. Lack of trust between the two nations due to historical and political reasons, inefficient institutional mechanisms and a rigid nature of the IWT has proven to be a huge roadblock for successful transboundary water governance (Kaushik, 2017).

Water conflicts between India and Pakistan

Water conflicts over the distribution of Indus basin dates back to the 19th century but at that time these were international conflicts between the provinces of Indian sub-continent, which were supposed to be resolved by the British India. The British India was able to resolve the first major dispute in 1935 through arbitration by the 'Anderson Commission'. When the demand for irrigation water increased over the next few years, new water related dispute emerged which was resolved again in 1942 by the 'Rao Commission'. With the partition of united India, the Indus basin was also divided between India and Pakistan in 1947 (Barrett, 1994; Rehman and Kamal, 2005); what left the control of Pakistan's irrigation water in the hands of India, geographically. Therefore, water conflicts between the two nations started soon after independence in 1948, when India claimed sovereign rights over the waters passing through its territory and diverted these waters away from Pakistan. This illegitimate control of rivers threatened war when India refused Pakistan's proposal of neutral arbitration to settle down the conflict. Later on, the World Bank offered its neutral services to resolve the conflict and both India and Pakistan agreed.

The proposal of joint use and development of the Indus basin as a single water resource was refused in 1952 over the concern of national sovereignty by both, what lead to the division of the Indus and its tributaries. According to this proposal, India was offered three eastern rivers (Ravi, Beas and Sutlej), while Pakistan was offered three western rivers (Indus, Jhelum and Chenab). India was also supposed to provide monetary fund's to construct canals and storage dams to replace Pakistan's irrigation supplies from the eastern rivers to western rivers. However, India refused to pay for the construction of storage dams, which was then settled through external finance with the help of the World Bank. Since Indus Waters Treaty (IWT) signed In September 1960, many controversies have arisen over the design and construction of different projects on both sides of the basin, some of which have been resolved and others are yet to be resolved (Barrett, 1994).

From December 2001 to June 2002, India was vocally considering pulling out of the treaty as one of the steps of hitting back at Pakistan for its alleged support of terrorist outfits targeting India, and in turn Pakistan has stated that it would be prepared to use nuclear weapons over a water crisis (Wirsing and Jasparro, 2006). A senior Pakistani diplomat, among other regional experts, confirms, -Water has become the core issue between India and Pakistan (Wirsing and Jasparro, 2006 and Sridhar, 2005).

Non-implementation over Indus Basin Treaty in true letter and spirit has threatened the regional and global peace and serious attention to resolve the issue between two rival nuclear states. Both the countries have conflict over the construction, alterations of various barrages and dams over rivers Chenab and Jhelum. In short, we can say that the International legal system has changed and evolved through modification in the United Nations but still needs to be revised according to the changing political situation or emergence of new states. The recent decision of ICA in the case of Indo-Pak water conflict over Kishangnaga and other projects have not been well received by Pakistan. According to the decision ICA upheld India's right to divert water from the Kishanganga Hydroelectric Project (KHEP) (Z. Hasan, 2012). In a partial award ICA permitted on 18 February to divert a minimum flow of water from Neelum/Kishanganga River for power generation (Bokhari, 2013). Reportedly, India got benefit of the situation and started construction of three other projects over River Chenab which will likely to further deteriorate the availability of water to Pakistan ("Water Row: Govt. objects to Indian hydel projects on Chenab", 2013). Further improvement in international legal system can be done while carrying out some modification in the charter of regional organization like SAARC.

Key issues of contention

Water sharing between the two neighbors has been characterized by intermittent conflict and long sustained cooperation. However, recent issues have brought the sustainability of the IWT under serious scrutiny. Twenty-seven projects undertaken by India in the Indus basin in Jammu and Kashmir have been questioned by Pakistan. This has resulted in delays in implementation, prohibitive increases in costs, and stalling of development in J&K. Three of the most contentious issues, the BagliharHydel Power Project (BHP), Tulbul Navigation Project (TNP), and Kishanganga Project are discussed below.

Baglihar

The 900 megawatt (MW) BHP on the Chenab River in Doda district in Jammu stands out as a key issue between India and Pakistan. It was also the first ever to be referred for international arbitration through the dispute resolution mechanism under Article IX of the IWT. Pakistan feared that the BhP would divert considerable downstream flows and could also be used to cause floods in the riparian areas. Similar objections were raised by Pakistan over Salal, a 480 MW hydropower project on the Chenab in 1978, that storage could be used for drying up flows as well as for flooding the lower riparian states. However, any attempt to flood Pakistan would inundate the Indian side of the Line of Control (LoC) first. Such action would also run counter to the rules of war and against the Geneva Conventions, inviting international condemnation. It is highly unlikely, therefore, that India would indulge in such an act and such fears are thus unfounded. India's agreement to make design changes in the Salal dam has resulted in severe siltage problems and India was wary of a repetition of the same. In response to Pakistan's objections over the BHP, India contended that as it was a run of the river project, the water utilized for power generation would be released back into the river stream and therefore there would be no difference in the quantum of water release. Both India and Pakistan tried to resolve the issue through bilateral talks. Pakistan's demand to shelve construction work until the issue gets resolved was not heeded by India, as the latter did not want a repetition of the TNP, which has been shelved since 1987. Since no breakthrough was achieved, Pakistan sought arbitration of a neutral expert under the ambit of the IWT to look into the matter. The report by the neutral expert, Raymond Laffitte, vindicated the Indian position that the BHP was not in violation of the Indus Waters Treaty. Design changes, including reductions in freeboard and pondage and increase in the height of the power intakes, were recommended. The neutral expert over- ruled Pakistan's objections over the use of gated spill- ways, as it is one of the most important techniques to handle the problem of sedimentation. The verdict on the BHP case will hopefully establish momentum for building such projects in the conflict-ridden state, to augment developmental work there.

Although, both countries tried hard to settle the issue by themselves but bilateral negotiation did not bear any productive result. So, first time in the history of IWT, on January 15, 2005, Pakistan asked for World Bank to appoint a neutral expert to resolve the differences over Baghliar Dam. After five months of the original request, Raymond Lafitte, Professor of Swiss Institute of Technology in Lausanne was appointed as a neutral expert to address the differences regarding Baglihar project.

In February, 2007, Lafitte delivered his final decision to both parties and also one copy of decision to World Bank. In his report he partly addressed some objections of Pakistan like, reduced the pondage capacity, increased 3m height of power intake and acknowledged India's right to construct gated spillway. Both countries agreed to follow the final decision of the neutral expert.

But, the dispute again got activated when, India filled the dam during the dry season in 2008 that seriously disturbed the livelihood and agriculture production of Pakistan. Pakistani media and local people blamed that India stole water having rights of Pakistan. The filing of Baglihar dam above Marala reduced the flow as low as 20000 cusec, whereas India obliged to maintain the minimum inflow at the level of 55,000 cusec. Pakistan lost about 2 MAF of water from August 25, 2008 to September 4, 2008 and it adversely affected Pakistan's wheat crop. President of Pakistan even raised the issue in his speech to the UN General Assembly. Pakistan strongly protested and claimed that India is violating the IWT. But this time, Pakistan decided to solve the issue by negotiation. Indian commission admitted that reduction was because of unavailability of any mechanism to pass the flow at the low level. He explained that this happened because we were expecting heavy rainfall during these days. Pakistan's Indus commissioner in an interview told that although "Pakistan felt that parameter and procedure mentioned in IWT were not followed during the initial filling of the dam. We have resolved the differences on the initial filling of the dam in a spirit of cooperation and good will and India gave us the insurance that it will be careful in future" (Muhammad Rashid 2013).

Tulbul Navigation Project

The Tulbul Navigation Project, called as Wullar barrage in Pakistan, is part of the composite dialogue within the framework of the peace process under-way between India and Pakistan (unlike the BHP, which was referred for international arbitration). The TNP originally envisaged the construction of 439-feet long and 40-feet wide barrage by India in 1984 on the River Jhelum, at the mouth of Wullar Lake, near Sopore in Kashmir. With a maximum storage capacity of 0.30 million acre feet (MAF), it was intended to maximize the utilization of water at India's largest fresh water lake, making the Jhelum navigable by regulating water storage in the Wullar through enhancing currents in the Jhelum during the lean months from November to February. Pakistan claims the TNP is in violation of the IWT, believing it could be used by India to control the river's flow as a geo-strategic weapon. The Indian stance is that the purpose of the barrage is to make the river navigable in summer and not to affect the outflows into Pakistan. The barrage, according to Pakistan, would impede flows into their Upper Chenab Canal and the Lower Bari Doab Canals. The case was referred to the Indus Waters Commission in 1986, but failed to be resolved. Before Pakistan could move to the International Arbitral Court, India stopped construction and the project has been shelved ever since 1987. The most recent talks in August 2007 in the fourth round of composite dialogue ended in conclusively. In 1991, a draft agreement was prepared, which allowed the construction of the barrage with certain technical stipulations—such as leaving 6.2 meters of barrage ungated, reducing general storage capacity by 30,000 acre feet—with due monitoring by the Indus Water Commissioners. However, the draft agreement was not signed, since Pakistan linked its resolution to the 390 MW Kishanganga Hydro- Electric Project, another unresolved issue between the countries, and demanded that India should forego its construction. The 1991 draft could be used as a basis for resolution as it asserted that the issue would be resolved within the scope of the IWT. Each contentious issue has to be resolved separately for giving resolution a real chance. The tremendous potential of waterways in J&K needs to be utilized and reaching a consensus over such projects is imperative.

Kishanganga

The Kishanganga Project entails a 75 meter high concrete dam at Gurez at about 8,000 feet to store 140,000 MAF of water and divert some flows through a 22 km tunnel bored into the mountain into the Madmati Nala, which empties into the Wullar Lake. Kishanganga, called Neelum on the other side of the LoC, is a tributary that flows into the Jhelum near Nowshera (close to Muzaffarabad). Inter-tributary transfer is allowed under the IWT. Pakistan's objection is that the water is not transferred into the same tributary Neelum, although it finally gets into the Jhelum. It also fears that the project would flush the Wullar Lake. India informed Pakistan about the project in 1994, while Pakistan contends that the construction of a dam on the Neelum near Nowshera had been underway for irrigation purposes and those 133,000 hectares were already being irrigated at that time. Pakistan's Water and Power Development Authority (WAPDA) does not show this as one of its projects, and there is no evidence to substantiate this claim. According to India, the work on the Kishanganga Project commenced well before the Neelum project, while Pakistan insists to the contrary. Determination of the "existing use" of water that will get affected and the date that is to be taken into account for the same are the major issues of the dispute, among others. The water sharing environment in South Asia is fast deteriorating. The Pakistani frustration at Indian inflexibility was evident when it referred the matter of Baghliar Dam on

River Chenab to the World Bank in January 2005. The verdict by a neutral expert, appointed by the bank ultimately settled the issue in February 2007. The decision accommodated both the parties and each country felt that its respective stance had been addressed and vindicated. The problem did not end there; within four years, the two countries are back for arbitration over the water issue and the bone of contention this time is construction by India of the Kishanganga Storage-cum-Hydroelectric Power Project on River Neelum (Indians call it Kishanganga), which is a major tributary of River Jhelum. Iftikhar (2011) points out that: "The matter is sensitive because not only the dam will curtail the flow of water for agriculture, but Pakistan is also constructing the Neelum-Jhelum Hydroelectric Project on River Neelum, downstream of Kishanganga Project." Pakistan's fundamental objection to Kishanganga is that it involves diverting the water of Neelum River through a 21km long tunnel towards the Wullar Lake to generate 330MW power. This is manifestly not allowed by the IWT. Iftikhar indicates: "This diversion is against the provisions of the IWT and has not only serious consequence for the 969MW power generation capability of Neelum- Jhelum Hydrolectrical Project, but will also reduce the water supply for agriculture in the areas of Azad Kashmir, which are dependent on the Neelum River flow. It is estimated that the diversion of water towards Wullar Lake will reduce flow into Pakistan by 27 percent (Ibid). According to the available data, it is estimated that, "the dry spell is likely to extend to eight months per year. The lack of water is going to have an adverse impact on the agriculture in over thousands of acres in Azad Kashmir, which are dependent upon the flow of River Neelum, besides causing damage to the environmental aspects of flora and fauna nurtured by the rivers flow in the Neelum Valley" (Ibid). Kazi (2011) supports the view that, "the proposed Kishenganga project violates the treaty in a most glaring way. Firstly, the hydroelectric plant is not located on the Kishanganga but way off the channel at the end of a long tunnel that discharges into another tributary. And, secondly, the recipient tributary ultimately outfalls upstream of the Wullar Lake, and this completely changes the patterns of the flows of both Kishanganga and Jhelum Rivers"(Muhammad Rashid 2013).

Objectives of India on Kishanganga Project

The Indian objectives over the construction of Kishanganga hydropower projects are:

- To augment power output of Uri Hydel Power Project (480 MW) by additional regulating water.
- To augment supplies in the Wullar Lake for use during the lean period.
- To utilize the hydroelectric potential of J&K for the states of Punjab, Haryana, Himachal Pradesh, Chandigarh, Rajasthan and Delhi (Ammad Hafiz Mohammad).

Factors which can lead to conflicts over water resource sharing between India and Pakistan

There are various factors which may lead to conflicts between states or groups who share scarce resources. Most conflicts arise when there is perception that one group is unduly benefiting at the expense of another. This is made worse when resources being shared are scarce, and are required by a lot of people. The Pakistan-India conflict over the water resource is one example. Various factors which lead to conflicts over water sharing will be briefly analyzed below;

Population growth

Population growth is a major factor which puts pressure on resources. Population growth leads to the over-utilization of resources, and in case these resources are scarce, the population needs are not met. In such circumstances, this may lead to the development of conflict. Water is a scarce resource in many countries. When population growth exhausts the available water resource or the growth rate does not match the increase in water resources, then population needs will not be met, leading to conflict. The population will be unable to acquire safe water for consumption and adequate water for agriculture, especially in agrarian economies. In such cases, political instability may occur as citizen's fight for their right to access a water resource. This conflict may begin at a local level and gradually escalate to a matter of international concern as in the case of Pakistan and India.

Weak treaties

Weak treaties are another major source of international conflict. Sometimes, treaties are used when sharing resources to ensure all parties acquire a reasonable stake in the resource. Treaties which are weak are those which may be ambiguous, those which do not anticipate future trends and those with loopholes among others. Weak treaties are bound to generate conflicts over time, as each party to the treaty analyzes their benefits from the treaty and seeks ways of maximizing benefits. When one or more parties realize that the treaty does not favour them, they are likely to rescind their decision to follow the treaty.

However, one mistake which often occurs when making treaties, and is the cause of conflict between Pakistan and India, is the inability to project future trends and needs. When the Indus treaty was made in 1960, adequate projections on the water needs of both countries, in decades to come, were not properly done. It was therefore impossible to factor into account exceptions where either country would be allowed to construct dams in the various rivers, and their repercussions to those relying on such rivers for agriculture. It is necessary for treaties to factor in dynamic nature of the world in order to avoid future conflicts over water resource sharing.

Inadequate water conservation measures

When many countries discover a resource, they exploit it until it gets depleted without understanding the consequences of depletion of the resource. Water resources are no exception, and unless they are conserved, they are likely to be depleted or used ineffectively. Many poor countries do not conserve water although it is a scarce resource. Such countries are unable to meet the population needs when these water resources dry up, or have declining levels. As it will later be discussed, Pakistan loses millions of cubic meters of water daily due to lack of water conservation efforts. When such losses occur, the country is unable to satisfy its citizens' water demands. The inability to meet this need is blamed on other factors and this may create conflict between two or more nations.

Declining water levels

The water capacity in Pakistan has been declining over the years and it poses a threat to the survival of its population within the next decade. Pakistan had water crisis during 2009 due to the reduction of its water capacity. In 2009 its water capacity was 1200 cubic meters while in 1950 it was 5000 cubic meters. This figure is expected to reduce to 800 cubic meters over the next decade. Scientists warn that Pakistan will face a water disaster within the next three years if interventions to ensure availability of water are not implemented.

Reduction of available water from India's Baglihar Dam

As has been stated, there is a great concern that the construction of the Baglihar Dam will deprive Pakistan of water. Pakistan is of the opinion that further reduction in water capacity can be attributed to India's construction of the Baglihar Dam. Scientists explain that over 320,000 acre feet of water will be lost from the construction of this dam. This will adversely affect agricultural activities such as the production of wheat in the province of Punjab. In addition, irrigated land around Ravi and Chenab rivers is set to be adversely affected due to the reduced water capacity.

Climate change

Climate change has had severe impacts on available resources. Environmental destruction has led to unpredictable and adverse weather conditions across the world. Such weather conditions include drought, floods, heat waves and others. In economies which heavily rely on agriculture, these conditions may cause heavy losses. When drought or winter occurs, and there is a limited water resource, this may lead to conflict over this resource especially if a nation has not taken enough water conservation measures. The latest dispute involving Pakistan and India relates to construction of a dam, and Pakistan argues that climate change will bring harsh winters, which will reduce the river flow as a consequence of diversion of the river by India.

Poor political leadership

Leadership in any country entails the distribution of resources. All leaders should ensure that available resources are distributed and used for the welfare of the majority population in the nation. When there are good leaders, even scarce resources are effectively used and conserved to ensure that they satisfy the country's needs. However, in cases where the leadership is weak, the available resources are misappropriated or used for the benefit of a few. This leads to wastage, and the majority population does not have access to such resources. In this case, conflict over the limited water resource is likely to occur. The dispute between India and Pakistan can be partly blamed for weak leadership which is hesitant in solving the issues present.

Nuclear nations

Like China's acquisition of the bomb, India and Pakistan's evolution into regional nuclear powers changed the stakes of total war forever. These declared nuclear states will now have to carefully weigh every decision to wage war. In particular, the perception that India directly threatens the survivability of Pakistan may convince Pakistan to use nuclear weapons as a last resort. In fact, the nuclear doctrines of India and Pakistan paint a scary picture that supports the possibility of nuclear exchange if certain red lines are crossed.

India's nuclear doctrine is much different from Pakistan's. The National Security Advisory Board published India's draft doctrine in 1999. India, unlike Pakistan, does not have any stated nuclear red lines. In fact, it proclaims a retaliatory, no first-use policy with the goal of nuclear deterrence. Therefore, concern arises from the possibility of a nuclear strike from Pakistan. If initiated, the outcome of a nuclear volley would be catastrophic, leaving the countries devastated and regional security in shambles.

Pakistan's nuclear doctrine is shrouded in secrecy. However, there are a number of public statements by senior Pakistani officials that help clarify the picture. Major General Khalid Kidwai, in a late 2000 interview, illuminated critical elements of Pakistan's nuclear doctrine. First and foremost, it is obvious that Pakistan's nuclear doctrine is directed at India. Second, he plainly laid out the red lines that, if crossed, would cause Pakistan to use nuclear weapons against India. These scenarios include the loss of a large part of Pakistan's territory, destruction of a large part of Pakistan's military, economic strangulation, or other attempts to politically destabilize Pakistan.

The looming tensions over water resources highlight the importance of the economic strangulation red line. This red line seems to be the most likely to be crossed; however, it is important to note that this red line reportedly consists of two parts–stemming the water from the Indus River and simultaneously blockading key Pakistani ports. However, it is unknown whether Pakistan will wait until both are accomplished. If it perceives that India is posing a clear and present danger to its survival as a state, it may resort to the use of nuclear weapons. Therefore, it is clear that the problem should be resolved before it spirals out of control, given the many ongoing tensions over aspects of the Indus Water Treaty that challenge the relevance of the treaty (jamesf.brenan).

Evaluation of the Treaty

The Indus Water Treaty 1960 is criticized in both the countries. It is considered as a successful treaty for the conflict-resolution between the two countries that have otherwise been locked in conflict. The treaty remained in place despite the three wars. Though the people of both countries criticize the Treaty, still it is relevant. The Treaty has some causes of the opposition as well as some factors of its survival.

Causes of the opposition to the treaty

i) Water sharing

Indus water treaty myth : According to Haris Gazdar, Indus Treaty is a myth. "A myth has grown that the IWT is a model of good neighbourliness in an otherwise conflict-ridden bilateral relationship. It is common for contemporary commentators to repeat analyses such as, "the IWT is perhaps the most successful confidence-building measure (CBM) between the two countries [having] remained intact all these years, surviving two wars and several phases of conflict". Such judgments are about the political and technical basis of the IWT. The admirers of the treaty appear to be unaware that the terms of the treaty actually require virtually no cooperation between the two parties"(Gazdar 2005).

Ramaswamy Iyer argues, —the thrust of Haris Gazdar's article is that the Indus Treaty is an 'unequal' one; that Pakistan has failed to look after its riparian rights and entitlements; that the division of the waters was more or less on the lines sought by India. In appearance, it is a scholarly paper, but it fails to rise above a nationalistic and partisan approach. In India, many feel that the allocation of 80 percent of the waters to Pakistan and 20 per cent to India was an unfair settlement. It is foolishly accepted by the Indian negotiators; and many in Pakistan argue that the territories that went to India under Partition were historically using less than 10 per cent of the waters, and that the Treaty was generous to India in giving it 20 per cent of the waters. Both are fallacious arguments.

According to Iyer, Haris Gazdar may be surprised to know that his criticisms of the Treaty from the Pakistani point of view (unequal, poorly negotiated, negligent of riparian rights, not in the national interest, etc) will be fully endorsed by a strong body of opinion in India, but from exactly the opposite point of view, namely, the Indian one! There are many in India who feel that the Treaty is unfair to India, that our negotiators did a bad job, that they gave away far more water to Pakistan than that country was entitled to under any fair sharing principle, and that the Treaty should be repudiated or renegotiated. When such voices were raised in 2002, Ramaswamy Iyer wrote against them. He argued that when a Treaty emerges from prolonged intercountry negotiations by teams acting under governmental briefing, and the Treaty is approved and signed at the highest levels, it must be presumed that it was the best outcome that could be negotiated under the given circumstances, and that we are then precluded from saying that it was unfair, unequal, etc. (Iyer 2005) Gazadar characterizes the treaty as a myth. However, the international view of the Treaty is as a great example of successful conflict-resolution.

ii) The Kashmir issue

The Kashmir issue has appeared to be the major contention. Kashmir is located at the northwest of India and the northeast of Pakistan. Several important river tributaries flow through or originate from this land, pass through India, and reach Pakistan. For this reason, Kashmir occupies a strategically important geographical location that is crucial for India and Pakistan in order to own the rivers as an upper riparian state. Both nations claim ideological rights over Kashmir. Pakistan owns 33% of Kashmir and has named it Azad Kashmir. The remaining territory of Kashmir, and where the tributaries of major rivers originate, is in the possession of India and is named the territory 0f Jammu and Kashmir (Qureshi, 2017).

Haris Gazdar argues that pending the settlement of the Kashmir dispute, India actually had no riparian claim on the western rivers to begin with. According to Ramaswamy Iyer, Haris Gazdar puts forward the strange proposition that given the disputed nature of Jammu and Kashmir, India had no riparian rights at all over the western rivers that flowed through that territory, and that only the eastern rivers were up for sharing. In any case, the two governments did negotiate on the Indus system including both the western and the eastern rivers and arrived at an allocation that has been enshrined in a Treaty, and that is an implicit recognition of Indian rights (Iyer 2005).

All those projects are in the state of Jammu and Kashmir. There is much unhappiness in the state at the fact that the restrictions placed on India in relation to the western rivers make it virtually impossible for J & K to derive any benefits by way of irrigation, hydroelectric power, and navigation, from the waters of the Jhelum and Chenab rivers. Successive J & K governments and legislatures have complained that the treaty did not take care of the interests of the state. That feeling is shared by the people, media, academics and others in the state. From time to time there have been calls for a scrapping of the treaty.

J & K has huge hydro potential that needs to be

exploited for the benefit of the state and the country as a whole. There is much unhappiness in the state regarding the restrictions placed on the western rivers to derive limited benefits by way of agricultural use and generation of hydroelectric power. It is because of this realisation that a number of political leaders and legislators in J & K have pointed out the huge loss the state is suffering annually. On April 3, 2002, the J & K assembly cutting across the party affiliations called for a review of IWT (Siyad 2005).

Since 1947, Pakistan has demanded a United Nations (UN) administered plebiscite in the Jammu and Kashmir Valley on the allegiance of Kashmir to either India or Pakistan. Despite initially being agreed in 1948 that a plebiscite would be held in Indian side of Kashmir, the Indian authorities never facilitated it. Since then, Kashmir has generated a geopolitical and strategic rivalry between Pakistan and India. This issue has caused the failure of the cooperation and peace process dialogue that has taken place between both states at any moment in their history (Qureshi 2017).

iii) Adversarial Situation Created by Treaty

Pakistan is apprehensive of the structures in question enabling India either to reduce water flows to Pakistan or to release stored waters and cause floods. The Pakistani objections are thus partly water-related and partly security-related. The Indian position is that the security fears are misconceived as India cannot flood Pakistan without flooding itself first and that its capacity to reduce flows to Pakistan is very limited (Iyer, 2005).

iv) Divergent approaches

The Indian engineers would tend to plan and design techno-economically sound projects that would yield the best benefits in the given physical circumstances. Fortunately, the need for techno-economic soundness is recognised in the treaty. On the other hand, in their examination of the Indian plans and designs, the Pakistani engineers with protecting Pakistan's interests, would tend to start from the treaty provisions and limitations as the governing and paramount considerations, and treat techno-economic considerations as secondary. They may possibly be negatively inclined and may try to find grounds for rejecting the Indian proposals. They may suggest changes, modifications or alternatives that may appear techno-economically less sound or less attractive to the latter.

Pakistan tends to accuse India of planning works that are violative of the treaty, withholding information, and not cooperating in a resolution of the difference, and India complains about what it perceives as Pakistan's negativism and deliberate obstruction of any effort by India to utilise even the limited rights given to it on the western rivers.

There is a further political dimension to these differences. Pakistan is perhaps not keen on letting these projects go forward because (a) they are in what it regards as disputed territory, and (b) the benefits of the projects would go to J & K under Indian auspices. Hence, (presumably) the stalemate.Tulbul, Baglihar, etc, might not have proved so difficult to resolve if they had been located not in J & K but elsewhere. Pakistan allowed Salal project to proceed under certain conditions, but not the Baglihar or Kishenganga projects.

v) Differences over Projects

The Pakistani position is that these projects constitute violations of the treaty by India. India denies Pakistan's allegations. The differences over these projects arise from different approaches to, and interpretations of, various provisions of the main text of the treaty. The Article III (4) of the treaty basically precludes the building of any storages by India on the western rivers, except to a limited extent carefully laid down in Annexures D and E, which also specify technical conditions relating to engineering structures and features, such as limits on raising artificially the water level in the operating pool, pondage levels, crest level of the gates (where a gated spillway is considered necessary), location of intakes for the turbines, and so on.

vi) Technical treaty

The first reason is the density of technical details in the treaty, which provides ample opportunities for differences among engineers. It is interesting to compare this treaty with the Mahakali treaty between India and Nepal, or the Ganges treaty between India and Bangladesh. The latter two are relatively nontechnical documents that are easy to understand, even for non-engineers. On the other hand, while the main part of the Indus treaty is fairly slim and not too dense, the devil is in the detail: the treaty is accompanied by several Annexures and Appendices of a highly technical and opaque nature. It is these Annexures and Appendices that determine the overall character of the treaty. Facetiously speaking, one could say that this is not a treaty between two governments, but a treaty between two sets of engineers. The engineers on the two sides can have a field day disagreeing on the meaning and precise application of the various technical features and criteria that the Annexures and Appendices contain. The treaty provides a happy hunting ground for technical disagreements.

The differences are over 'run-of-the-river' projects and 'storages'. The 'run-of-the-river' means the absence of storage. The treaty prohibits storages by India on the western rivers except to a limited extent, but permits run-of-the-river schemes subject to certain conditions. The conventional engineering view is that a diversion barrage or a run-of-the-river hydroelectric project, unlike a dam and a reservoir, does not create any storage. However, even run-of-the-river projects involve structures, and any structure on a river does raise the water level and create a minimal storage. The question then becomes one of the level and acceptability of that storage, and a difference of opinion on this is possible, and has, in fact, occurred. Even a run-of-the river project can be a big project involving a big dam. What India regards as 'run-of-the-river' could be in Pakistan's view a 'storage' project.

vii) Nature of Division under Treaty

The second reason is the nature of the division of waters under the treaty. Having allocated the western rivers to Pakistan, the treaty aims at restraining and not facilitating Indian projects on those rivers. It is essentially negative towards Indian projects - particularly, big projects - on the western rivers, with some limited permissive provisions. India wants to use those permissive provisions to the full. It is aware of the dissatisfaction in the state of J & K, and would like to remove that grievance. It, therefore, formulates projects such as Salal, Tulbul, Baglihar, Kishanganga, and so on. However, the treaty requires India to send all the technical details of such projects to Pakistan in advance, and that is when the trouble starts. The treaty gives Pakistan virtually a veto power over Indian projects on the western rivers, which Pakistan tends to exercise in a stringent rather than accommodating manner (Iyer 2005).

viii) Terrorism

The dissatisfaction in some quarters in India with the water-sharing proportions, and the sense of frustration at the stalling of projects, were aggravated in 2002 by the harm that Pakistan was perceived to be inflicting on this country through what came to be known as 'cross-border terrorism'. In India, after the terrorist attack on Uri Army base on September 18, 2016, the demand is made not only to abrogate the Indus Treaty, but also to withdraw the Most Favored Nation status of Pakistan (The Indian Express 2016). Indians want to scrap all types of ties.

Current issues and challenges over the use of Indus Rivers Water

Although the Indus Treaty has been an emblem for maintaining water dispute and achieving the bilateral relations, but last one and half decades witnessed that the treaty has been under strain. The growing economies and the energy needs are nurturing a different set of challenges. Though, water is technically not a core issue between the two countries, differences over the use of water of the rivers is a core issue (Iyer 2005). The Treaty allows India to tape water for run-of-the river projects, on western rivers. However, India has constructed many projects on western rivers, which Pakistan claims as the violation of the Treaty and considers as the threat to its economic security, as the stoppage of water from western rivers could devastate Pakistan's agriculture.

Indian stand over projects

India says that the construction of projects is endorsed by the treaty and all projects are within the limitations of the Treaty's criteria. India replied, citing the norms of the treaty and Indian experts have expressed frustration over long delays in approval of these projects due to objections held by Pakistan, as around 27 projects on the western rivers have been questioned by Pakistan (Ibid). Indian analysts and media are of the view that the provision of neutral experts should be the last option and not the recourse for each and every project that India proposes. The reference does cost time, money and efforts, in terms of delaying the projects, thereby increasing the cost of not only construction but also related expenditures in not making use of the hydro potential (Chandran, 2010).

Pakistani Apprehensions over the Projects

First, Pakistan, as lower riparian has apprehensions over the projects such as Salal, Baglihar, Kishanganga, Wullar Barrage, Uri Nimo-Bazgo etc. and it considers them as the

150

existential threat to its inhabitants, as stored water can flush out the land and property. Secondly, Pakistan also fears that these projects will reduce the water flow in critical times, especially during the sowing seasons. From a security point of view, some strategic analysts in Pakistan are of the view that the Indian intentions are directed towards flooding Pakistan during military action and that flood waters could destroy Pakistani defences. Pakistan has also certain economic and defensive apprehension on the construction of projects, especially on Jhelum and Chenab River.

In 2008, after filing of the Baglihar project and subsequent reduction of the water flow in Pakistan, the project has drawn serious concerns and gained critical attention in Pakistan's political circles. With regard to Wullar Barrage, it has also incurred political and strategic voices from Pakistan, as it fears that with the construction of the Wullar Barrage in Indian side of Kashmir, India could close the gate of Wullar Barrage during a warlike situation, enhancing the ability of Indian troops to enter Pakistan (Akhtar, 2010). The project is also frequently criticized in farming communities of Punjab and Sindh. The technical difficulties in interpretations of the Treaty can be attributed to political motives rather than to differences over technical and engineering aspects of water management. Some non-state actors, especially radical extremist groups from two countries have their vested interests in the complex issue of water sharing and the treaty. Some are of the view that if the gap between water availability and requirements widens, terrorist operations and recruitment in the region will increase (Waslekar, 2005).

Analysis over current water sharing issues

Control of water from western rivers has received considerable attention from both the sides. It is because of the construction of the projects on western rivers, Pakistan fears that India is exercising 'hydro hegemony' on these projects and it will use these projects as a bargaining tool with Pakistan to settle other related issues. In addition, the political mobilization on dam construction on the western rivers has stimulated anti-Indian sentiments among farmer associations, military consortium, politicians, and fundamentalist groups in Pakistan. But in reply to Pakistan's apprehensions on western rivers, Indian position is that it is not violating the spirit of the treaty. Secondly, Pakistan's security fears are misconceived as India cannot flood Pakistan without flooding it first within its territory.

Conversely, India's concern is to improve its energy efficiencies and economy, for which it is endeavoring to utilise the full power potentialities. Its booming economy, waves of globalization, overwhelming urbanization push India to generate more and more electricity from hydro-power projects on Himalayan Rivers (The Observer Research Foundation 2011). Its peak power demand in the year 2007-08 was 108,886 MW, while the peak power demand met was 90,793 MW; there was a shortage of 18,093 MW or 16.6 percent of peak demand. The projects on western rivers are a crucial part of India's plan to close that gap. The hydro-power sector is also an attractive revenue earner for Himalayan states, which are underdeveloped in the industrial sector as compared to other states. Therefore, the exploitation of hydro power from Himalayan Rivers is the only source to boost their industrial sector (Ibid).

In 1960, both governments had agreed to sign the Indus Water Treaty, but public reaction to the treaty was very different. People in Pakistan criticised the loss of three eastern rivers to India, although Pakistan received a huge amount of financial aid in lieu of this loss even though this loss imposed heavy financial and ecological penalties upon Pakistan (Allouche 2005). In 1964, political circle in Pakistan criticised President Ayub Khan, and used the term as 'selling' the historical rights of the country over the common rivers (Choudhury, 1968). While in India, the public often criticised the loss of its three western rivers to Pakistan and the treaty makes it impossible for India to utilise the full power potentialities on three western rivers (Verghese, 2005). The outcomes of the on-going disputes have broader implications not only for future water development but also about India-Pakistan relations. The Indus Treaty has served both the countries and stood with the test of time, but the growing economies of both countries and the energy needs are nurturing a different set of challenges. Multiplying problems related to acute water supply have also put on serious burdens on the Indus Basin Rivers. Exploitation of water with the last drops means the violation of the treaty.

In 1960, it was hoped that water dispute settlement would pave the way for resolving the Kashmir dispute (Khan 1967). In fact, at the time of signing of Indus Treaty Jawaharlal Nehru the Indian Prime Minister, before coming to Pakistan had expressed in the Indian parliament that he was ready to resolve any issue including Kashmir(Choudhury 1968). Similar views and hopes were also expressed by Muhammad Ayub Khan the Pakistani President (Ibid). Hitherto, three wars have been fought between India and Pakistan over multiple issues, but the dispute still remains unresolved and problematic. Until and unless the Kashmir issue is settled, both countries will not be able to develop good relations in the future. If, the countries came up with an agreement to settle the Kashmir dispute, nothing will prevent them from building good relationships (Ali, 2011).

Water disputes add to the importance of Kashmir

On Kashmir issue, Pakistan and India fought war in 1948. As described before, the area was under Kashmir rule by Hindu Maharaja at the time of partition. India wanted Kashmir to include Kashmir in its territory but majority of

153

that area consisted of Kashmir Muslims. First this appeared to be the problem but as time passes it was clear that India wanted Kashmir because all rivers pass from Kashmir to Pakistan. When India was unable to find an alternative, they took this issue to the UN-Security Council in January 1948. Months later, on 21st April the UN passed a resolution. The resolution had many objectives like an immediate ceasefire and the pull out of all external forces from Kashmir, among others. After resolution India tried not to implement this resolution over Kashmir because India wanted all Kashmir land under its control (Muhammad, 2015).

The Indus Water Treaty of 1960 was another attempt to resolve the water issue. Before the division of the subcontinent, it was noted that the rivers would be divided, so in 1942 (before either country gained independence) a judicial commission was appointed to deal with this issue but neither party accepted the recommendations and so the case was sent to the London Commission in 1947 for final review. No final decision came even after the countries gained independence. In fall 1947, both countries faced monsoon conditions, and the chief engineers of both the counties signed a temporary "Standstill Agreement". According to this agreement, water allocations at two points on the river were frozen until March 31, 1948, allowing discharges from headworks in India to continue to flow into Pakistan. This agreement expired on 1 April 1948, but India didn't stop water flow.

The Indus Water Treaty addressed this problem. Water is the heart of the problem between both countries even now, because the head quarter of the Indus is mainly in Kashmir and India is the upstream country and Pakistan is the downstream. At any time the upstream country can reduce the flow of water to downstream by constructing dams on head quarter. This is a form of "hydro politics". Kashmir is an area covered by huge mountain ranges and has been a disputed area for more than 60 years. This area sometimes referred to as the, "Switzerland of the East" due to its scenic valleys and snow-capped mountains. Due to climatic changes, its glaciers melted and became the source of water in the region. From early on, both countries expressed their own ownership of Kashmir. It is based on the hypothesis that India is unwilling to resolve the Kashmir issue because of Pakistan's dependence on water from the Indus basin. Pakistan depends on the water flowing through occupied areas of Kashmir into Pakistan for a range of purposes including agriculture, industry, daily use, drinking and also hydroelectric power generation.

Geographically, three of the five key rivers and the Indus River proper pass through Kashmir on its journey to Pakistan. But it also has some issues because of the situation in Jammu Kashmir. If India restricts the water or makes any dam on these rivers it will directly affect the economy of Pakistan because its agricultural and industry largely depend on this water. After that it also leaves bad effect on the relation of both countries. Any conflict over the treaty (1960) directly affects Jammu Kashmir, and on the other hand any tensions and battles over water in Jammu Kashmir directly put pressure on the Indus Waters Treaty and the increasing ongoing tension between the two countries.

It seems India's dams and upper riparian status as potential means to economically squeeze or starve Pakistan, or alternatively to flood it, possibly for military purposes. From the Indian side, it sees Pakistan as making it virtually impossible for them to exploit effectively the Treaty's no consumptive uses, especially hydropower production (Verghese, 2005). As India labours to find more water and be able to use it, it watches carefully as the three western Indus rivers flow from its territory to Pakistan. The opportunity to tap the Jhelum and the Chenab rivers would provide windfall gains not only to India's side of the Line of

Control (LoC)in Kashmir, but also to its three desperate states of Punjab, Rajasthan and Haryana (Muhammad, 2015).

Pakistan-India Water Wars

Indian Water Terrorism

Two problems occurred; Pakistan did manage to build a link canal system for optimum utilization of its rivers and constructed the Mangal and Tarbela Dams but failed to construct any new dams, resulting in loss of waters during the monsoons and the mountaintops. Even the link canal system, over a period of time deteriorated through silting. This negligence also compounded the problem of flash floods and wreaked havoc in the country. On the other hand, India constructed numerous dams, some of them illegally. Reportedly, it also compromised the Pakistani Indus water Commissioner, who wilfully neglected to counter Indian machinations of water terrorism. Resultantly, India is in a position to deprive Pakistan of waters during crucial seasons to create a drought or open the spigots to flood Pakistan. Allegedly, India also bribed certain Pakistani politicians to oppose the construction of the vital Kalabagh Dam and other dams to keep Pakistan deprived of water and energy. Chairman Wapda was forced to resign for advocating Kalabagh dam in his series of columns in local media.

There are some serious emerging violations of IWT as India plans to construct 155 hydropower projects in Kashmir and India is not sharing any information pertaining to the detail design, structural drawings, and design calculations of the upcoming projects. India began building major hydropower projects in Kashmir in 1970s and now has 33 projects at various stages of completion on the rivers in Kashmir. Currently, the most controversial dam project is the proposed 330 megawatt dam on the Kishanganga River, a tributary of the Indus. Its construction began in 2007. Earlier in 2013, the International Court of Arbitration decided that

"India shall release a minimum flow of 9 cumecs [cubic meters per second] into the river below the Kishanganga Hydroelectric Plant at all times. The judgment also dictated that any time at which the daily average flow in the river immediately upstream of the Kishanganga Hydroelectric plant is less than 9 cumecs, India shall release 100 percent of the daily average flow."

Current Imbroglio

Today Pakistan and India are locked in a bitter water conflict. Though diplomatic exertions have prevented a major escalation, both countries are entangled in legal battles as more dams and power projects come up in Indian side of Kashmir. In Kashmir itself, politicians and civil society groups of all hues have been demanding a review of Indus Water Treaty, which has been labeled "detrimental" to the region's economy. Pakistan and India are dangerously energy-starved and nowhere close to an agreement on disputes over Kashmir. The intertwining impact of climate change and population pressures offer a forecast on their water conflict that is anything but encouraging.

Indian troops in Kashmir are wreaking havoc to make the lives of the Kashmiris miserable, while they are also orchestrating false flag operations in which terror attacks are carried out in Kashmir of India and Pakistan is getting the blame so that Pakistan's position becomes weak. Under the leadership of Indian Prime Minister Narendra Modi India is determined legitimately to bring back Azad Jammu Kashmir and Gilgit Baltistan which were part of India before Pakistan's aggression in 1948 from Pakistan.

There is a dire need for launching a comprehensive campaign to highlight the importance of water storage, prevalent water issues between Pakistan and India, India's water terrorism and implication for Pakistan and needs for early resolutions. Despite the reservations expressed by the current Minister for Water and Power, Pakistan should continue lobbying that India has been violating the IWT and India should be compelled to abide by the IWT in its true letter and spirit since water is the "lifeline" issue for Pakistan and this could trigger a war between two nuclear weapons equipped states, India and Pakistan. In case India raises the issue at official level, then Pakistan must seek arbitration and intense involvement of World Bank, International Court of Justice and other relevant international forums to resolve hydro related issues with India, after necessary preparation (Hali, 2018).

Status of disputes between Pakistan and India over water sharing

Present status of the dispute

The dispute between Pakistan and India over water has continued over several decades. Currently, the dispute revolves around the construction of a hydro-electric plant along a tributary of Indus, which is Kishanganga River. Although India is defending its raising of several issues over the project, Pakistan explains that India is planning to have adverse effects on Pakistanis who rely on the river. Pakistan explains that this would reduce the capacity of the river by more than 30 percent during winter as a result. When this happens, Pakistan's plan to construct its own dam will be adversely affected. However, the dispute is about to be solved through arbitration, as both parties are hopeful to see this mechanism work.

Can the conflicts be transformed into armed conflicts in future?

Terrorism

Pakistan is one of the countries which has become the breeding ground of a plethora of terrorist activities against India. There are many terrorist groups which operate in Pakistan and some of these include Tehrek-e-sahaba, Lashkar-e-Taiba and Tehrek-e-taliban terrorist groups. These groups have committed various terrorism acts through

158

suicide bombing, booby-trapping, arming vehicles, armed assaults and others. These acts have been serious and have led to many fatalities. Between 2006 and 2009, over five thousand fatalities were attributed to these groups. This is a very high fatality rate in any country. However, most of these attacks are political in nature and they aim at discrediting the government. As a result, policemen and the public have been the major targets.

Since terrorist activities are clearly established in Pakistan, it is clear that terror attacks can occur anytime. Although the terrorist activities follow political causes, it is very easy to alter the cause and motivate terrorists to carry out attacks due to the India-Pakistan water crisis. Such terrorists may be brainwashed into believing that they are carrying out terrorism for the good of their nation. If a charismatic leader who believes in terrorism emerges, he or she may easily convince them to attack Indian targets. This shows that it is important to resolve the Pakistan-India water crisis as soon as possible.

War

The conflict between Pakistan and India over water resources has been developing for a long time. Dialogue has apparently failed to solve this crisis which relates to the Indus treaty. Since this conflict has lasted several decades, leaders may get frustrated and resolve to use force to achieve their objectives. There are many scholars who are of the opinion that India is intentionally flouting the Indus treaty in order to force Pakistan to take military action against it. In such circumstances, India is of the view that it will win the resultant war and put the water crisis matter to rest. The water crisis should therefore be solved before leaders resort to taking this cause of action which may adversely affect both countries.

It has been discussed that terrorism is a real threat to India by Pakistan, and the water conflict may degenerate into a terrorism war if terrorists are of the opinion that it is a real cause worth defending. Any terrorist activity against India by Pakistan may easily lead to war between the two countries. This is because it will be perceived that the government supported the attack. Other countries which are either enemies of Pakistan or India may also influence the perception that the government supported these terrorist attacks. This may lead to a full-scale war between the concerned countries hence the need to resolve the water crisis.

There has not been yet any war on water issues between nations at the global level. With climate change wrecking huge impact on the availability of water as IPCC report predicts, the growing water scarcity and non-availability of drinking water for survival and water for agriculture and other purposes may be in near future a great issue of conflict between nations and violent conflict between variety groups within a state of society. The possibility of war between nations cannot be simply ignored. But the fact remains is that water can very much amplify the causes of war on other political issues. It can at best act as a catalyst to ignite the already smouldering issues or conflict as found in case of India and Pakistan on issues of Kashmir and terrorism. Water can be used as a strategic contrivance on the upper riparian nations to build pressures on the opponent. Recently on the issue of cross border terrorism sponsored by Pakistan, there was news that India might stop supply of water on the rivers flowing to Pakistan. Hence water can be used as a military weapon.

Reasons for the water crisis in Pakistan

According to Pakistan's Economic Survey (2011-12), the agrarian economy is heavily dependent on river water provided by melting glaciers. The survey also highlighted that during the period 2011-12, the availability of water for both kharif and rabi crops was respectively 10 percent and 19.2 percent less than normal. Also water availability for Rabi crop was 15 percent less than 2010-11.

This Economic Survey also highlighted the excessive wastage of water from the irrigation system due to the improper lining of waterways. As a consequence, the agriculture, livestock and fisheries sectors were adversely affected. According to the World Bank and Needs Assessment Report, 2011, the total damages caused to these sectors were $1,840 million while reconstruction costs were estimated to be about $305.6 million. Damages to agriculture, livestock and fisheries sectors accounted for 49.33 percent of total damages of all the sectors during that period.

Pakistan has one of the world's largest glacial reserves in the Karakoram-Hindukush-Himalaya ranges supplying fresh water to the Indus River System, the world's largest irrigation system. Fears of this supply getting affected by climate change have been voiced since the 1990s. With global average temperatures rising, it was feared that glaciers would be melting at an alarming rate. However, a separate study found that Karakoram glaciers and ice caps, as a whole, were losing mass less quickly than once feared, offering some respite to the effected region. This fact was noted by the National Plan of Pakistan 2012-13.

The same National Plan mentioned that the Integrated Irrigation Network of Indus Basin is under serious threat of water logging, hydro-salinity, adverse effects of pollution and contamination of surface and ground water. Consequently, the Plan suggests that an overall environmental management plan and process for approval and implementation be put in place. Hence, one can infer that more than anything else, it is inadequate water policies and loopholes in the regulations for management of water systems, that are acknowledged as the causes of the water crisis in Pakistan. Its impacts on various sectors including agriculture and allied activities have also been documented.

The Pakistan Economic Survey 2010-11, categorically acknowledges that water related issues are a serious threat in Pakistan. It states that, 'the existing water resources in the country are under threat due to untreated discharge of municipal and industrial wastes to rivers and other surface water bodies. The majority of the population of Pakistan is exposed to the hazard of unsafe and polluted drinking water.' These issues are testimony to the limitations of existing water management policies and regulations in Pakistan.

Water Crisis in India

Like Pakistan, India too faces acute water shortage. This has been stated in various government documents, including the Draft Water Policy of India -2012, which listed several causes of the precarious water situation in India. The policy document states that water stress in large parts of India can be attributed to population growth, urbanization and changing lifestyles, improper addressing of water governance, mismanagement of water resources, and the threat of climate change. Many of these are also leading to salinity of both groundwater and surface water.

Interestingly, it also highlights that while multi-disciplinary water resources projects are planned and implemented, they suffer from problems of fragmentation and ignore optimum utilization, environmental sustainability and holistic benefits to the people (Draft National Water Policy of 2012). These issues, besides others raised in this draft make many of the earlier National Water Policies inconsequential (Verghese 2011).

When we move from the broader national scenario and look specifically at water quality of Indus basin on the Indian side, we find that several studies have been conducted to test the quality of water. One such physico-chemical water quality analysis was conducted in Harike Wetland, a site at the confluence of the two rivers–Sutlej and Beas (Ramanathan 2012). The study revealed the deterioration in water quality towards Sutlej River resulting from untreated effluents and municipal wastes from townships and industries situated on its banks. A gradual increase in temperature, electrolytic conductivity, high proportion of total dissolved solids, alkalinity, hardness, high levels of calcium and magnesium were observed in Harike waters. Thus, both long-term water security in the region and more immediate local concerns, offer compelling reasons for India and Pakistan to cooperate.

Significant parties to the conflict and current context

Indian Government

On 18th September 2016, four gunmen ambushed an Indian military base in Uri, a small town located in Kashmir near the line of control. Seventeen Indian soldiers were killed in an attack in what was reported as the deadliest attack on the security forces in the valley in two decades. India blamed terrorist groups based in Pakistan for the attacks. Post Uri attacks, the current government led by Prime Minister Modi made public announcements about setting up an inter-ministerial commission to review the IWT (Retrieved October 23, 2016). The government also suspended the Indus water commissioners' meetings indefinitely. The commissioners on either side of the border met regularly in the last 69 years to discuss potential disputes.

Pakistani Government

The Pakistani Government initially reacted with a degree of restraint upon learning about India's stance on the water issue. There was no official response from the government, but Sartaj Aziz, the Advisor on Foreign Affairs to the Pakistani Prime Minister said if India were to pull out of the treaty, Pakistan will proceed to the International Court of Justice. As of today, Pakistan has stated that the abrogation of treaty will be considered as an act of war. The water conflict is being used to entice tensions by groups on both sides of the border. Hafiz Saeed leader of Jama'at-ud-Da'wah, a terrorist organization has vowed water jihad against India, blaming India for the flood crisis in Pakistan (Hafiz Saeed, 2016). The Pakistani Government recognizes that being a lower riparian country, the leverage lies with India. Pakistani Government understands that the water from Indus forms the lifeline of their economy and is far more important to Pakistan than to India. They have requested the World Bank which played a key role in the signing of the original treaty to mediate in the dispute.

Mediator

The World Bank acted as a mediator between India and Pakistan post partition to develop the Indus Water Treaty. Amid reports of India considering reviewing the IWT, Pakistan has approached the bank to help settle the dispute. The bank has agreed to fulfill its obligations in a timely fashion under the purview of the treaty while remaining neutral. They play an important role specified in the treaty vis-a-vis establishment of court of arbitration to settle disputes and facilitation of appointment of three judges. There are also reports of Pakistan having approached the International Court of Justice to help settle the matter but no details were available regarding these claims (Pakistan approaches International Court of Justice 2016).

Perspectives of the Parties and Framing of the issue

Indian Government

India's framing of the issue is illustrated in Prime Minister Modi's recent statement after the Uri attack "Blood and Water cannot flow at the same time." As the treaty is based on mutual trust and cooperation, India believes that the treaty should be revisited in the light of current events of terrorism allegedly perpetrated by forces originating from the Pakistani side. From the Indian perspective, the areas of interest are twofold.

First, IWT treaty acts as a bargaining chip for India to use against Pakistan in other matters such as border disputes in Kashmir and terrorist activities. As Indus River originates in the Kashmir region and the fact that 90 percent of Pakistan's agricultural economy depends on the Indus basin, India expects to use its upper riparian status to control the flow of water and use it as leverage during negotiations on important matters related to Kashmir.

Second, India feels it has underutilized its requirement as entitled in the treaty. Even though the rivers flow from India to Pakistan, the IWT grants Pakistan control to 80 percent water in the entire basin. This reason justifies India's need to review the terms of the treaty. India can utilize about 20 percent water on the western rivers (allocated to Pakistan). India is allowed to construct Run-of-River (ROR) power plants with specific design constraints on western rivers for power generation and is allowed to use specific amounts of western river water for domestic non-consumptive purposes as mentioned in the treaty. Some of the proposed projects along western rivers have been shelved due to Pakistan's objection. The Indus water basin constitutes a major source of water to the Northwest regions namely Punjab, Rajasthan and Haryana. Punjab produces about 20 percent of India's wheat making the basin a significant contributor to India's agricultural needs. During current times of droughts, there have been talks to completely maximize the opportunity afforded by the treaty even if it impacts Pakistan gravely.

Pakistani Government

Pakistan has framed the issue of conflict on the context of International Law. The bone of contention has been India's construction of dams and hydro projects on the rivers allocated to Pakistan. Pakistan has constantly accused India of constructing projects that violate the terms of the treaty that affect the water supply in Pakistan. In recent times amid reports of India reviewing the Indus Water Treaty, Pakistan has approached The World Bank to mediate the issue. Pakistan's position has been to exercise the terms of the signed treaty and prevent India from building dams and hydro projects on the western rivers that would reduce the quantity of water flowing into Pakistan.

Pakistan's interest has been to ensure continued access to water originating from the western rivers of the Indus. If Pakistan's access to the western rivers were cut off or even reduced, the impact on agriculture, water security and human consumption would be catastrophic. To illustrate the point further, about 90 percent of Pakistan's food and 65 percent of its population depend on agriculture along the banks of the Indus basin. Recent reports from the International Monetary Fund states that the per capita water availability is at the scarcity threshold whereas the water intensity rate is one of the worlds' highest, thus making Pakistan one of the world's most water stressed countries in the world (Kaushik, 2017).

Indus River is a time bomb

Basically, the Indus River is a water time bomb which can explode at any second if India and Pakistan do not cooperate on the issue. Any military confrontation in the region would inevitably lead to an even more extreme water scarcity and trigger irreparable climate changes. The ever-rising water demand has led to pollution, water scarcity, shortages and worsened relations between India and Pakistan. Such factors as rapid population and economic growth have also been making matters worse. The nature of the growing tension between Islamabad and New Delhi increases the difficulty to start cooperation on water issues between the two nations. Therefore, any amicable solutions are almost impossible at this point.

However, the UN experts still hope the nations will find peace for the sake of their own futures. But the longer

Islamabad and New Delhi wait, the more difficult it will be prevent the water catastrophe. It also does not help that climate change only worsens by the day. Also China and Afghanistan seem to be rapidly gravitating towards the Indus River for their own benefit. That means we could end up having a four-nation conflict instead of the current two nation one (Tikhonova, 2016).

Implications of these conflicts on regional and national development of these states

There are various implications which the water conflict between India and Pakistan has on these states. Most are adverse implications and they are related to the hostility and suspicion between these countries, which hinders cooperation on essential economic matters. Some of these implications will be discussed below in more detail;

Water conservation

Water is one of the most important resources which India and Pakistan rely on in achieving economic development. This is because both countries rely on agrarian economies which form a large proportion of their GDPs. For these two countries to achieve greater economic prosperity, they should cooperate in implementing moves aimed at conserving the water resources. Since these rivers flow between Pakistan and India, it is necessary for both countries to implement simultaneous actions aimed at conserving water and using it effectively to meet the needs of each country. However, there is suspicion and hostility between these countries, and they have been unable to develop uniform policies aimed at achieving water conservation. As a result, there is a lot of water wastage which increases costs to the government and decrease water available for agricultural activities. This has a negative impact on both the economies of Pakistan and India.

Fight against terrorism

The Indian Prime Minister is of the opinion that the best

way to fight terrorism in the region is through collaborative efforts between Indian and Pakistan. Since both countries face similar terrorist threats and they border each other, the fight against terrorism will only be won after a joint approach is used by both countries. In fact, foreign secretaries of both countries have met and strategized on how terrorism would be fought by both countries. However, the water dispute is threatening to erode these efforts due to hostility and suspicion which are brought about by the dispute. If the dispute is not resolved and this dual-approach in fighting terrorism is neglected, then terrorist activities are bound to rise. The high number of terrorist attacks in these two countries will increase when this happens and an unprecedented wave of terror may be seen leaving a trail of destruction (http lawteacher).

Way out for cooperation in sharing water resources

In order to resolve this and other conflicts which involve the sharing of resources, countries concerned should cooperate to ensure that they all benefit from the use of such resources.

Effective policies by countries

In order to ensure that India and Pakistan both benefit from the rivers, both countries should implement policies which favour their mutual use of the rivers. Pakistan should allow India to use rivers which complement its goal and vice versa, as long as national interests are not affected. For instance, when both countries are constructing dams, mutual consultation will enable then to draft policies which favour both countries and reduces destructive effects of this construction to the other country. Just as the two countries are stressing on collaboration to fight terrorism, they should also collaborate to ensure that they both achieve their objectives regarding the availability and use of the water resource.

Dialogue

Dialogue is the most effective way in which the dispute between India and Pakistan over water can be resolved. Other measures such as aggression or violence will only lead to losses among both countries. It is imperative that the issue is sorted soon in order to prevent further conflict or bloodshed which may occur as a result of the conflict, as has been seen. Since 1960 Indus Treaty has proved to be ineffective in solving the current dispute, both the Pakistan and Indian leaders should hold dialogue and develop a new treaty which will solve the present stalemate. The various issues which have been brought under consideration are relatively complex and may have been unforeseeable when developing the initial treaty. It is therefore necessary to alter the treaty to reflect the current concerns while safeguarding the interests of both countries. Since these rivers under consideration flow in both countries, it is clear that India and Pakistan are dependent on one other and none can exist independently.

Mediation

Mediation is another successful strategy which may be used to end the conflicts between Pakistan and India. For mediation to be a success, it should involve a mediator who is neutral to concerned parties. Both Pakistan and India should choose a leader who comes from a country which is neutral to both countries' interests. The proceedings should be held at a neutral country or on a rotation between both countries. Both countries should choose representatives who will argue their case to the mediator. The mediator will then make a decision on India's decision to build a dam, on the basis of evidence provided. Decisions which are made in such cases are binding to both Pakistan and India.

Water conservation

It has been discussed that water conservation is a problem faced by both Pakistan and India. However,

Pakistan appears to have greater problems as far as water conservation is concerned. Water conservation is important since it will enable both countries reduce reliance on the rivers, which are scarce resources and instead take advantage of rainfall and sea water to mitigate the citizens' needs. It has been discussed that Pakistan loses millions of cubic water to the sea due to lack of water conservation initiatives. It has also been discussed that Pakistan faces a looming water disaster. Water conservation will enable Pakistan have more water for use in agriculture, and ensure that citizens have access to water. It will also reduce disputes which arise from the use of rivers by India and Pakistan since poor water conservation is one of the factors which have worsened the crisis.

Development of a new treaty

The establishment of a new treaty is another way in which the India-Pakistan conflict may be resolved. It is clear that the conflict is solely related to the Indus Treaty which forbade India from constructing a dam within Chenab River without permission from Pakistan. However, when the treaty was initially established, future projections on water needs for both countries were not adequately assessed. For instance, the surge in population to hundreds of millions, decades later was not factored in when establishing the treaty. Since the modern world is dynamic, it is necessary to reconsider the contract and factor in these changing factors. India and Pakistan should re-negotiate the treaty afresh and clearly explain how the water may be used by both countries to achieve mutual benefit. The new treaty should project future trends as far as water consumption is concerned to avoid other future conflicts relating to water use (Sarvat N. Hanif 2013).

Room for cooperation between both countries

As aforementioned, there have been many concerns raised by Pakistan on Indus Water Treaty and there is room for further negotiations. Citing Article XII of IWT, B.G. Verghese, an India based expert on water issues, has proposed Indus II that will be largely based on the foundation of Indus I. Some on the Pakistan side, like F.S. Ajjazuddin, have articulated that the conflict is too important to be left to the two commissioners to discuss and refer to an arbitrator (in this case the Word Bank). He proposes the setting up a Joint Commission, whose structure is based on the belief that water resources are a common asset and that neither country owns them. Each country should see itself as a trustee of the resource for future generations. Rather than having two Commissioners from each country sit across the table and negotiate, the Joint Commission will be different in the sense that it would function as one body looking at the interests of both Pakistan and India (Ajazuddin, 2012).

But the crux of the matter is beyond this Treaty and is the water crisis faced by both the countries. The crisis cannot be attributed to any provisions of the IWT but is largely related to the mismanagement of water resources in general by each country and Indus River Basin in particular. Both these countries found themselves in such a crisis due to common factors like population growth, urbanization and ineffective polices dealing with these factors in order to tackle the water crisis. The fear of the melting glaciers of the Himalayas is adding to the woes of the existing water stress.

Therefore, at the first instance what these countries need is, to deal with their current water management problems and then create spaces for cooperation wherever possible, including those that can help deal with climate change. Thinking of Indus II or even abrogation of the same cannot guarantee any solution to the existing water crisis these two countries are trapped in.

The first step by each country should be to recognize the water problems of not only its own people but those of its neighbour, for the simple reason that these issues transcend national territories or borders drawn by states. Action or inaction of either country would impact the situation in the other country and more so in Pakistan, which is a lower riparian country. Even if the existing treaty were to be abrogated, Pakistan will still continue to have normal lower riparian rights over the rivers flowing into its territory under international law.

The next step would be for India to allay Pakistan's fears with regard to the Indus Treaty. In April 2012, India's Indus Water Commissioner G. Aranganathan, speaking to Time, had clarified that "there was no question of interrupting or reducing Pakistan's water supply". He had said that India was not preventing the flow of water to Pakistan. After filling the reservoirs in the initial stages—of the Tulbul navigation project on the Jhelum—the waters would only be used for running the turbines (Niharika, Madhana 2012). Such clarifications can build confidence and it is important for India to continue to take further steps to address Pakistani concerns.

Pakistan on its part must acknowledge that the Indus Treaty is an example of successful conflict resolution between the two rival countries, which have otherwise fought three wars after independence and have locked horns on various issues over the years. Therefore, it is time that both countries end their shrill and clichéd stances that restrict fresh approaches in dealing with challenges as existential as water scarcity.

Building on the stability of the IWT both nations should go beyond just conflict resolution over Indus water sharing and develop partnerships in the water sector by setting up institutional mechanisms and building joint capacity to tackle the water problem.

The current institutional mechanism in the two countries is similar in many respects and it will not be difficult to bring the relevant levels of administration to partner with their counterparts in the other country. Both Central and State Governments in these countries have been entrusted with the responsibilities of development, conservation and management of water. Like India, it is the Federal Government in Pakistan which is responsible for the overall policy formulation in this area. Besides, it provides technical assistance to the states/provinces on irrigation, multipurpose projects, groundwater exploitation and exploration, flood control, water logging and so on. Furthermore it is the State/provincial Government which has the responsibility of using and controlling this precious resource (Madhana, 2012).

A partnership between the governments of two Punjabs can go a long way in ensuring that the common problems are viewed from a holistic perspective and not from a standpoint of suspicion and uncertainty. While this may seem like a difficult proposal to push, given the history of the bitter and violent partition along this part of the border, the fact also remains that the two Punjabs share common climatic conditions, similar water management practices, nonstringent water policies and water intensive crop cultivation. Once both sides come to an agreement that they could each benefit from the others' innovations and practices in dealing with water scarcity; and are transparent about developments, this process can become a template for cooperation in other areas of mutual interest.

The improved bilateral relations in recent months provide an opportune moment for this cooperation to take shape. Addressing the water management issues in the Indus river basin on both sides of the border can improve the status of water availability and water quality (Gill, 2010) in both countries and bring India and Pakistan closer to achieving the MDGs. At a political level, the water issue is important for the politically dominant province of Pakistani Punjab and finding synergies may be a way of reaching out to those sections of the population who have apprehensions with regard to India's stand on water and are in some senses the driving force behind the continuing hostility. By driving home the point that policy failures and not India is responsible for the water crisis. Pakistan can begin to concretely address its water security problem (Maini, 2011).

The purely technical and juridical aspects of the water issue can be augmented by focusing also on greater interaction and enhanced dialogue between important stakeholders on both sides, some of whom include farmers, researchers and students of various water and agricultural universities. Some of the possible areas of cooperation are discussed below.

Conducting joint studies on receding glaciers by both countries

Various independent studies have been conducted on receding Himalayan glaciers by agencies worldwide. Appreciating the source of the problem, both the countries could cooperate on conducting research on the specific impacts of the receding glaciers. This would help these countries to come up with solutions on River Basin Management, instead of harping on the provisions in the treaty itself. Once the fundamental problem of water stress is taken care of through joint efforts, the problems in the Treaty will become immaterial (Rana, 2012).

Greater interactions between farmers' groups of both the countries

On 7-8 May 2012, when a business delegation from India visited Lahore to participate in the second Amanki Asha Indo-Pak Economic Conference, the idea of exporting farm produce to Pakistan was seriously discussed. One of the farmers, Rattan Singh Randhawa, who was part of the Indian delegation, echoed the sentiments of many when he said that: "In a village only those neighbours, who exchange household goods or farm equipment with each other, have good relations. It is the same with nations" (Rana 2012). Frequent interactions of a similar nature will thus not only strengthen Indo-Pak trade ties, but also give a fillip to cooperation between the agricultural sectors of both countries. Further, if there are more exchanges for farmers of both countries such as those facilitated by the Two Punjab Centre which is part of the Centre for Research in Rural and Industrial Development (CRRID) Chandigarh and Aman Ki Asha, it would contribute towards improved relations in other areas as farmers can more easily arrive at consensus on shared issues and problems (Maini, 2007).

Finding common ground in combating desertification

India and Pakistan can also join hands for fighting environmental degradation in their shared desert region along the border. Desertification can easily lead to agricultural losses resulting in food shortages. This phenomenon is already visible in both India and Pakistan. With collaboration, both countries can protect agricultural lands vulnerable to desertification through water conservation measures and modern irrigation techniques. Both countries have already shown interest in protecting communities and farming operations that lie on the desert's fringes. For example in the case of Pakistan, a collaborative project between Pakistan's Integrated Rural Awareness and Development Organization and the One-UN Joint Program on Environment aims to build check dams, rehabilitate ponds in the area of Nagar Parkar, and construct earthen embankments to help store water and promote conservation. Similarly, in Rajasthan's Churu district, the Bhoruka Charitable Trust, an Indian NGO, is encouraging villagers to build and renovate water tanks, ponds, and dug-wells to preserve potable water. Efforts of both countries in the Thar Desert can be shared as best practices and this sharing could go a long way as a confidence building measure (Panuganti, 2012).

Effectively utilizing the SAARC platform

There should be more emphasis towards greater interaction and cooperation within South Asian Association for Regional Cooperation (SAARC) countries on issues like water management and agricultural growth. The SAARC, from its very inception has focused on regional cooperation in the spheres of agriculture and rural development. The Technical Committee on Agriculture and Rural Development (TC-ARD) conducted a number of meetings on the application of statistics on agricultural research, exchange of scientific and technical information and so on. It has also deliberated on various demand-driven areas such as 'Water Resources Management' and 'Water for Agriculture' in SAARC countries (http 2012). More concerted action in these areas using the space provided by the regional body can contribute to improving bilateral relations.

Greater collaboration between the two Punjabs

In this context, a substantial start could be made by accelerating cooperation between the two Punjabs. The two Punjabs share a similar culture and face similar problems. They can be a good starting point for collaboration on the problem of water shortage. The two premier agricultural institutions of the region, the Punjab Agricultural University, Ludhiana and the University of Faisalabad in Punjab province of Pakistan can collaborate. Training can be provided to Pakistani students on understanding the hydrological data, water management techniques, restoration of water bodies, watershed management practices, and improving the quality of groundwater, and restoring the water tables through rainwater harvesting. The two countries can learn from each other in the policy sphere as well. "For example in 2009, India promulgated the Sub-Soil Water Preservation Act and discouraged its farmers from planting a nursery before 10 May and sowing before 10 June each year, thus bringing down the irrigational requirements of canal

176

water and maximizing the use of monsoon rains. This actually helped in raising water levels in the Indian Punjab" (Maini, 2012). Such knowledge can easily be disseminated between farmers across the border. There is limited awareness in India about the innovative techniques being used by the farmers in Pakistan; however, we believe that similar knowledge can be offered by them to the Indian side as well.

World Bank officials play mediator in two months of diplomatic negotiations:

Signaling a major shift in its position on talks with Pakistan on the Indus Water Treaty (IWT), India has accepted an invitation to attend a meeting of the Permanent Indus Commission (PIC) to be held in Lahore in March 2017. According to official privacy to the development, the move came after two months of diplomatic negotiations, with World Bank officials playing the mediator in encouraging Pakistan to extend an invitation and for India to accept it.

The news closely follows the visit of World Bank chief Executive Officer Kristalina Georgieva to New Delhi, where she met with Union Finance Minister Arun Jaitley, week after her visit in January to Islambad, where she met Prime Minister Nawaz Sharif. Official acknowledged that the holding of the next annual round of the PIC, which was a "positive" sign, given that India had announced it was "suspending" the talks after the Uri attacks in September.

According to senior government officials at the time, the decision to suspend the talks was taken when Prime Minister Narendra Modi held a meeting with key officials, including National Security Adviser Ajit Doval and Foreign Secretary S. Jaishankar, to "review" the IWT. At the time, tensions with Pakistan were high, as the government considered all retaliatory measures after the army camp attack, in which 19 soldiers were killed. "Meetings can only take place in an atmosphere free of terror," a senior official briefing the press about the suspension of the Indus talks had said.

Asked if the scheduling of the talks now in March despite the previously decision meant a climb down in India's position or whether terror attack had in fact decreased in the past few months, the Ministry of External Affairs did not offer an official comments. "It is a regular bilateral meeting of the permanent Indus Commission, which implements the Indus Water Treaty", a senior official told The Hindu, denying that there was any "shift" in India's positions.

In November, another controversy erupted over the World Bank decision to constitute a court of Arbitration to look into complaints from Pakistan over India's construction of Kishanganga and Ratel river water projects. India said the World Bank decision was biased in Pakistan's favour, threatening to "take step" against it. Eventually, the matter was resolved after it was taken up at the heighest levels between the World Bank President Jim Young Kim, who also spoke over the telephone to Jaitley and to his Pakistan counterpart Ishaq Dar. This was followed by visit to India and Pakistan by World Bank expert Lan Solomon and then Georgieva.

In an exclusive interview to The Hindu, Georgieva said: "Our contribution is to help the countries better understand each other's concerns and address them. We have seen that the treaty has served the two countries very well and survived difficult moments" (Hindu 3 march 2017).

Conclusion

Water as a sign of life is essential to maintain the daily life routine. Water as a limited resource is under stress due to the high population density, climate change, urbanization and poor management. Competing demand on a limited resource contribute in arising acute water conflicts and disputes among the users whose livelihood mainly depend on it. In case of the international rivers the situations become more complicated. The rivers cross political boundaries, sometimes difficult to manage because of the poor political relationship.

Indus River is shared between four riparian countries. Pakistan and India are the two major countries dependent on Indus water flow. The 1960 agreement of Indus Water Treaty was signed between Pakistan and India for sharing the Indus water resource. This agreement was based on the amputation surgery of Indus River that gave the right of three eastern tributaries (Ravi, Beas and Sutlej) of Indus to India and western tributaries (Jhelum, Chenab, Indus) to Pakistan. Now, because of the high population density, climate change and high water demand both countries are facing water stress situation and trying hard to get as much water as they can. Construction of dams, hydropower units and navigational project is a need to meet the future challenges of water and energy crisis. Building of such infrastructure without considering the value and norms of other creates conflict among both countries. The reason behind this conflict is the lack of cooperation because of the poor political relationship and distrust among both countries. In case of international river basin cooperation and coordination is necessary for regional stability and sustainability.

In the beginning of 19[th]century there was only one political issue in the Indian subcontinent, i.e. to get independence from the British rule, but after independence, the sub-continent faced more grave geopolitical issues, which includes the distribution of Indus river water as well. The dispute over the water of the Indus Basin between India and Pakistan is notable not only for its size, significance and complexity but also in that it was brought to conclusion by a comprehensive Treaty. The dispute lasted for twelve years from 1948 to 1960 but fortunately the World Bank's intervention brought the parties together and guided them towards a solution. The resolution of dispute was made with the landmark agreement of Indus Water Treaty. This monumental treaty was the outcome of eight years of discussions and negotiations between the governments of two countries under the aegis of the World Bank. In fact, the Indus River, a basic source and a powerful stimulant to economic development of the shareholders and has also linked the riparian countries and their people together. On the other hand, water sharing mechanism is a complex issue which has multiple parameters and addressed economic, social, political and ecological gains. Under these circumstances any suggestion is to be honestly implemented on the existing Treaty with spirit of good will and cooperation. The Article VII (I) of the Indus Water Treaty states that the two parties recognize that they have a common interest in the optimum development of the Rivers and calls upon both sides to cooperate, by mutual accord, to the fullest possible extent, in undertaking engineering works in the Rivers (IWT 1960). Moving forward on Indus Basin rivers dispute with particular thinking or mind set can never see the end of path. The complexities involved in the water sharing issue such as lack of political will, geographical based stands, high level of mistrust between the people of two countries, and linkage of Kashmir issue and deep buried hostilities offer formidable obstacles to minimise the issue. Therefore, any move forward on the use of water between two countries will need a deep analysis of mindsets on both sides.

The Indus Water Treaty is a comprehensive document that gives major to minor details of sharing transboundary waters and tier mechanism for resolving differences and disputes. It seemingly served to prevent wars on water disputes between India and Pakistan. But the wars so far fought between the two countries were in fact indirectly water wars, as each remained endeavoring to control head waters of Indus Basin and that too in an era when both the countries were water surplus. With rapid population growth on both sides of border, Pakistan has entered into the category of water scarce countries owing to its inherent arid and semi climate, whereas India despite being the second wettest country of the world has also become water stressed. Being amongst the thickly populated countries of the world, food security is their major concern together with cheap energy to sustain industrial growth. Climate change implications have further added to these concerns like accelerated glaciers melting, may benefit only India. Sharing of waters under droughts also remains unaddressed. Under these circumstances, India being the upper riparian is trying to get more and more quantity of waters flowing though its territory taking advantages of the subjective clauses and/or self-serving interpretations of the Treaty. The quantum of work completed, initiated or planned on the head waters of Pakistan has added to its apprehensions that India will use the structures on western rivers as strategic, political and economic tools. In sharing of transboundary waters, not only quantity but timing of flows is also of extreme importance. Violations of the timing for filling of Baglihar dam, duly mentioned in the Treaty, have strengthened these apprehensions. Climate change, environmental concerns, and using state of the art data sharing mechanisms are the issues least tackled in the treaty. That may give rise to multiple dimensions to differences and disputes. The Court of Arbitration is, in fact, not a Court of Justice but facilitator for arbitration. Trust deficit is already there and both the countries are nuclear powers. The international community is therefore required to frame and implement universal laws based upon equitable and fair sharing of transboundary waters all over the world for avoiding water wars.

In conclusion, it is imperative for the political

leadership, civil society and other important stakeholders in the water issue to exhibit confidence, to counter propaganda and ensure that both countries deal with the challenges posed by the water crises in the region jointly. They must refrain from pointing fingers at each other. The challenges posed by water scarcity should unite the two countries and not divide them and cause hostility.

The Pakistan-India water dispute has been continuing for the last several decades. This dispute is attributed to the Indus treaty made in the 1960s which set out how Pakistan and India would share water resources. One of the clauses was that India would not construct a dam in rivers which belonged to Pakistan without express permission from Pakistan. However, India flouted this rule by constructing a hydro-electric plant in Doda district along Chenab River without due consultation from Pakistan. Pakistan saw this as an economic and political threat since it depended on waters from this river for agricultural purposes.

However, this conflict has adversely affected both countries by limiting development through cooperation. It also poses a danger of encouraging terrorism between the two countries especially if terrorists find it a cause worthy of their intervention. This conflict may also degenerate into war, especially if a terrorist activity occurs as a result of the conflict or if leaders intentionally provoke each other in a bid to resolve the dispute. This may lead to a regional war and may cause very many fatalities.

In order to mitigate the threats caused by the conflict, it is imperative that action is taken to prevent further escalation of the conflict. There are various ways in which the dispute may be resolved and one of the most effective ways is use of dialogue and mediation. Dialogue and mediation enable concerned parties to discuss issues and present them to a neutral mediator who makes a binding decision on issues raised. Another means is the re-negotiation of the treaty.

Since the treaty was made many decades ago, and it overlooked certain societal changes which occur over time, a new treaty which replaces the current one may be developed by Pakistan and India. However, this treaty should predict future trends which may cause further disputes in future.

Finally, water conservation is an important policy which should be embraced by Pakistan and India to reduce expenses on water costs and prevent the depletion of the water resource. These measures should be embraced by all countries with resources, since they will prevent future problems or conflicts which are associated with possession of resources.

References:

- Akhtar Shaheen, "Emerging Challenges to Indus Waters Treaty: Issues of Compliance and Trans-boundary impacts of Indian hydro projects on the Western Rivers", Institute of Regional Studies Islamabad (2010).
- Ali Raja Nazakat, Faiz-ur-Rehman and Mahmood-ur-RehmanWani, 2011"Indus Water Treaty between Pakistan and India: From Conciliation to Confrontation".
- Allouche Jeremy, "Water nationalism: An explanation of the past and present conflicts in Central Asia, the Middle East and the Indian Subcontinent? PhD diss., University in Geneva (2005).
- Ammad Hafiz Mohammad "Water Sharing in the Indus River Basin: Application of Integrated Water Resources Management" 2000.
- Arora, R.K. 2007, "The Indus Water Treaty Regime", New Delhi: Mohit Publications.
- Article VII, Indus Water Treaty, (1960).
- Ajazuddin F. S. speaking at a Conference on "The Software of Peacebuilding," New Delhi, August 25, 2012.

- Barrett, S., (1994) "Conflict And Cooperation In Managing International Water Resources‖ CSERGE Working Paper London Business School And Centre For Social And Economic Research On The Global Environment, University College London And University Of East Anglia.
- Bokhari, Ashfak. "Kishanganga verdict a tilt in India's favor." The Dawn, February 13, 2013.
- B.G. Verghese, "Fuss Over Indus-I: India''s Rights Are Set Out in the Treaty," The Tribune (Chandigarh), 25 May 2005.
- ChandranSuba, "Indus Waters Governance-II: From 'Letter and Spirit' to 'Letter vs Spirit'", Institute of Peace and Conflict Studies (19 July 2010).
- ChoudhuryGolamWahed, Pakistan's Relations with India: 19471966. (London: Pall Mall Press Ltd., 1968).
- Draft National Water Policy of 2012, Ministry of Water Resources, Government of India.
- Gazdar, Haris (2005). 'Baglihar and Politics of Water: A Historical Perspective from Pakistan' Economic and Political Weekly, Vol. 40, No. 9 (Feb. 26 - Mar. 4), p. 814.
- Gill, M.S. "Water crisis of east and west Punjab." The Hindu, May 28, 2010.
- HaidarSuhasini, The Hindu. 3rd march 2017.
- Hafiz Saeed blames India for Pakistan floods, calls it ... (n.d.). Retrieved October 23, 2016, from http://timesofindia.indiatimes.com/india/Hafiz-Saeed-blames-India-for-Pakistan-floods-calls-it-waterterrorism/articleshow/42116443.cms.
- Hali M Sultan, 2018, "Pak-India Water War", Pakistan Today.
- India suspends Indus commissioners' meetings | The Third Pole. (n.d.). Retrieved Octobe r23 2016 from https://www.thethirdpole.net/2016/09/26/india-suspends-indus-commissioners-meetings/.

- Iyer, Ramaswamy R. (2005). 'Indus Treaty: A Different View,' Economic and Political Weekly, Vol. 40, No. 29 (Jul. 16-22), p. 1075.
- Jason Gehrig with Mark M. Rogers Edited by Dennis Warner, Chris Seremet, and Tom Bamat, "Water and Conflict in Corporatingpeacebuilding into Water development", United States Conference of Catholic Bishops. Published 2009.
- Kaushik k. Aditya, "Regulating Water Security in Border Regions: The Case of India and Pakistan", August 1st, 2017.
- Khan Muhammad Ayub, Friends not Masters: A Political Autobiography (London: Oxford University Press, 1967).
- Madhana, Niharika. "Water Wars: Why India and Pakistan Are Squaring Off Over Their Rivers," Time, April 16, 2012.
- T.S. Maini, "South Asian Cooperation and The Role of the Punjabs" (New Delhi: Siddhartha Publications) 2007; and T.S. Maini, "Now let's tackle the tougher issues," Tehelka, (May 15, 2012), http://www.tehelka.com/story_main52.asp?filename=Fw1 50512Now.asp.
- Maini T.S. , "Indo-Pak water issues: Room for cooperation," The Daily Times, July 26, 2011.
- Maini T.S., "Now let's tackle the tougher issues," Tehelka, 15 May, 2012 http://www.tehelka.com/story_main52.asp?filename=Fw1 50512Now.asp (accessed August 20, 2012).
- Muhammad TayyabSohail, Huang Delin, Aqsa Siddiq, FarwaIdrees, Sidra Arshad, RehanMuhammad, February 9, 2015, "Evaluation of Historic Indo-Pak Relations, Water Resource Issues and Its impact on Contemporary Bilateral Affairs".
- Muhammad Rashid Khan University of the Punjab, Lahore South Asian Studies A Research Journal of South Asian Studies Vol. 28, No. 1, January – June 2013,

185

pp.213-221 Crucial Water Issues between Pakistan and India, CBMs, and the Role of Media.

- Niharika, Madhana, "Water Wars: Why India and Pakistan Are Squaring Off Over Their Rivers," Time,(April 16, 2012), http://www.time.com/time/printout/0,8816,2111601,00.ht ml (accessed August 20, 2012).

- Pakistan approaches International Court of Justice, World ... (n.d.). Retrieved October 23, 2016, from http://www.dnaindia.com/india/report-pakistan-approaches-international-court-of-justice-world-bank-overindus-waters-treaty-225943.

- PanugantiSreya, "Desert Solitaire: Why India and Pakistan Should Collaborate to Combat Desertification," Stimson, April 10,2012,http://www.stimson.org/spotlight/desert-solitaire-why-india-and-pakistan-shouldcollaborate-to-combat-desertification-/ (accessed August 20, 2012).

- Qureshi Dr. Waseem Ahmad, 2017, "The Indus Basin: Water Cooperation, International Law andthe Indus Waters Treaty".

- Ramanathan A.L. (ed). National Workshop on Water Quality (Including Drinking Water).Book of Abstracts. Jawaharlal Nehru University. February 2002. New Delhi, available at http://jnuenvis.nic.in/publication/water quality.pdf.(accessed 16 October 2012).

- RanaYudhvir, "Farmers teach India Inc ways to mend ties," Times of India, (May 7,2012), http://articles.timesofindia.indiatimes.com/2012-05-07/india-business/31609560_1_aman-ki-border-villagesindia-and-pakistan (accessed August 20, 2012).

- Rehman, H., and Kamal, A., (2005) "Indus Basin River System - Flooding and Flood Mitigation" Ministry of Water and Power, Islamabad,Pakistan.Available from http://www.riversymposium.com/2005/index.php?elemen.

- Sarvat N. Hanif, 2013 "Acess to water catalyst for cooperation, peace building".
- Siyad A. C., Muhammed (2005). 'Indus Waters Treaty and Baglihar Project: Relevance of International Watercourse Law,' Economic and Political Weekly, Vol. 40, No. 29 (Jul. 16-22), p. 3146.
- Tariq Sardar Muhammad, 2004, "Managing the Indus Waters: Alternative Strategies".
- The Indian Express, September 30, 2016.
- The Observer Research Foundation (2011): "Reimaging the Indus", 15-17. Availabale at: http/www.orfonline.org.
- TikhonovaPolina. November 4, 2016. "India vs. Pakistan water Conflict Poses Global Threat".
- Vaid Manish &MainiTridivesh Sing, "Indo-Pak Water Disputes: Time for Fresh Approaches" Chapter-4, peace print: South Asian Journal of peace building, vol.4, no-2, 2012.
- Verghese B. G., "It's Time for Indus-II." The Tribune 26 (May 25, 2005).
- Verghese, BG, "Water issues in South Asia," ORF Discourse, Vol. 5, Issue 8, April 2011.
- Waslekar s, "The Final Settlement: Restructuring India-Pakistan Relations, Strategic Foresight Group Mumbai (2005): 55.
- Wirsing and Jasparro, 2006 and Sridhar, 2005)Wirsing, R.G and Jasparro, C., (2006) "Spotlight on Indus River Diplomacy: India, Pakistan, and the Baglihar Dam Dispute". Asia-Pacific Center for Security Studies. Available from http://www.apcss.org/Publications/APSSS/IndusRiverDiplomacy.Wirsing.Jasparro.pdf).
- World Bank. 'South Asia Water: Water Resources Management,' available at http://web.worldbank.org/WBSITE/EXTERNAL/COUNTRIES/SOUTHASIAEXT/0,,contentMDK:22022926~page PK: 146736~piPK: 146830~theSitePK: 223547, 00.html.

- ZaheerulHasan . "Indo-Pak Dispute over Kishanganga Project." Pak Tribune, October 30, 2012.
- https://www.lawteacher.netzthe-India-Pakistan.
- http://www.saarc-sec.org/areaofcooperation/cat-detail.php?cat_id=44# (accessed August 20, 2012).

Chapter-IV

Resolutioning Water Conflict and Peace Building : Issues and Challenges

Introduction

"Water wars are coming!" the newspaper headlines scream. It seems obvious-rivalries over water have been the source of disputes since humans settled down to cultivate food. Even our language reflects these ancient roots: "rivalry" comes from the Latin rivalis, or "one using the same river as another." Countries or provinces bordering the same river (known as "riparians") are often rivals for the water they share. As the number of international river basins (and impact of water scarcity) has grown so do the warnings that these countries will take up arms to ensure their access to water. In 1995, for example, World Bank Vice President Ismail Serageldin claimed that "the wars of the next century will be about water."

Of course, people compete-sometimes violently-for water. Within a nation, users-farmers, hydroelectric dams, recreational users, environmentalists-are often at odds, and the probability of a mutually acceptable solution falls as the number of stakeholders rises. Water is never the single-and hardly ever the major-cause of conflict. But it can exacerbate existing tensions. History is littered with examples of violent water conflicts: just as Californian farmers bombed pipelines moving water from Owens Valley to Los Angeles in the early 1900s, Chinese farmers in Shandong clashed with police in 2000 to protest government plans to divert irrigation water to cities and industries. But these conflicts usually break out within nations. International rivers are a different story (Wolf, 2006).

Conflicts over water-a precious resource, the supply of which is growing sparser and the demand for which is ever mounting-have been much talked about by experts. Growing populations and extending development would render conflicts between water rich and water-scarce nations inevitable. Upstream states that control the flow of water to downstream states would use this valuable resource as a key diplomatic and strategic tool to coerce the downstream nations into submitting to its demands. According to the 2002 United Nations World Water Development Report, there were 507 conflictive events over water during the previous fifty years. Thirty-seven among these involved violence, of which 21 consisted of military acts (18 between Israel and its neighbours). "Some of the most vociferous enemies around the world have negotiated water agreements [concerning international rivers] or are in the process of doing so," says the report. Global warming would act as a catalyst to water-conflict scenarios, with decreasing rainfall and increasing evaporation in some areas that have made the regular climate patterns erratic. Intermittent phases of flooding and droughts causing massive human suffering would pressure governments into turning off the taps to its neighbours.

The Indus River, whose basin cradled one of the oldest civilizations of the world, sustains Pakistan today. Both India and Pakistan depend on snow-fed rivers that rise in the Himalayas. Pakistan depends on the Indus for its survival and sustenance. The Indus, moreover, passes through Jammu and Kashmir, which is in dispute between the two countries. The history of water sharing between India and Pakistan has been marked by exceptional cooperation and intermittent conflicts over the interpretation of the water sharing treaty that forms the basis for this cooperation. The Tulbul Navigation Project and the Baglihar, Kishanganga, and Salal hydroelectric power projects are a few contentious issues between the two countries revolving around the Indus Waters Treaty (IWT). The incongruities in interpretations of the IWT have been attributed to political motives, rather than differences over technical and engineering aspects of water management (Sridhar, 2004).

Pakistan, India and the Indus Water Treaty

Islamabad has asked the World Bank to honour the Indus Water Treaty executed between India and Pakistan in 1960. This is in response to Prime Minister Narendra Modi's remark that India is free to use the water which flows into the sea. This is not correct because according to the treaty India cannot use more than 20 percent of the Indus Water. The World Bank spent many years to persuade New Delhi and Islamabad to reach an agreement. According to the treaty, India could draw water from the Ravi, the Beas and the Sutlej while Pakistan from the Indus, the Chenab and Jhelum. Even though both countries felt that they could utilise the water which was flowing through their country, they refrained from doing so because of the treaty. In fact, the Indus Water Treaty is an example before the world that it held the ground even when the two countries went to war.

Modi's off-the-cuff remark has created consternation in Pakistan, forcing it to appeal to the World Bank to "fulfill its obligation" relating to the treaty. In a letter to World Bank President Jim Young Kim, Pakistan finance Minister Ishaq Dar has said the treaty did not provide for a situation where in a party can 'pause' performance of its obligation and this attitude of the World Bank would prejudice Pakistan's interest and rights under the treaty. Pakistan does not want any alternation in the treaty. In its reaction, the World Bank has admitted to have paused its arbitration in the water dispute between India and Pakistan, saying it is doing so to protect the Indus Water Treaty. India would take no unilateral step to stop the water going unused into the Arabian Sea. However, there is a case where the two countries should sit and hammer out another treaty because the old one is outdated. Then it was thought that the water given to Rajasthan would be utilised by the rest of the country because the state, part of the desert would not be able to do so. But this has turned out to be wrong. The state has utilised the water allotted to it and wants more. When Prime Minister Modi wants to have good relations with Pakistan and has wished his counterpart Nawaz Sharif on this birthday, Modi would not take any step which would harm Pakistan. There were enough of provocation from Islamabad like the attacks on Pathankot and Uri that killed many civilians to act unilaterally. Even otherwise, it is in the interest of both countries that peace should prevail in the region both would benefit.

The Indus water treaty can be replaced with another treaty but the consent of Pakistan is necessary. When it has not been willing to allow getting electricity from the run of the river it is difficult to imagine that it would agree to the use of rivers in the Indus system even through water from them is pouring into the Arabian Sea without being used for either irrigation or hydroelectric projects.

There is a tendency in Pakistan to link everything with Kashmir, which is a complicated problem and it would take many years to solve. The revision of Indus Water Treaty, which can satisfy both the countries, would add to the peace prospects. The only point to be taken into accent is how the two countries can come closer to each other (Nayar, 2017).

Water Woes

With winter setting in, the corresponding rains have not yet arrived. The result has been a shortage of water for agriculture, for which it is nothing less than lifeblood. However, while agriculture is suffering, the water shortage has also meant that canals have to be closed. As a result, production of hydro-electricity will go down; with the result that load shedding will increase. While electricity has been cut off for the domestic consumer, it has also been absent for the tube wells that are the fallback of the farmer. The shortfall is now 4025 MW, and this is the time that a callous administration has decided to shut down further releases from the Mangla Dam. When one considers what was said by PML (Q) Senator Muhammad Ali Durrani to the participants of a protest walk in Bahawalpur, it becomes clear what the real problem is. Senator Durrani has accused India of a plot to turn the Bahawalpur civilisation into a Death Valley. Senator Durrani wanted the federal government to build pressure upon India to obey international law, as well as the Indus Waters Treaty which it was violating to divert water for its own use. Senator Durrani was particularly eloquent, because in that area river water is not just used for agriculture, but also domestic use, and thus Indian diversions do not just prevent agriculture, but they also affect living in the area.

That India is behind this mischief is indubitable. Its shifting of the waters of Kashmir, which it has, down South, all the way to Rajasthan, is too well known. Also, in the most recent attempts, it has made diversions for the Wullar Barrage and now the Baglihar Barrage, which are not only causing crippling shortages in Pakistan, but are also in violation of the Indus Waters Treaty. At the same time, the Pakistani government, in its eagerness to restart the composite dialogue, has not only virtually let these violations go by default, but has also dragged its feet on the eminently feasible Kalabagh Dam project. This has not been conveyed to India that Pakistan was making a sacrifice at the altar of federalism, because federating units had manufactured objections to the project, but that Pakistan did not need either large storages or any more hydel.

Therefore, the Government of Pakistan must abandon its present spineless attitude, and tackle the problems of the citizens in right earnest. Not only does this mean electricity load shedding, but also gas load shedding. Even one is enough to make life a misery during winter. Combined, they make more misery for those already rendered miserable. The

Government of Pakistan must also take up not just with India, but with the international community, the guarantees and promises it has made, and stop its strangling of Pakistanis, not just Pakistani agriculture. This issue is of prime importance, and must not be placed on the backburner at anyone's bidding.

Conflict Factors in The Indus River Basin

The geo-political and geo-economic factors of the Indus waters conflict can be grouped together in pairs as follows: relative locations and riparian claims, the unnatural patchwork pattern of political boundaries and surface features for agriculture and water availability, climate change and water supply, population density and patterns of settlement for the land utilisation, and internal pressures and foreign relations of the parties. Some of these elements also contributed towards conflict transformation ultimately leading to an accommodation. Most particular among those was the changing domestic political and economic situation and nature of external relations. Each of these factors is connected to the economic and security interests of the riparian are bounded in the control of the Kashmir territory. The relative conflict potential of these factors in generating an inter-state dispute over the control of the Indus rivers system has been assessed by using the pair comparison method. The question whether the boundaries in the Indus basin were drawn on the basis of the location of water resource access or not, is also dealt with in detail.

1.Geographical Location and Riparian Rights

The Indus is a multinational basin, shared by four nation states; China, India, Pakistan and Afghanistan. The Chinese territory of Tibet contains the origin of the Indus and the Sutlej rivers characterizing China as the upper-most riparian of the Indus basin. Afghanistan contributes the Kabul River, a tributary to the Indus River. The other five tributaries to the Indus river system are the Jhelum, Chenab, Ravi, Sutlej and

Beas which originate in Indian and Pakistani parts of Kashmir and the Himachal Pradesh of India. A major area of the basin is shared by the modern states of Pakistan and India and as a result, these two countries have been getting engaged in large-scale development programmes and, consequently, indulging into conflict of interest. India's portion of the basin, including the disputed territory of Jammu and Kashmir, contains the headwaters of all five rivers of the Punjab. The conflicts between the upper and lower riparian of the basin and the agreements that emerged from them have centered on the Punjab [East and West Punjab or Indian and Pakistani Punjab] and the territory of Jammu and Kashmir. If all the riparians are considered in a wholesome picture, India is the middle riparian and is supposed to adhere to the principle of 'community in resource utilisation' of international rivers. If exclusively India and Pakistan are considered, India enjoys an obvious advantage of being an upper riparian and is expected to invoke 'absolute territorial sovereignty' and Pakistan would favour 'absolute territorial integrity' principle.

2. Surface Characteristics

The Indus river system which originates in Tibet constitutes its headwaters in the Western Himalayas. Excluding the uppermost portions and its longest tributary (the Sutlej River), the Indus River flows through mountainous and difficult terrain until it emerges on to the Punjab plains. Given the nature of the terrain and the scant population in that region, the area contains a number of hydro-strategic sites for dam construction. Such projects would have inherent potential for the water-based conflicts. The likelihood of the conflict, however, depends upon the decisions made in the upper parts of the basin for resource development. One can thus safely say that the conflict potential is at best latent, and that its activation is contingent upon developments in the catchment areas (Indian side of

Kashmir and the mountainous parts of the Indian Punjab) of the basin (Basheer, 1969).

Another aspect of the Indus system which is necessary to be mentioned here is the peculiar geographic nature of the Kashmiri territory. This beautiful landscape consists of high mountain ranges, snow-covered peaks and dense forests with heavy snow falls in winters and high precipitations in the rainy season. The enchanting scenery of the valley is bestowed with a number of streams, lakes and rivers which latterly join Indus River to formulate a gigantic system with massive flow of waters. The melting of snows on the sky-scrapping peaks in the summer season and the showering of the rains in the valleys during monsoon provide a permanent natural source of waters flowing from Kashmiri terrain into the banks of Indus River. This system of six rivers gives life to the predominantly arid, agrarian economy of Pakistan and part of the Indian Punjab. The socio-economic life cycles of the agricultural civilization on the both sides of the border have flourished along the banks of river Indus.

Kashmir shares its borders with China, India, Afghanistan and Pakistan. The topography of the Kashmir territory can be divided into following mountain ranges, which enfold a number of valleys, lakes and rivers.

Karakorum Range

This snow-covered mountain range is situated to the north of the main Himalaya and Ladakh ranges leaving Aksai Chin and Depsang plains along Chinese border. Twelve peaks with an elevation above 7,000 meters, including the famous K2 (28,250 feet) and Rakaposhi (25,550 feet) are the hallmark of this range. The other peaks are: Saser Kangri (25,170 feet), Slataro Kangri (25,400 feet), Sia Kangri (24,480 feet), Masher broom (25,660 feet), Gasher broom (26,470 feet), Kunjat Sar (25,459 feet), Dastagil Sar (25,868 feet), Haramosh (24,270 feet), Kampiri Diwar (23,434 feet) and Ishkuman (18,467 feet). The Karakorum-range forms a part of trans-Himalaya. Its average elevation is over 3,000 meters.

The Karakorum-range has some of the biggest glaciers of the world, outside the polar region. Most prominent among them is the Siachen glacier which has a length of 72 and breadth of 10 kilometres.

Ladakh Range: The Ladakh range lies to the south of Karakorum and north of the main Himalaya ranges. It has an average elevation of over 3,500 meters. There are a number of prominent rivers in eastern Ladakh that drain into the Indus River and into the famous Salt Lake. Drainage of the Karakorum and Ladakh ranges forms the major source of water of the main Indus River originating in Tibet.

Great Himalaya: The great Himalaya-roof of the earth-passes through Bhutan, Sikkim, Nepal, Tibet, Himachal Pradesh, Jammu and Kashmir and touches its lower peak, Nunkun (23,410 feet). the mountain range of great Himalaya branches off at the Nanga Parbat Massif (26,660 feet) and runs along an arc passing to the south of the Kashmir valley to Murree and Margalla hills encircling Islamabad valley (Pakistan's capital) from its north, west and south sides. The great Himalaya drains in Tibet and gives birth to the mighty Indus River which flows down towards west, passing through Kashmir territory along with Ladakh range. The river then turns to south near Gilgit and passing through the whole of Pakistan drains in Arabian Sea at Karachi.

The Jammu and Kashmir valley bears origins of three out of five Punjab's rivers— Jhelum, Chenab and Ravi. While Beas and Sutlej collect drainage of the Indian territory of Himachal Pradesh but both rivers were main source of irrigation in Pakistan's province Punjab, well before partition of the subcontinent to the signing of the Indus Water Treaty in September 1960 between India and Pakistan.

The geography of the Sutlej River is less complicated than that of the Indus. The Sutlej acts as a transverse

Himalayan stream, apparently exploiting an ancient fault-line in its gorge below Shipki La. This course brings it to Inner Siwaliks at the Bhakra site about 1,200 feet above the sea level. But the rim-station on the Sutlej is at Rupar, where it cuts through the last foothills and emerges onto the plains. From Rupar to Mithankot, Sutlej falls only 560 feet over a distance of almost 550 river miles, making an average gradient of one foot per mile.

Michel in his book, The Indus Rivers, makes reference to two dam sites on River Chenab and Jhelum: "The Chenab and the Jhelum each offers a dam site within Jammu Kashmir." The Chenab site is at Dhaingarh to the north of Riasi, where India has constructed Salal dam in the late 1970s. The dam is approximately 50 kilometres upstream from Pakistan's Maralla headworks. The second site on the River Jhelum where it leaves Lake Wullar and cuts through the Pir Panjal Range is an ongoing issue between India and Pakistan. Pakistan has constructed dam on the course of the Jhelum where the Salt Range meets the Siwaliks near Mangla. The Mangla Dam is built under the Indus Basin Project, after signing the Indus Waters Treaty with India in 1960. The dam, located at the rim-station, includes the Kishanganga and Kunhar tributaries of the Jhelum in its storage.

The above mentioned geographic details emphasize a remarkable feature of the Indus river system i.e., catchments area of the entire river system is found in the disputed territory of Jammu and Kashmir. Where water fall is above 20 feet per mile and when it leaves the Kashmir territory, at various rim-stations of its tributaries, the water fall reduces to one foot to only six inches per mile in the rest of the basin. These two amazing characteristics signify the hydro-strategic importance of the Kashmir territory for the riparians as the Kashmir is the only territory suitable to develop water resources for the benefit of the inhabitants of the entire Indus basin (Aloys, 1967).

3. Climate and water supply

The Indus basin is classified as arid or semi arid, except for its upper most area. The per annum precipitation may exceed sixty inches along the south-facing slopes of the Himalaya, but it decreases rapidly south-westwards, so that Lahore, some 25 miles from the foothills, receives about twenty inches. The rainfall in the region of Pakistani Punjab is characteristically torrential and unreliable and this trend increases south westwards.

The climatic condition of the region does not provide any uniform delineation between the plains of upper and lower Indus basin. There are climatic changes over this vast region but the variation over the 63 miles from Karachi to Thatta, indicates beginning of the change from coastal to an inland station. This is despite the fact that the climatic change which still receives some maritime modification is much greater than that over the 61 miles from Thatta to Sukkur or over the 251 miles from Thatta to Hyderabad. In fact, in any given season, differences in temperature between Hyderabad and Lahore (693 miles apart) are smaller than those between Thatta and Karachi.

In any monsoonal region, differences in elevation are more significant than latitude especially within the first 20 miles from the sea. The plains of Indus are pretty much a climatic unit except in the coastal and sub-mountainous zones, because the gradient of the Indus plains is less than one foot per mile. Of the Indus plains meteorological stations, Jacobabad, northwest of Sukkur, experiences the highest temperatures and the lowest average annual rainfall. But on an afternoon in June, when it may be 120F in Jacobabad, it is likely to be 110F or even 115F in both Hyderabad and Multan, and not much cooler in Faisalabad or Lahore. On the other hand, the winter differentials are greater and are reflected to some degree in the natural vegetation and cropping patterns. Light frosts are experienced in Lahore and occasionally even in Multan, though never in Hyderabad or Karachi. Winter rainfall is not unknown in Jacobabad, though it gets at least 3 of its 4 inches in the months of June, July and August (Basheer, 1961).

The Punjab Government realised that the flowing water in the rivers goes unused as it flows down into the Arabian Sea before the maturing season of Rabi crops and the sowing season of Kharif crops. While shortage of water, on the other hand, was adversely affecting the agricultural production. The canals network was useless without proper upstream storage. The Punjab Government formally requested the Centre to locate sites for dams to store water for irrigation during lean months and to produce electricity as well. The British Government started locating probable dam sites on the river Indus and all its tributaries (UNECAFE).

The first proposed dam had to be on the convergence of the rivers Indus and Soan. The High Dam Authority called it Makhed Dam—now famous as Kalabagh Dam, with a storage capacity of 15 MAF. The second dam on the Indus was proposed at Tarbela. It offered 9.3 MAF storage along with an off-channel storage capacity of 30 MAF.

Two more dam sites were located on the river Jhelum; first on the mouth of Wullar Lake; and second at Mangla near Mirpur. While on the river Chenab, the proposed dam site was located at Dhiangarh. On the Sutlej a gorge had already been under study since 1907 at Rupar. The second dam site at Sutlej was proposed at Bhakra with 8 MAF storage capacities. It was further decided to connect the waters of the Chenab and Ravi by constructing a tunnel under Marhu Pass, from where it could be distributed to Sutlej Valley Canals through that was at this juncture of the history that Indian subcontinent was partitioned resulting in the splitting of Punjab into West and East Punjab. The proposals to meet the deficiency of Sutlej Valley Canals were being framed. The West Punjab was given to Pakistan while East Punjab was awarded to India. Almost all the catchment areas of the Indus Rivers were gone under the Indian control which threatened the Pakistan's interests.

4. Domestic Scenario and External Relations

According to the Indian Independence Act 1947, legal understanding was that the treaty obligations relating to territories contained in the Dominion of India and Pakistan would be obligatory only in relation to a third state and did not include bilateral Indo-Pakistani relations. The question was whether two states which formerly were part of the same legal entity have obligations to each other? Nijim notes that Pakistan's membership to the UN was also a similar question. India's membership was kept continuing while Pakistan had to apply for the consideration (embassy 1958). Consequently, India invoked the principle of absolute territorial sovereignty relating to its claims over the international rivers flowing through its land. A new status quo had emerged. The relevant matter was the question of state succession.

Since the Indian Independence Act included nothing about the status of the rivers and canals, a standstill agreement was concluded between provincial governments of Indian and Pakistani Punjab on 18 December 1947, to be terminated on 31 March 1948 with the end of the fiscal year in both countries, subject to further extension. Meanwhile, bilateral relations were further strained as the ongoing conflict over Jammu and Kashmir took a new turn since India airlifted its troops there on 26 October 1947, in an effort to capture the princely state (Akbar 1988).

Consequently, no negotiations regarding water conflict were held or even attempted. India on 1 April 1948, cut-off the flow of water to Pakistan from the Upper Bari Doab and Dipalpur canals systems. The intended effect of this action was to deprive the West Punjab of irrigation water at the

201

critical time of sowing of the Kharif crops and to deny Lahore of its prime source of municipal water, and to assert propriety rights over the power supply from a hydroelectric plant on the upper Beas.

The apparent reason attached to the termination of water flow was Indian urge to bring more lands, in East Punjab, under cultivation but at the same time it feared that if the status quo was maintained a precedent would be established which Pakistan might later invoke as a right. Another possible Indian intention might have been forcing Pakistan to withdraw its claims over Kashmir territory.

In sum, there was hardly any declaration of riparian rights in favour of Pakistan notwithstanding later writings by Pakistani sympathizers. The Agreement needs to be evaluated in the context of prevailing conditions of that time. Being the lower riparian, Pakistan was forced to request for the restoration of water. Short of war declaration, Pakistan held an unfavourable bargaining position. This accounts for the haste with which the Agreement was signed and turned to be totally unfavourable for Pakistan. From Pakistan's point of view, there was no specific provision as to when negotiations should be resumed or for how long the Agreement was to be binding.

IWT Related Issues and Challenges
Hydrological Shock

Pakistan faced the first hydrological shock when Eastern Rivers were given to India which prior to the Treaty were irrigating close to 5 million acres of most productive agricultural land in the West Punjab of Pakistan. Pakistan at the time of signing of this Treaty was to a large extent dependant on agro based economy. Agricultural sector contributed over 75percent of GDP. Denial of irrigation water to over 5 million acres of land meant economic strangulation of Pakistan. To overcome this hydraulic shock, Pakistan has to undertake massive Indus Basin Replacement

Works. These works constituted the largest single civil engineering contracts ever awarded in the history of the world. Water has to be transferred over massive inter-river main canals with aggregate length of 61,000 km, 12 barrages, a network of secondary and tertiary canals with total length of 1.61 million km and two large dams one on River Jhelum and the other on River Indus known as Tarbela Dam which even today stands as world's largest volume dam (Tariq, 2014).

Operation &maintenance cost of replacement works

Though the Indus Basin works were completed within ten years period, the time frame allowed under the Treaty, the perpetual operation and maintenance cost of these mega structures was prohibitive along with the cost of safety monitoring and surveillance of large barrages.

High hazard potentials

The Indus Basin replacement works were located either on main river channels or across the direction of flood flows thus rendering them vulnerable to flood damages. These massive hydraulic structures having high hazard potentials are perpetual source of worries and require a very high degree of competent operation, maintenance and surveillance.

Damages to Deltaic region

The sediments brought by the Basin Rivers were mostly deposited in the lower deltaic region close to the coast. With construction of dams, barrages and canals as required under the Treaty, most of sediments which used to flourish the delta were trapped in these hydraulic structures. This destroyed the large track of coastal land rendering it none located along the coastal belt had to be abandoned with millions of people losing their livelihood.

Twin menace of water logging and salinity

The Indus River System brings in some 33 million tons

of salt hydraulic structures and networks of canals, almost 30 million tons of salt get deposited annually in the basin. In addition to that the network of unlined canals excessively charged the ground water aquifer with the result that over 100,000 acres of land in the basin was getting water logged annually. Billions of rupees worth Salinity Control and Rehabilitation Projects (SCARP) were undertaken in the affected areas of the basin to control this twin menace of water logging.

Annual Desilting Cost

The Himalayan Mountains are geologically young and the geological formation is highly erodible. With steep slopes and high flow velocities the rivers which originate from the Himalayan ranges carry enormous sediments which get trapped in the storage dams, barrages and network of canals constructed as a result of the treaty. To maintain the discharge capacity of the canals annual desilting has become essential resulting in closure of canals over prolonged periods and incurring heavy desilting cost annually together with loss of storage in the dams and barrages.

Future challenges for Pakistan

Climate change impacts

a) Impacts on Glaciers: The climate models predict that due to temperature rise in the Himalayan-Karakorum-Hindukush (HKH) region the glacier world melt and some 30 to 40 percent additional water would become available for certain period of time. Pakistan, therefore, would deserve reasonable percentage of this additional water to be given to it. These models also predict that after 30 years the water availability in the basin would decline by 20 to 30 percent.

b) Climate change impacts and global warming would result in more severe hydro meteorological events. In the absence of reliable real data Pakistan would face myriad management challenges.

c) Monsoon pattern change: It is anticipated that climate change would impact the existing monsoonic pattern and changes thus brought about would have severe implications on the agriculture. With global warming the existing agro-climatic zones would undergo major changes with changed cropping pattern and more likely would necessitate replacement of existing crops with different varieties. Pakistan therefore needs to prepare itself for future climate change impact challenges and should start initiating adaptation plans for combating violent hydro-meteorological events, living with less water, ensuring food security and creating a resilient society.

Reliable hydro-meteorological data

Most of the water resources of Pakistan are generated outside the territorial domain of Pakistan. It is therefore vitally essential for Pakistan to have access to reliable real time hydro meteorological data for management of extreme events along with judicious management of its water resources.

Storage facilities allowed to India on western rivers

India is constructing a number of hydropower stations on the Western Rivers with storage facilities incorporated in design for flushing sediments. The cumulative effect of these storages can have extreme negative impact on Pakistan's irrigated agriculture. India's capacity to hold back substantial amount of water particularly during lean flow periods could have disastrous effects on Pakistan's agricultural productivity thus impacting Pakistan's food security efforts.

Over extraction of transboundary aquifer

Due to extremely low tariff for electricity for tube wells in the bordering states of India, the farmers are over extracting ground water thus mining transboundary aquifer impacting the ground water availability to farmers in the West Punjab of Pakistan. Such depletion of ground water on the Pakistan side would severely impact irrigated agriculture where over 50 percent of water comes from underground aquifer.

Transboundary pollution

India's untreated effluent both agricultural and industrial entering Pakistan is polluting the ground water aquifer, contaminating the rivers and fresh water bodies, degrading the agricultural land and has increased water borne diseases impacting large cross-sectors of population both in terms of their health and livelihood. More cooperation is urgently called upon to ensure transboundary untreated effluents are controlled and international declarations are fully respected by riparian countries. Similarly within each country similar steps would be required to ensure untreated effluents both agricultural and industrial are strictly controlled and strict penalties are imposed on the violations.

Population pressure on water resources

With rapidly growing population, multi-sectoral demand of water would grow manifold resulting in myriad management and water governance issues and challenges. Pakistan therefore, needs both hardware and software along with effective demand side and supply side management of scarce water resources of the country.

Decline in transboundary flows

Over the years it has been observed that Transboundary Rivers entering Pakistan are continuously indicating decreasing flows. This is contrary to the expected enhanced flow to enter Pakistan due to glacier melting as a result of temperature rises in Himalayan region. This fact needs to be seriously probed and researched.

India's latest policy document

India's latest thinking on transboundary waters is amply reflected in a recent report by Institute of Defence Studies in India (IDSA, 2010) on water security elaborates the increasing attention to water issues within a broader geographical context.

While reviewing India's bilateral water relations with neighbouring countries, country by country, the report notes that if not managed well, riparian issues will lead to increased conflicts. It calls for a paradigm shift from the historical supply side considerations in domestic and international agreements, and past investments focused on water sharing among competing interests, to one that focuses on benefit-sharing. It stresses that rivers can no longer be viewed as a "soft-component" of a country's foreign policy. Rather they must be seen as intricately linked to development goals and domestic needs impacting bilateral relations. The report goes on to say that while it is important to adopt sensible riparian policies and 'healthy rivers' schemes, there is a need to re-evaluate existing treaties and reframe them based on current hydrological knowledge and future mutual needs. India's geographical contours place multiple upper, middle and lower riparian systems within its borders thus placing it at the epicentres of riparian politics. Therefore, collaborative riparian management will be crucial for setting many of the water induced conflicts in the region; greater hydro-diplomacy both internally and across national borders will need to balance the region's growing water needs with larger security concerns.

Public perceptions in India on IWT

The Indian public is generally divided on the IWT. To broadly sum up the Indian views, five broader constituencies can be demarcated. These constituencies are briefly described below:

a) First Constituency: This constituency is in favour of Indus II under article VII and XII of the IWT for a joint development of the Indus Water Basin. This is in line with what David Lilienthal had suggested way back in 1950's.

b) Second constituency: This constituency favours a new Indus Treaty and considers the IWT as a partitioning treaty. The treaty should be based on new hydrological relationship.

c) Third Constituency: This constituency catering to the pressure group in Indian Kashmir asking for unhindered use of Indus, Jhelum and Chenab rivers–the three western rivers allocated to Pakistan under the IWT.

d) Fourth Constituency: This constituency considers war over water not an option and suggests India should use water as coercive tool and bargaining instrument for larger politico strategic objectives of India.

e) Fifth Constituency: This constituency is of the opinion that India should first exploit all the potentials permissible under the treaty and then ask for more and ask for review of the treaty.

A Way Forward
IWT Provisions

So far both India and Pakistan have been exploring the dispute related clauses to their respective advantages. Both countries searching for grey areas to hinder each other's development efforts. No country has looked seriously into other articles of the Treaty which have much larger connotation for cooperation and development with benefit accruing to both the countries and population across the Line of Control (LOC). Both countries therefore need to look into the article 6 & 7 of the Treaty and exploit the potential available there for larger cooperation.

Capacity Building of Commission rates

The first tier of dispute resolution mechanism under the Treaty is the offices of the two Commissioners. Unfortunately these Commissioners so far have failed to resolve the disputes and have been referring the disputes to international experts or International Court of Arbitration at a heavy financial cost and delays in implementation of projects. It is therefore envisaged that if we strengthened the technical and legal capacity of the offices of the

Commissioners on both sides, we can address the issues more expeditiously and more economically with much reduced ill-feelings on both sides.

Credibility of data exchanged

The mistrust and reliability of data exchanged is a serious issue and can be addressed through the technology available now. In case both countries jointly share the cost a more reliable data can be retrieved by both the countries through satellite and telemetry system. Similarly cooperating with international organization such as ICIMOD and WMO, both climate change impacts on monsoon pattern change and glacier behaviour can be assessed more reliably for better water management.

Catchment management

The catchment management is a crucial issue in ensuring the water availability. A joint catchment management authority would lead towards greater cooperation and surety against resource preservation.

Disaster management

Climate change impacts would affect the hydrological cycle – more violent hydro meteorological events are inevitable. To cope with such events joint mitigatory and adaptation plans can be worked out to create more effective disaster management institutions to cope with floods, droughts, landslides, etc and create resilient societies in both the countries.

Joint research studies

Water, food, energy and livelihood security under climate change would be excessively impaired. To meet these challenges there is tremendous scope where joint research can be carried out for not only the benefit of both countries but for the region as a whole (Tariq 2014).

Indus Water Treaty rides out latest crisis

The 1960 World Bank-mediated Indus Water Treaty

between India and Pakistan is considered one of the great success stories of water diplomacy, especially as it has survived the India –Pakistan wars of 1965, 1971, 1999 and much bad blood during and after the wars. Tension between the two countries is again at a peak following a terrorist strike in Kashmir, and some Indian commentators are speaking of re-engaging on the treaty as a non-military option to pressure Pakistan.

On September 18, 2016 an attack was carried out on an army base in the Garrison Town of Uri, 75 kilometers North-West of Kashmir's summer capital Srinagar, near the Line of Control (LOC) that effectively divides Kashmir between India and Pakistan. Eighteen Indian army personnel and four terrorists were killed in the attack, and India has blamed the attack on militant from Pakistan.

India and Pakistan have long been embroiled in diplomatic face-offs over Kashmir and have fought three wars, but have so far managed to uphold the treaty that provides mechanisms for resolving dispute over water sharing.

Just two days before the Uri attack, an Indian author on water disputes, Brahma Chellaney, wrote that, "India should hold out a credible threat of dissolving the Indus Water Treaty, drawing a clear linkage between Pakistan's right to unlimited water inflows and its responsibility not to cause harm to its upper riparian". Officially the Indian government has said little. In response to a question, the spokesperson of India's Ministry for External Affairs, Vikas Swarup, merely said, "For any such treaty to work, it is important that there must be mutual cooperation and trust between both the sides." He avoided going into the details.

The World Bank – which negotiated the treaty and setup an adjudicator in case of disputes- has not made an official statement either. A World Bank spokesperson said, "The World Bank's role in the Indus Water Treaty is limited and strictly procedural." Putting this into perspective, Ashok Swain, who teaches at the Department of Peace and Conflict Research, Uppsala University, Sweden, said that World Bank is co-signatory for certain, provisions of the Indus Water Treaty and its role is limited to a dispute regarding the implementation of the treaty, not its ation.

On whether India can create any problem for Pakistan by stopping water, Swain said that India does not have the enough storage facility to create supply problem immediately for Pakistan. "It has to raise its dam structures and that will take time. There is also another angle to it. India, even if it wants to, cannot take the water out of Kashmir valley. So the water of the three rivers (Indus, Jhelum and Chenab) will remain in their basin and India cannot divert that to other areas due to geographical reasons. India can stop the supply for some time, but cannot divert it".

Uttam Sinha, a research fellow at New Delhi based Institute for Defence Studies and Analyses (IDSA) also disagreed with those asking for scrapping the treaty. "For sending message to Pakistan, we do not necessarily need to go to the extent of scrapping the Indus Water Treaty. We can even send a strong message to Pakistan by using the water of western rivers of Indus basin for irrigation, electricity and storage of up to 3.6 Million Acre Feet (MAF), well within the norms laid down in the treaty".

Azeem Ali Shah, a Lahore based researcher with the International Water Management Institute (IWMI), told, "A unilateral withdrawal from the Treaty will bring World Bank into the dispute. It will also incite further anxiety among Pakistani people and might lead to violence."

The former Chief Minister of the Indian state of Jammu and Kashmir, Omar Abdullah, tweet, "will stick my neck out and say that nothing will happen to Indus Waters Treaty. It survived four wars and a Jammu and Kashmir Assembly unanimous resolution." Jammu and Kashmir Assembly had

211

passed a resolution in 2003 asking India and Pakistan to review the treaty which had not considered the developmental needs of the state, which mostly hosts the three rivers allocated to Pakistan.

"Such statements in favour of scrapping the treaty can only be treated as mere propaganda, not a diplomatic option," Medha Bisht, who teaches International Relations at South Asian University, told. One major reason for this is that India is itself a middle riparian country for two of the six rivers mentioned in the treaty. The Indus and Sutlej flow from Tibet, and there is no treaty between China and India to manage the relationship. One senior Indian commentator has even claimed that that China has indicated it would act to divert water from India if India decided to divert waters from Pakistan. Such a scenario, though, would lead to flooding and huge damages to all three countries. This highlights that, more than anything else, such treaties survive not just because of trust or goodwill, but because they serve the interests of the entire nation involved (Parvaiz, 2016).

India suspends talks on Indus water pact

Indian Prime Minister Narendra Modi held a meeting of senior officials from the water resources and External Affairs Ministries and the PMO to discuss the government's options on the India-Pakistan Indus Water Treaty in the wake of the Uri attack.While the meeting decided to suspend further water talks and increase the utilisation of rivers flowing through Jammu and Kashmir to maximise India's share, there was no decision on either reviewing or abrogating the 1960 treaty official sources said.

The government decided to suspend talks on the Permanent Indus Commission, the dispute redressed mechanism that has met 112 times, until "terror comes to an end". According to Article Viii_of the Indus Water Treaty, the commission must meet once a year, alternately in India and Pakistan. The last meeting was held in July 2016.

According to the sources, the Prime Minister held the meeting as "things have been difficult with Pakistan", adding that, hence, "this was the appropriate time to review arrangements under the Indus Water treaty again" (Haidar 2016).

Will approach U.N. if India violates Indus Water Treaty

Sartaj Aziz, foreign Affairs Adviser to Prime Minister Nawaz Sharif, said on 27 September, 2016 that Pakistan would approach the United Nations and the International Court of Justice if India suspends the 58-year-old Indus Waters Treaty, insisting that the revocation of the treaty could be taken as an "act of war"."The international Law states that India cannot unilaterally separate itself from the treaty". Aziz said while briefing the National Assembly on the issues. He said a unilateral revocation of the treaty could pose a threat to Pakistan and its economy. "This Indian act can be taken as breach of international peace and hence giving Pakistan a good reason to approach the United Nation Security Council," He said Pakistan was considering drawing attention of the international community on the dangers of such an action (Hindu, 2016).

Withdrawing Indus Water Treaty is not a solution to punish Pakistan as it will only bring global condemnation

India needs to remember that the 1960 Indus Waters Treaty is an international agreement. Unilateral withdrawal from it will bring global condemnation, and the moral high ground, which India enjoys vis-a-vis Pakistan in the post-Uri period, will be lost. This will give the regime in Pakistan to turn the tables. The uniqueness of the treaty is it is the only international water treaty co-signed by a third party-the World Bank. India's open withdrawal from the treaty will automatically draw the World Bank into the dispute-and in support of Pakistan. If India decides to withdraw from the treaty, Pakistan can also take India to International Court of Justice and, in all likelihood, win the case. The World court's decision in 1997 on the case concerning Gabcikovo-Nagymaros project on the Danube River between Hungary and Slovakia clearly establishes the importance of respecting international water agreements.

If India decides to ignore international norms and treats the Indus waters as a weapon to punish Pakistan, it will unfortunately lead to huge human insecurity in the neighbouring country. At the same time, this will make India's own dams and reservoirs in the river system genuine military targets for Pakistan to retaliate. That will be a huge risk to take. Certainly, there are not many viable options available for Prime Minister Modi to successfully inflict retribution on Pakistan for the Uri attack to openly take credit for it. If he decides to sacrifice the Indus Water Treaty as a face saver, it will impose a huge cost on India itself (Swain, 2016).

India's Prime Minister Modi inaugurates hydro project in Kashmir, amidst Pakistan protests

India's Prime Minister Narendra Modi inaugurated a hydroelectric power plant on 12 may 2018 in the state of Jammu and Kashmir, amid protests from neighbour Pakistan which says the project on a river flowing into Pakistan will disrupt water supplies. The 330 megawatt Kishanganga hydropower station, work on which started in 2009, is one of the projects that India has fast-tracked in the volatile state amid frosty ties between the nuclear-armed countries. "This region can not only become self-sufficient in power but also produce for other regions of the countries," Modi said in the state's capital Srinagar. "Keeping that in mind we have been working on various projects here in the past four years."

Pakistan has opposed some of these projects, saying they violate a World Bank mediated treaty on the sharing of the Indus River and its tributaries upon which 80 percent of its irrigated agriculture depends. "Pakistan is seriously concerned about the inauguration (of the Kishanganga

214

plant)," its foreign ministry said in a statement. "Pakistan believes that the inauguration of the project without the resolution of the dispute is tantamount to violation of the Indus Water Treaty (IWT).

India has said the hydropower projects underway in Jammu and Kashmir are "run-of-the-river" schemes that use the river's flow and elevation to generate electricity rather than large reservoirs, and do not contravene the treaty (Chitrakar, 2018).

Seeking an 'amicable solution' to water dispute between India, Pakistan: World Bank

The World Bank, which is holding talks with a Pakistani delegation regarding the water dispute with India, has said that they are seeking an amicable solution, said a report in the Dawn. A Pakistani delegation, headed by Attorney General Ashtar Ausaf Ali, arrived in Washington on Sunday, a day after Indian Prime Minister Narendra Modi inaugurated Kishanganga Dam, which Pakistan fears will reduce its share in the waters of the Indus and its tributaries.

The Indus system of rivers comprises three western rivers-the Indus, Jhelum and Chenab – and three eastern rivers-the Sutlej, Beas and Ravi. The controversial Kishnaganga dam is built on the Neelum river, which is a tributary of the Jhelum river. "Senior World Bank officials are meeting with a Pakistan delegation at their request to discuss issues concerning the Indus Waters Treaty", a World Bank spokesperson, Elena Karaban, told Dawn.

Recently, Aizaz Ahmed Chaudhry, Pakistan's envoy in Washington, at a news conference said the water dispute was "hugely important for us as we are an agricultural country and water is our lifeline". He added: "As a lower riparian country, we have the right to have unfettered access to the water that flows into Pakistan from the upper riparian areas". Islamabad argues that the dam violates the conditions that the treaty places on the construction of a structure that can

215

hinder the flow of a river. The treaty, which distributes the water of the six Indus valley rivers between Indian and Pakistan, fixes the height and the storage capacity for all such dams.

Pakistan says that the Kishanganga dam is higher than the suggested height and has a wider pondage area than stipulated in the treaty. India on the other hand says that it had corrected both about two years ago, when Pakistan first raised the objections. Islamabad rejects the Indian claim, saying that the dam inaugurated "still violates the suggested conditions and is against the spirit of the treaty" (Free Press Kashmir, 2018).

Kishanganga Dam dispute: Stand down, accept India's offer, World Bank tells Pakistan

The World Bank has asked Pakistan to withdraw its stand on referring the Kishanganga Dam dispute to the International Court of Arbitration (ICA) and accept India's proposal on appointing neutral experts to examine the issue. In a fresh communication to the Pakistan government, World Bank president Jim Yong Kim asked it to stand down from its stand on the matter, Pakistan daily the Dawn reported (Finance Express 2018).

The bank had on November 10, 2016 even picked a US Chief Justice, the Rector of Imperial College, London, and the World Bank President for appointing chairman of the court to resolve the dispute over the dam. India says there is difference between it and Pakistan over the design of the dam and, therefore, the matter should be addressed by some neutral experts. A source privy to the development told the paper that Pakistan believed that acceding to India's proposal of referring the dispute to neutral experts or withdrawing from its stand would mean closing the doors of arbitration and surrendering its right of raising disputes before international courts. "It will become a precedent and every time a dispute emerges between Pakistan and India, the latter

216

will always opt for dispute resolution through neutral experts".

On December 12, 2016, the World Bank president had informed Pakistan through a letter to then finance Minister Ishaq Dar that he had decided to "pause" the process of appointing the ICA chairman as well as the neutral experts. Dar had lodged a strong protest with the World Bank telling it that Pakistan would not recognise the pause. He had asked the bank to play its due role in the matter. Pakistan believes that on the one hand the World Bank has tied its hands from raising the dispute at the ICA, and on the other, it has not blocked the Indian effort to complete the construction of the dam. The World Bank did not even heed to Pakistan's concerns when provided with satellite images during a number meetings with the bank even denied Pakistan the opportunity to stay the construction of the dam (India TV, 2018).

In May 2018 a high-powered Pakistani delegation led by Attorney General Ashtar Ausaf Ali, met with Kristalina Georgieva, World Bank Chief Executive Officer, and the regional management for South Asia. During the meeting, held at Pakistan's request to discuss issues regarding the Indus Waters Treaty and opportunities within the treaty to seek an amicable resolution, "several procedural option" for resolving the disagreement over the interpretation of the treaty's provisions were discussed, the bank said. "While an agreement on the way forward was not reached at the conclusion of the meeting, the World Bank will continue to work with both countries to resolve the issue in an amicable manner and in line with the treaty provision", the Bank had said in a statement at the end of the talks.

Prime Minister Narendra Modi had in May 22 inaugurated the 330MW Kishanganga hydroelectric project in Jammu and Kashmir. Pakistan had protested the inauguration claiming that the project on a river flowing into

Pakistan will disrupt water supplies. The project, at located at Bandipore in North Kashmir, envisage diversion of water of Kishan Ganga river to underground power house through a 23.25-km-long head race tunnel to generate 1713 million units per annum (Zee News, 2018).

Win some, lose some, Indus Waters Treaty continues

India has asked the World Bank not to rush in to resolve a dispute with Pakistan over the Kishanganga and Ratle hydropower projects. Indian officials told a World Bank representative in New Delhi on January 5, 2017 that any differences over the projects can be resolved bilaterally or through a neutral expert.

On January 5, World Bank representative Ian H Solomon met officials of India's External Affairs and Water Resources ministries in New Delhi in an effort to break the deadlock. The Indian delegation, led by Gopal Baglay, joint secretary in the Ministry of External Affairs, made a detailed a presentation on the two projects to support their argument that neither project violated the IWT.

After the meeting, a government official told journalist that the Indian side had described the objections raised by Pakistan as "technical", and therefore they would be best resolved by a neutral expert. Pakistan has dismissed this suggestion earlier, and is seeking a full court of arbitration. The World Bank had agreed to a court of arbitration and then to the appointment of neutral expert, leading to objections by both countries. That was when both processes were suspended.

Under the IWT, India is allowed only non-consumptive use of water from the three western rivers in the Indus basin – Indus, Jhelum, and Chenab. The Kishanganga and Ratle projects are on the western rivers. They are run-of-river hydropower projects that do not hold back any water, though Pakistan's objection is about the height of the gates in the dams from which water is allowed to flow downstream. The three eastern rivers – Ravi, Beas and Sutlej – are reserved for the use of India.

The Pakistan government approach the World Bank in September 2016, saying the design of the Kishanganga project was not in line with the criteria laid down under IWT, and sought the appointment of a court of arbitration. Since the Kishanganga project has been going on for years, the "inordinate" delay by Islamabad to approach the World Bank would give India more time to complete its projects.

However, Pakistan's Finance Minister Ishaq Dar wrote to the World Bank on December 23, 2016, stressing that it was not withdrawing its request to set up a court of arbitration. This was followed by a call from the outgoing US Secretary of State John Kerry to Dar, saying that the US would like to see an amicable solution to the transboudary water row (Gupta 2017).

Conflict Resolution and Peace Building
India-Pakistan Dialogue

The Institute of Peace and Conflict Studies organized a two and a half day India-Pakistan dialogue on Conflict Resolution and Peace Building in Bangkok from 5-7 October 2009, with support from the Ploughshares Fund. The aim of this dialogue was to provide members of the strategic community on both sides with a common platform to discuss issues that plague Indo-Pak relations and reflect on the possibilities of charting alternative course in the near future. The significance of this Track II initiative was further reinforced by the stalling of the composite dialogue process at the Track I level in the aftermath of the Mumbai attacks. The discussions, spanning over eight sessions, touched on a number of issues which are of critical importance in the bilateral relations ranging from analyzing Confidence Building Measures (CBM's), cross LOC interactions, the Siachen dispute, sharing of the Indus river waters, possibility of forging a common strategy for Afghanistan, expansion of Indo-Pak trade, the challenge posed by religious radicalism and terrorist violence to evolving better joint mechanisms for countering terrorism. The discussions, not only brought out the Indian and Pakistani perspectives on the issues highlighted above but also helped put forth key recommendations which will contribute towards addressing some of the key impediments that have constrained a forward movement in some key areas of concern in Indo-Pak relations such as Siachen, enhancement of Indo-Pak trade, expansion of CBM's.

Pakistani Perspective

The Pakistani perspective was that CBMs have successfully worked in the areas of military, nonmilitary and cross LOC in Kashmir. In the military sphere, the cease fire has been holding since 2003 (26 Nov), and the establishment of better communication channels between DGMOs were the other positives. The impediments have been the role of the intelligence agencies on both sides, lack of contact between senior military officers, and infrequent contacts at the highest political levels. The new issues adding to mistrust are terrorism, water disputes and Afghanistan. Two non-controversial issues amenable to negotiating new CBMs are environment and agriculture. A question repeatedly posed was what has been the cost of the status quo. There were references to institutional weakness in Pakistan hindering the expansion of CBMs. It was also debated whether the dialogue needs to move beyond the core issue, i.e., resolution of the Kashmir issue, and progress can be enhanced on non-core issues; thereby increasing mutual trust and an attempt made thereafter to address the core issue.

Indian Perspective

The Indian perspective was that the CBM process has followed a stop-go pattern, interrupted by incidents of blatant aggression and provocative terrorism against

India which was seen in India as being aided and abetted from Pakistan. Nevertheless, CBMs like the ceasefire along the LoC have held, nuclear CBMs were negotiated and non military CBMs like increased road and rail connectivity were important. To bridge the trust deficit, resolution of issues like Siachen, further discussion of nuclear doctrines and policies as mentioned in the Lahore Agreement and a relaxation of visa and trade restrictions would provide a fillip to confidence building.

Expanding the CBMs across the LOC

Indian Perspective

The Indian prespective was that the CBMs across the LOC were welcome, but they have thrown up functional problems due to the varied needs of the people on both sides of the line of control. These problems arose from the restricted number of contact points on both sides of the LOC despite local demands, and new crossing points not being opened up like between Kargil and Skardu. There were further problems regarding modes of payment, as barter of goods was being employed.

Additionally, travel restrictions across the LOC need to be reduced to facilitate the movement of people. The human issue of divides families, particularly Hindus and Sikhs, and the historic links between Jammu and Sialkot, as also between Ladakh and Skardu need to be recognized. An additional and powerful bonding modality can be the exchange of students and access to medical facilitie.

Pakistani Perspective

The Pakistani perspective was that these CBMs were welcome. They did not impinge on the resolution of the core issue, for which other steps needed to be taken like making the LOC irrelevant, demilitarization, self governance and autonomy. The change of status in Gilgit and Baltistan appeared to be a step towards crystallization of the existing boundaries. On the negative side, the cycle of dialogue and its frequent interruption by acts of terrorism within India remained intact. Cross-LOC CBMs can only be a subset of India-Pakistan CBMs. The approach to CBMs has to be incremental, and should not overload the capacity to build on what has already been achieved before introducing new ideas. Means have to be found to link these CBMs, and create some common ground between the people on both sides of the LOC to address the issue of greater autonomy.

Optimizing river water use
Reviewing Indus Water Treaty after 50 years
Pakistani Perspective

Pakistani presentations recognized that the Treaty had functioned successfully and did not need to be abrogated. There was, however, an impression in Pakistan that they were denied their fair share of water. This was becoming a sensitive public issue. Pakistan proposed joint watershed management as the inevitable solution to maintain sustainable flow in the upstream states to control floods and soil erosion. Greater transparency regarding hydrological data of all upstream areas including 3D data was demanded. It was also conceded that public discourse on water in Pakistan was being shaped by ill-informed public articulations based on rumour and rhetoric. Because Pakistan was reaching levels of water distress, corrective measures like meetings between officials dealing with water on the two sides, and more informed public discourse was essential.

Indian Perspective

The Indian presentation underscored the success of the IWT which had served well by dividing the Indus basin waters and enabled each country to move forward and accomplish a first green revolution. However, India has been able to utilize no more than a fraction of its prescribed share of the waters of the three western rivers, owing to political objections from Pakistan, while the latter has no access to the upper catchment of the three rivers allocated to it as these lie in Indian Kshmir. Hence, the need to avail of Article 7 of the Treaty titled "Future Cooperation" in order to maximize utilization of the potential of the three western rivers to mutual benefit in a sustainable and optimal manner through joint survey and development of the upper basins of the three western rivers in view of the threats and uncertainties emanating from gathering climate change. There would be no more potent means of making "boundaries irrelevant" in J & K and binding the two parts of the erstwhile princely state as well as India and Pakistan in a common cause for the greater good of all concerned.

Water-related issues as an entry point for dialogue and cooperation, and a pathway for peace building

Sharing an ecosystem, such as river basins or other water resources, creates complex interdependencies between parties. Based on these interdependencies, environmental problems can provide incentives for cooperation and collective action across political boundaries and ethnic divides. In many instances, parties whose relations are otherwise characterised by distrust and hostility – if not open violence – have found that environmental issues, such as shared water resources, are one of the few areas in which they can sustain ongoing dialogue (Conca, 2005).

This leads to the question of whether environmental cooperation could be harnessed for peace building aims. There are several pathways along which environmental cooperation could contribute to peace. Working together on solving common problems can help replace distrust, uncertainty and suspicion with shared knowledge and a tradition of cooperation. The interdependencies created by shared water resources can further reveal mutual benefits of cooperation. In another ideal scenario, cooperation over environmental issues could lead to the internalisation of shared norms, the creation of an economic regional identity

223

and regional interests (Carius, 2003).

Some of the specific characteristics of environmental issues further support the argument that environmental cooperation could translate into broader forms of long-term cooperation and solutions. The ramifications of environmental cooperation can therefore encourage local and non-governmental participation and constitute "high" and "low" politics (Dabelko, 2006). Since water management, in particular, requires horizontal coordination between different economic sectors, as well as vertical coordination efforts from local to international levels of society, water cooperation offers particular opportunities for spill over of positive impacts. Still, it cannot be expected that environmenttal cooperation per se will contribute to peace. The way in which cooperative processes are designed and implemented remains critical for their peace and conflict impacts. In this regard, considering aspects of ownership, transparency, participation and power relationships are of utmost importance.

Environmental cooperation could be introduced at different levels of society with the aim of contributing to peace. Social interest groups can take advantage of ecological interdependence across territorial borders to facilitate cooperation between academia and civil society actors. This can bring changes in the attitudes, values or perceptions of individuals. Over time, regular interaction at the societal level may translate into changes of behaviour and help lay the foundation for changes at the political level (Carius,2006). However, such spillover effects from the individual/personal level to the social/political level do not occur automatically, but require coordinated action to bring about the structural change that is necessary for peace (Anderson, 2003).

At the governmental level, regional water cooperation can range from sharing data and conducting joint research, to infrastructure projects to institutionalise cooperation mechanisms. The latter often take the form of joint water commissions or river basin organisations that, at best, manage the water resource cooperatively. Institutions play a large role in this by providing predictable and stable behaviour of the actors, a normative and organisational frame for long-lasting/enduring interaction–which also reduces the costs of cooperation–and for increased information exchange, which leads to transparency. The change of behaviour towards compliance with mutually established rules or norms usually provides opportunities for conflict transformation. However, to guarantee equal participation and mutual benefits from cooperative management, even when power is unevenly distributed, disadvantaged negotiation partners must be given the means (information, trained staff and financial support) to act as an equal partner. Existing power imbalances between parties might otherwise further manifest in the institutions created to solve these disparities (Kramer, 2008).

Water and post-conflict peace building

Indus Waters Treaty

Consisting of twelve articles, the IWT allocated the Eastern Rivers to India. However, because some of these tributaries meander back and forth across the Indo-Pakistani border before making their final departure from India and receive additional tributaries from inside of Pakistan, the treaty permitted Pakistani farmers residing along these tributaries the right to use the water (in articles II and III,). The treaty allocated the Western Rivers to Pakistan, but it preserved India's right to use the rivers in Jammu and Kashmir to generate hydropower, meet municipal demand for water, and support the agricultural sector (in article III). Although the Western Rivers flow through the disputed territory of Kashmir, mediators and leaders were vigilant in writing a treaty that excluded discussion of this dispute.

India and Pakistan were in effect able to separate this macro political conflict from the management of their international river (Lowi, 1993).

Another unique feature of the IWT was the fact that the World Bank was a signatory to several provisions. The World Bank was responsible for operating the Indus Basin Development Fund, which coordinated funding from the donor community and India to construct the hydrological infrastructure specified in article V of the treaty. The World Bank was also involved in the provision, stipulated in article X, that permitted the extension of the transition period should war occur. This covered sharing the canal waters during the transition period. The IWT's mechanisms for conflict resolution underlie the role for the World Bank.

Permanent Indus Commission

An analysis of existing treaties revealed that the majority establish river basin commissions to implement the accord and facilitate future cooperation (Conca, Wu, and Mei 2006). These institutions are especially important for post-conflict states because they provide interested states with cooperation mechanisms to manage their disputes. The institutional capabilities needed to facilitate cooperation are the same in post-conflict states as in other riparian states. There is, however, a difference in that post-conflict and developing riparian states can use the help of a neutral mediator to design an effective river basin commission capable of facilitating negotiations and averting conflict.

With the assistance of the World Bank, the IWT (in article VIII) established the Permanent Indus Commission (PIC) to implement the treaty and negotiate issues that arise over the development of the shared river system. Headed by two commissioners, one Indian and one Pakistani, the PIC was given sufficient capabilities to perform its functions.

The commissioners have the ability to communicate directly with one another, which enables them to schedule meetings, arrange maintenance work, and exchange hydrological and meteorological data. Commissioners also hold meetings on a regular basis, which permits them to negotiate the design of hydrological infrastructure and coordinate their work in cleaning the river. The commission's work year ends on June 1, and it is required to submit an annual report summarizing its activities to member states. To complete this report, the PIC must hold its meeting by May 31 every year. Since 1960, the PIC has met every May to finalize and submit its annual report. Meetings have been held even when member states lacked any official diplomatic relations, which demonstrate the commission's resiliency and ability to avoid the frequent tensions in the macropolitical environment (Zawahri, 2009).

During the 1960s, the PIC was busy implementing the treaty, managing the distribution of canal waters, exchanging hydrological data and flood warnings, maintaining drainage systems, and gathering data on the construction of hydrological infrastructure. The PIC conducted many tours of inspection, visiting hydroelectric plants, dams, drains, and flood embankments (PIC 1962, 1963, 1964). In response to requests from Pakistan, the commissioners negotiated the construction of wireless stations for transmitting flood warnings. The commissioners were responsible for maintaining India's extensive drainage systems inside both India and Pakistan. The Indian commissioner requested that Pakistan construct a drainage siphon under the Fordwah and Eastern Sadiqia canals along the Sutlej River in eastern Pakistan. Timber floating from India into Pakistan on the Ravi and Chenab tributaries was another issue the commissioners managed.

Over the years, the PIC's role has not changed. What did change was the increasing demand for it to negotiate issues as the riparian states increased their use of the shared river system. Commissioners negotiated the amount of agricultural land India is permitted to irrigate from the Western Rivers. For Pakistan, this was an important issue because it directly influenced the quantity and quality of water in these rivers. The more land India irrigated in Jammu and Kashmir, the less the quantity and quality of the water Pakistan would receive. The commissioners also negotiated the way flood warnings are delivered to Pakistan. In their 1989 agreement, India agreed to deliver them via broadcast, telephone, and wireless services (Gupta, 2002). The commissioners negotiated, modified the design, and oversaw the construction of several major hydrological structures along the Indus River system. These structures include the Dulhasti (390 megawatts (MW)), Lower Jhelum (105 MW), Salal I and II (combined 690 MW), and Uri I (480 MW) dams in Jammu and Kashmir.

The PIC has been relatively insulated from political pressure against cooperation. The deterioration in bilateral relations in 2001–2002 illustrates this point. After a series of terrorist attacks against India by militants suspected of being based in Pakistan, relations between the two states deteriorated significantly. Political and economic elites demanded that the Indian government abrogate the IWT or, at a minimum, cancel the PIC's annual meeting. Despite substantial domestic pressure, the PIC proceeded with its meeting (Zawahri, 2009).

Since 1960, the PIC and the riparian states' foreign secretaries have succeeded in managing all but one issue. Recently, Pakistan invoked the neutral expert mechanism to address a difference that arose over India's construction of the Baglihar dam. Because the two states have accepted the expert's decision, it can be argued that the IWT has facilitated the peaceful management of the Indus River by India and Pakistan (Salman 2008).

Factors affecting success

A combination of factors affected the Indian

government's ability to settle millions of rural refugees in eastern Punjab by using the waters of the Indus River system effectively. Within the Indian government, there was a general perception that the refugees in eastern Punjab were potential contributors to economic development (Rao, 1967). There was also political will, strong intervention, and commitment on the part of the government at both the provincial and national levels, which was critical to securing the necessary financial resources and appropriate rehabilitation package (Voutira and Harrell-Bond 2000). In fact, the central government provided eastern Punjab with the most comprehensive rehabilitation program received by any Indian province (Menon and Bhasin 1998). The province also received the highest expenditure allocated for the development of infrastructure in the post-conflict setting (Chadha, 1986). The government's willingness to expend these resources certainly facilitated the successful outcome, but the fact that many refugees came from the highly developed canal colonies in western Punjab meant that they were experienced farmers capable of cultivating their allotments efficiently.

As for the transboundary consequences of India's development of the Indus River system, several factors contributed to the successful management of this issue. One of the most important factors appears to have been the presence of a neutral and legitimate mediator (Nakayama 1997; Alam 1998; Biswas 1999; Salman 2002; Weinthal 2000, 2002; Wolf, Yoffe, and Giordano 2003; Giordano, Giordano, and Wolf 2005). Scholars agree that the World Bank's mediation from 1952 to 1960 and its use of carrot-and-stick approach to persuade India and Pakistan to compromise were critical to the signing of the IWT (Salman and Uprety 2002; Nakayama 1997; Alam 1998; Biswas 1999).

The World Bank also performed an important function in organizing the international donor community to underwrite the treaty's implementation and enable the construction of hydrological infrastructure to support the establishment of an agricultural sector in the post-conflict Indus River Basin (Gulhati, 1973; Salman, 2002). The donor community and India funded the necessary hydrological infrastructure that allowed Pakistan to draw on the Western Rivers to meet its domestic needs for water. India also received financial support totaling US$200 million to develop the irrigation potential of the Eastern Rivers (Swain, 2004). Coordination of the donor community cut the transaction cost of locating donors to fund the treaty's implementation and assisted with the reconstruction of post conflict economies. It also kept in check competing donor interests that might have prolonged, complicated, or even derailed the treaty's implementation. Therefore, it may be argued that the presence of a single agency with sufficient financial resources to fund the treaty's implementation facilitated the rapid and smooth development of hydrological infrastructure.

The fact that the IWT is clear, concise, and detailed could have contributed to the commissioners' ability to maintain peace. Negotiated and written by engineers, the treaty has meticulously detailed provisions for conflict resolution mechanisms, design limitations on hydrological infrastructure within Jammu and Kashmir, and the commission's ability to tour the entire river system. Moreover, the fact that the treaty focuses only on the Indus River system, and avoids discussion of Kashmir and other Indo-Pakistani disputes, might have also contributed to the commissioners' ability to manage water disputes.

In 1970, the World Bank completed the majority of its obligations under the IWT. Its only remaining role is to facilitate the selection process for the neutral expert or court of arbitration for the operation of the conflict resolution mechanisms. This remaining function is not sufficient to compel the states to alter their behaviour to ensure cooperation. In fact, experts have noted that a mediator has "little power to prevent any of the signatories from defecting that is becoming free riders, once a project is implemented" (Waterbury, 1990). Rather, India and Pakistan maintain cooperation with the IWT because it is in their interest. The treaty enables Pakistan to secure access to its only source of water, and India is able to develop the Eastern Rivers to support the agricultural sector in its north-western provinces (Swain, 2009; Zawahri 2009).

The Indus Water Treaty, not for revenge but for development and peace

Disappointing a number of television news anchors and so-called strategic experts, Indian Prime Minister Narendra Modi decided on September 26,2016 not to do hara-kiri on the Indus Water Treaty issues with respect to Pakistan while he employed usual rhetoric- "Blood and Water cannot flow together"- to placate his core constituency, India will however, stay and abide by the treaty. Modi now has plans to set up an inter-ministerial task force to go into the details and working of the treaty in order for India to exploit the maximum possible amount of water from the three western rivers of the system.

Anyone with basic knowledge of the treaty knows the procedural limitations of India unilaterally taking up any water development projects on these rivers in the absence of Pakistan's consent. Under the provisions of the treaty Pakistan can complain about any Indian project upstream and the World Bank has the power to appoint a "neutral expert" to decide. Even if India's projects upstream are within the provisions of the treaty, as was the case in the Baglihar Hydropower Project, Pakistan can delay India's plans for a long time if it decides to.

Thus the mandate of the inter-ministerial panel to find ways to exploit more water within the treaty is nothing but to deceive public opinion in India. If Modi is really serious about making better use of the Indus Waters, he should ask his ministerial panel to explore the possibility of how to make the treaty wider and better to meet the increasing water and energy needs of the region.

Festering problem

Much before the Uri attacks, water sharing in the Indus basin had become a major political predicament in the face of increasing water demand and climate change-related uncertainties. The Indus water treaty has stood the test of time for the last 56 years, but the deep mistrust between India and Pakistan has thwarted the implementation of a number of seemingly advantageous water development projects in the basin.

Though the treaty is over waters, it is designed primarily to split the river waters, it is designed primarily to split the river system into two, not to encourage cooperative sharing of its waters. David Lilienthal, who had suggested that his friend and the then World Bank president, Eugent Black, mediate between the two countries, had envisaged the agreement to be one that would treat the whole basin as a single unit so that the two riparian states could cooperate in more effective ways for the sustainable management of river and land resources.

But the Indus Water Treaty, in facilitating the partition of the river system between the two countries, has in fact contributed to reducing the scope of engagement between them. The treaty is not a marriage of two consenting adults to lead a life together, but has turned out to be a mutually agreed divorce settlement. Though the best possible use of Indus waters needs both the major riparian countries to work together for the development of water infrastructure, the treaty unfortunately, does not encourage any incentive towards joint basin management.

The frequent fight over the interpretation of the treaty

has also raised serious doubts over any peace dividend coming out of it for the two countries. Moreover, conflict over water sharing is not limited at the bilateral level between India and Pakistan only.

Domestic politics

Domestic politics in both India and Pakistan has impeded the implementation of several critical water development projects in the basin. The half-completed Yamuna-Sutlej canal in India and the long-planned Kalabagh Dam in Pakistan are clear testimony of the costs implicit in the lack of working cooperation over water sharing, not only between but also within India and Pakistan.

Recent plans to develop hydropower in Afghanistan part of the Indus basin have fuelled political sensitivity in the region. Speculation regarding Indian support to Afghanistan for a proposed 12 dams on the Kabul River, an Indus tributary with a combined storage facility of 4.7 million acre feet has added to Pakistan's water worries.

It is not only Pakistan that is worried about Afghanistan's planned cascade of dams on the Kabul River. Similarly, India is tensed about China's dam projects on the upstream of the Indus River. Even a small sized Chinese dam near Demchok, Ladakh, on the Indus has ruffled Delhi, and it suspects that China might soon go for building dams on the Sutlej upstream.

Lasting solutions

Climate change-induced glacier melting in the Himalayas threatens future water supply in the Indus basin. There is increasing global warming, but the rise in temperature in the Himalayas has been much higher than the global average. Thus, harnessing the Indus river system sustainably is a crucial issue for improving human develop-ment and contributing to regional peace and security in South Asia.

Considering the complex nature of future challenges in the Indus basin, there is a need for exploring options for basin-wide, cooperation. With the help of integrated development of the basin, there are possibilities of building more storage facilities across the Indus and its tributaries to ensure better use of the scarce water.

For appropriate and competent management of Indus systems, it is necessary to explore establishing an effective and independent river basin organisation. Involving all the four riparian states, this will have the capability of taking decisions on its own and remain out of the political control of any national government. Under an integrated programme of basin development, water projects can be situated at optimum locations, not withstanding geographic divisions along political lines.

Any prospect of integrated development of the Indus waters, which is the only long-term answer to the basin's growing thirst, have not yet materialised, basically due to lack of trust and confidence between the riparian countries; Thus, it is important for India to explore the possibilities for a new Indus treaty that can address fast-evolving water-sharing challenges in the basin.

Instead of the urge to take revenge against Pakistan, if India takes the opportunity to work for a comprehensive and integrated form of basin management, the benefit sharing of the Indus river system will not be limited only to water resources; it can have other peace-enhancing effects and significantly contribute to regional peace, security and development (Swain, 2016).

India can solve its water scarcity by correcting Indus Water Treaty

The inter-ministerial task force set up by Prime Minister Narendra Modi for correcting India's under-utilisation of its allocated share of waters under the Indus Waters Treaty (IWT) has just held its first meeting. The water-related issue facing India, however, is much larger: The continued absence of institutionalised, integrated policy-making in India, which has prevented proper management of the country's increasingly scarce water resources. Indeed, India stands out for its lack of a national action plan to build water secrity.

Scarcity

When the Indian Republic was established, the framers of its Constitution did not visualise water scarcity in the decades ahead, given the relative abundance of water resources then. Therefore, they left water as a state-level subject, than making it a federal issue. Similarly, the IWT, under which India big-heartedly agreed in 1960 to the exclusive reservation of the largest three of the six Indus system rivers for Pakistan, was negotiated in a period when water shortages were uncommon in most parts of India.

Accountability

The startling fact is that the responsibility for water issues is so fragmented within India's central government that 12 different departments or ministries deal with different segments of water resources. To promote clear responsibility and accountability in national water management and to facilitate integrated policy-making, India must end its present fragmented approach on water issues. As for India's under-utilisation of its IWT allocated water share, the task facing the task-force is formidable.

Although the IWT permits India to store 4.4 BCM of waters from the Pakistan reserved rivers, a careless India has built no storage. And despite the treaty allowing India to built hydropower plants with no dam reservoir, India's total installed generating capacity in Jammu and Kashmir currently does not equal the size of a single new dam in Pakistan like the 4,500-megawatt Diamer- Bhasha, who is financing for construction, was approved recently.

Background

Against this background, the task force set up by Modi,

with his principal secretary as its chairman, may be a step in the right direction. But constituting this committee is hardly an adequate response to fixing the anomaly in India's under –utilisation of its water share. Made up of senior bureaucrats who are already busy attending to other tasks, the committee cannot by itself remove the bureaucratic hurdles in the proper utilisation of water resources. India's political negligence on this issue has been so deep and extensive that it can be remedied only through hands-on political direction and in coordination with the state chief ministers.

More fundamentally, water scarcity is a looming challenge across India. The water wars between various Indian states are highlighting how the competition over shared water resources is sharpening in an alarming manner. India must treat water as a strategic resource for its own well-being. If the current compartmentalised approach to managing water resources persists, water shortage are going to exact growing economic and social costs in India (Chellaney, 2016).

Floods in India and Pakistan Offer a Chance for Peace-Building

South Asia's rivers are again in furious flow with India's northern state of Kashmir hit by the worst floods in 50 years. Its capital, Srinagar, has been overwhelmed by the deluge, with road links to the rest of India washed away and villagers marooned on rooftops. India's Prime Minister Narendra Modi, has declared a national disaster. However, with crops and livestock affected seriously, a state that was re-emerging from years of conflict has suffered a cruel setback.

On the Pakistan side, the flooding has been equally devastating with more than 300 dead, 2.3 million people affected as cotton fields are intentionally flooded to save cities. The people in this region have been here before only four year ago and an epic flood engulfed large swaths of

Pakistan, displacing 20 million people across the country, leading the UN to describe it as the worst humanitarian disaster of its time.

In response to the 2010 floods, a younger generation of India and Pakistani leaders joined hands and created a platform to foster bilateral cooperation on shared risks and vulnerabilities. Chief among these was climate change and its manifestation in extreme weather events such as the floods, which the world meteorological organisation (WMO) mentioned as climate change.

The efforts of these young Indians and Pakistan have led to meetings in Lahore, Delhi and Davos, starting a conversation around the climate risk faced by both countries and challenging politicians to unite around the shared necessity of climate action.

Action is now needed more than ever. Climate change is both a challenge as well as an opportunity for these two nuclear nations. It is a risk that can no longer be ignored, and has to be managed. How to deal with the shared resource of its river waters and what to do when they break their banks in an era of climate change is a key challenge for both India and Pakistan. At the upstream end this will require improved bilateral cooperation on transboundary water management in the Indus river basin. At the downstream end this will need shared expertise and collaboration on improving disaster-risk management.

With new Prime Ministers at the helm in both countries, there is a unique opportunity to exercise leadership. Both Modi and Nawaz Sharif are from Border States and have shown remarkable willingness to engage in peace-building, despite persistent acrimony from their armed forces.

Acknowledging that the deadly floods are not an act of god but a symptom of climate change would be a first step towards acknowledging a common vulnerability. This could pave the way to a new era of pragmatic cooperation, embracing basic data sharing at a decentralised state level, encouraging border states to cooperate on climate change, water and disaster risk-management strategies. This may seem far-fetched, but existing initiatives have demonstrated a local will for cooperation, it is now for leaders to act. The stormy monsoon will have a silver lining if they can deliver a climate peace divided to both people (Ali, Mehera 2014).

Indus Water Treaty made peaceful cooperation possible between India, Pakistan

Water cooperation is an essential feature of managing international water courses among riparian states. It requires riparian states to coordinate with one another through the sharing of information and the creation of joint cooperative mechanisms for the optimal utilization of water resources for mutual benefit. In this spirit, cooperation was established for the sharing of the Indus Basin between India and Pakistan with the signing of the Indus Water Treaty (IWT). Both states acted upon the treaty and cooperated with each other through the formation of a joint body–the Permanent Indus Commission. However, over time this cooperation mechanism deteriorated owing to the initiation of controversial dams by India (Qureshi 2017).

United States said the Indus Water Treaty (IWT) has served "a model for peaceful cooperation" between Pakistan and India, US Department of state reported. At a weekly briefing of the US state department, spokesperson John Kirby said: "The Indus Waters Treaty has served... as a model for peaceful cooperation between India and Pakistan for now 50 years." When asked whether the US has offered to mediate on the issue between the two countries, Kirby said the US "encourage India and Pakistan to work together bilaterally to resolve their differences." Without giving details whether the US government spoke to Indian officials about the water dispute, Kirby said the US was "in regular communication with the Indian and Pakistani government on a wide range of issues."

The latest dispute between India and Pakistan concerns the two hydroelectric power plants- Kishanganga and Ratle- that India is building on the Indus Rivers system. Pakistan believes that the projects violate the design parameters of the IWT, which provides specific criteria for such plants. In conflicting reports, official sources had earlier told the Dawn that the US administration has initiated the process for peacefully resolving the current water dispute between India and Pakistan without waiting for an invitation to do so. US secretary of state John Kerry had also called Finance Minister Ishaq Dar and discussed with him different options for an amicable settlement of the dispute.

The initiative stems from the fear the US administration shares with the World Bank that the dispute, if dragged, may harm the treaty that has effectively resolved water disputes between India and Pakistan for more than half a century. The IWT is a water-distribution agreement between India and Pakistan, brokered by the World Bank and signed in Karachi on September 19, 1960. It recognises the bank as the main arbitrator and suggests appointing neutral experts and a court of arbitration for resolving dispute (Dawn, 2017).

Conclusion

A new dispensation is, therefore, needed to enable a spatial and holistic development of the Indus basin as a single entity to serve the best interests of both countries. An integral exploitation of the entire river basin would permit its optimal development; indeed, making the distinction between upper and lower riparian states is meaningless for addressing generic issues like ground water pollution, environmental degradation and climate change that transcend national frontiers. An integrated river management system would, assess the total availability and demand for water in the Indus basin before planning the infrastructure to optimize water usage, flood control, redistribution of water from surplus to deficit areas, preserving water quality and so on.

Indeed, the agenda for negotiating an expanded Indus Water Treaty is straightforward. It could include schemes for further storages and interlinking canal systems to serve the needs of both irrigation and power generation, apart from flood control, navigation, fisheries, and tourism. It should appreciate that the state which gains advantages needs to recompense the state that suffers in consequence, which is relevant for beneficial measures like compensatory afforestation and providing relief and rehabilitation to the ousters displaced by the project. Further, the spatial development of the Indus basin could include creating new townships, agricultural markets (mandis), road and rail networks, and agriculture-based industries. An IWT-II would also function as a huge confidence building measure between India and Pakistan. Viewed in this perspective there would be fruitful opportunities for enlarging bilateral India-Pakistan trade, people-to-people contacts, and human security related cooperation in the spheres of education, public health, forestry and, in truth, almost every aspect of economic and social development in the Indus basin where there is mutual interest in proceeding ahead.

Incidentally, Article VI of the IWT provides for the regular exchange of data on river flows in the Indus basin and their utilization, which lays the foundation for greater India-Pakistan cooperation. More specifically, Article VII recognizes their "common interest in the optimum development of the rivers" by installing hydrologic observation stations, carrying out new drainage works, and "undertaking engineering works on the Rivers". This enunciation of principles permits the extension of the IWT to incorporate a more ambitious IWT-II to develop the Indus rivers basin for the benefit of both countries.

Article XII, moreover, allows this modification of the IWT "by a duly ratified treaty concluded for this purpose between the two governments." The present modality of dealing with each river waters dispute as it arises is irksome, time-consuming and tension-promoting. It is also expensive. For example, the disputes over the Baglihar and Kishanganga projects were only resolved by external intervention after prolonged and costly litigation. And this could recur with every project that India wishes to construct on the three Western rivers. It bears reiteration that the existing IWT allows India to build storages for non-consumptive purposes on the western rivers subject to conditions, these storages have not yet been constructed by India, but their need has accelerated with water shortages increasing.

The IWT is under stress and could become another cause for India-Pakistan tensions and conflict. A bleak conclusion has been reached that: "Given the overall political climate, it is unlikely that the two countries will agree to modify the treaty and convert it from a water portioning treaty into a water resource development treaty." Nevertheless, the need for a more comprehensive Indus Water Treaty that addresses these multifaceted problems cannot be postponed much longer. The greatest obstacle to the fruition of an IWT is the trust deficit between India and Pakistan, as also in J&K and Azad Kashmir with New Delhi and Islamabad respectively. As stridently voiced by a Pakistani writer the waters of the Western Rivers could be "gone forever—courtesy Treaty as were the Eastern Rivers courtesy Treaty I. Transmitted through India's interlinking River network they may discover one day Pak Indus waters slaking thirst of multitudes of people and millions of acres of parched lands in the water-starved Tamilnadu and Karnataka states 2000 miles away in the southern Peninsula leaving in the wake Pak lands bone dry."

The danger from voicing such extreme views is that it invites an equally strident reaction in India, and especially in

J&K, where the belief is popular that India needlessly "lost" 80 percent of the Indus waters to Pakistan, which was the lower riparian state. Further, this genre of permanent victimhood has led to suggestions that India should contemplate action under Article 62 of the Vienna Convention on the Law of Treaties, which permits countries to withdraw from a treaty of unlimited duration, on the grounds that a 'fundamental change of circumstances' has taken place, Luckily, such extreme beliefs are only confined to ideologically driven, fringe elements in India, but their views could not gain traction in the heated debate proceeding between India and Pakistan. A great deal depends here on the inclinations of the leadership in India and Pakistan. Apropos, IWT-I reached closure only when Nehru and Ayub reached agreement with each other. Another lesson worth remembering from the IWT-I experience is that the most critical negotiations were held outside South Asia in various Western capitals, which offers a useful precedent for future discussions.

Admittedly, water is an emotive issue; it raises irrational fears and encourages nationalist primitivism to be easily generated. Jamait leaders, for example, like Hafiz Saeed have routinely been whipping up anti-India sentiments on the Indus waters issue. So have several J&K leaders and conservative parties in India, drawing attention to the "unfairness" of the IWT schema. The need to allay such negative sentiments and move forward constructively to share a dwindling resource cannot be postponed much longer. A case exists therefore for educating public opinion about the benefits that would accrue to India and Pakistan by extending the ambit of the Indus Waters Treaty to maximize its benefits.

Due to the communal violence that plagued India and Pakistan in 1947–1948, millions of people crossed the border between the two new states in one of the largest exchanges of populations in history. The worst massacres occurred in western and eastern Punjab. To settle the more than 4 million refugees who crossed into eastern Punjab, the Indian government decided to use the waters of the Indus River's Eastern Rivers to enable it to rehabilitate its refugees through the establishment of an agrarian economy. India was able to effectively facilitate economic development and peace building in this conflict-torn province. The government's successful policies and programs also permitted the employment of refugees to construct the infrastructure necessary for turning eastern Punjab into India's granary, which helped to meet the nation's growing demand for food. The long history since India's independence permits us to assess this case and conclude that it truly represents a successful example of the effective management of a livelihood resource to contribute to peacebuilding in a post-conflict society.

Yet to implement these policies and projects, India had to draw on the same resource that sustained Pakistan's agrarian economy, which resulted in a transboundary dispute. From 1947 to 1952, the two riparian states negotiated two temporary agreements, but these failed to provide a stable solution. The direct mediation of the World Bank from 1952 until 1960 enabled the two states to avoid conflict over this natural resource and sign the IWT, which allocated the Indus main stem and the five easternmost tributaries between the states. India received the Eastern Rivers and Pakistan the Western Rivers. To finance the construction of hydrological infrastructure to shift Pakistan's dependence from the Eastern Rivers to the Western Rivers, the World Bank coordinated funding from India and a consortium of donors. The World Bank also operated the Indus Development Fund, which financed the implementation of these projects. To oversee the treaty's implementation and manage disputes arising from the development of the shared river system, the IWT established the PIC and provided it with sufficient authority to fulfill its task. Should questions, differences, or disputes arise, the states have extensive conflict resolution mechanisms to draw upon. For over forty years, the parties to the IWT have used the negotiation path to peacefully address all their Indus River disputes (Salman, 2008).

References:

- Anderson M.B and L. Olson (2003). Confronting war: Critical lessons for peace practitioners. Cambridge, MA: The Collaborative for Development Action.
- Ali H Saleem, MeheraMalini, September 2014, "flood in India and Pakistan offer a chance for peace-building".
- Aloys Arthur Michel, the Indus Rivers: A Study of the Effects of Partition (New Haven: Yale University Press, 1967).
- Basheer Khalil Nijim, The Indus, Nile and Jordan: International Rivers and Factors in Conflict Potential (Thesis submitted to Indiana University, 1969).
- Basheer Khalil Nijim, Use in Arid Regions, (Paris: UNESCO Arid Zone Research, 1961), Vol. XVII, No. 1, pp. 143-174 op. cit., p. 28.
- Carius A (2003). 'NaturschutzalsBeitragzurFriedensentwicklung' in Naturschutz (Aus-)Löser von Konflikten?. Documentation of a conference by the BundesamtesfürNaturschutz and the Heinrich Böll Foundation, 25th-27th November 2002 in Berlin. Bonn, Germany. p.26.
- Carius A (2006). Environmental cooperation as an instrument of crisis prevention and peacebuilding: Conditions for success and constraints. Berlin, Germany: Adelphi Consul.

- Chadha, G. K. 1986. The state and rural economic transformation: The case of Punjab, 1950–85. New Delhi, India: Sage Publications.
- Chellaney Brahma. 30. Dec.2016. "India can solve its water scarcity by correcting Indus Water Treaty".
- ChitrakarNavesh. 2018. "India's Modi inaugurates hydro project in Kashmir, Pakistan protests", Reuters Staff.
- Conca K. et al. (2005). 'Building peace through environmental cooperation' in The Worldwatch Institute (Ed.). Op. cit.
- Conca, K., F. Wu, and C. Mei. 2006. Global regime formation or complex institution building? The principled content of international river agreements. International Studies Quarterly 50 (2): 263–285.
- Dabelko G.D (2006). Analyzing environmental pathways to peace. Paper presented at the annual meeting of the International Studies Association, Town & Country Resort and Convention Center, San Diego, California, US, 22nd March 2006. Available at http://www. allacademic.com/meta/p99621_index.html.
- Dawn, dawn.com. January 04, 2017, 10.27 pm. "Indus Water Treaty made peaceful cooperation possible between India, Pakistan".
- Embassy of Pakistan Let the Reader Judge, Washington, D. C., July 22, 1958; See Nijim, op. cit., p. 38.
- Finance Express, June 5, 2018, 11.17 am. "Kishanganga Dam dispute: Stand down, accept India's offer, World Bank tells Pakistan."
- Free press Kashmir, May 23, 2018. "Seeking an 'amicable solution' to water dispute between India, Pakistan: World Bank.
- Gulhati, N. 1973. Indus Waters Treaty: An exercise in international mediation. Bombay, India: Allied Publishers.
- Gupta Joydeep, Ebrahim Zofeeen, January 06, 2017, "Win some, lose some, Indus Water Treaty continues."

- HaidarSuhasini, The Hindu, September 27, 2016, "India suspends talks on Indus Water Pact".
- India Tv. June 5, 2018, 11.34. "Kishanganga Project: World Bank backs India, asks Pakistan not to take the matter to ICA".
- Kramer Annika, 2008, Regional Water Cooperation and Peacebuilding in the Middle East.
- Lowi, M. 1993. Water and power: The politics of a scarce resource in the Jordan River Basin. Cambridge, UK: Cambridge University Press.
- Menon, R., and K. Bhasin. 1998. Borders and boundaries: Women in India's partition. New Brunswick, NJ: Rutgers University Press.
- M.J. Akbar, Nehru: The Making of India (London: Penguin Group, 1988), pp. 443-444.
- Nakayama, M. 1997. Successes and failures of international organizations in dealing with international waters. International Journal of Water Resources Development 13 (3): 367–382.
- NayarKuldip, January 9, 2017, "Pakistan, India and the Indus Water Treaty".
- ParvaizAthar, September 25, 2016, "Indus Water Treaty rides out latest crisis".
- Qureshi Dr. Waseem Ahmad, 2017, "The Indus Basin: Water Cooperation, International Law andthe Indus Waters Treaty".
- Rao, U. B. 1967. The story of rehabilitation. New Delhi, India: Ministry of Information and Broadcasting.
- Salman 2008. The Baglihar difference and its resolution process—a triumph for the Indus Waters Treaty? Water Policy 10:105–117.
- Sridhar Seema, 2004, Kashmir and Water: Conflict and Cooperation
- Swain, Ashoka. 2004. Managing water conflict: Asia, Africa and the Middle East. London: Routledge.

- Swain Ashok. 2009. The Indus II and Siachen Peace Park: Pushing the India-Pakistan peace process forward. Round Table 98 (404): 569–582.
- Swain Ashok. 23September 2016. "Withdrawing Indus Waters Treaty is not a solution to punish Pakistan as it will only bring global condemnation".
- Swain Ashok, September 30, 2016, "The Indus Water Treaty, not for revenge but for development and peace".
- The Hindu, September 27, 2016, "Will approach U.N. if India violates Indus Water Treaty."
- UNECAFE, Multiple Purpose River Basin Development, Part 2B, p. 70.
- Voutira, E., and B. Harrell-Bond. 2000. "Successful" refugee settlement: Are past experiences relevant? In Risks and reconstruction: Experiences of resettlers and refugees.
- Zawahri, N. 2008a. Designing river commissions to implement treaties and manage international rivers: The story of the Joint Water Committee and Permanent Indus Commission. Water International 33 (4): 464–474.
- Zee News, June 05, 2018, 03.59pm. "Kishanganga dam dispute: World Bank asks Pakistan to accept India's demand".
- Waterbury, J. 1990. Dynamics of basin-wide cooperation in the utilization of the Euphrates. Paper presented at the conference "Economic Development of Syria: Problems, Progress, and Prospects," Damascus, Syria.
- Wolf Aaron T, Annika Kramer, Alexander Carius, and Geoffrey D. Dabelko, 2006, Water Can Be a PathWay to Peace, not War.

Chapter-V

Conclusion

Owing to the complex geographical setup of Indus Basin, hostilities between India and Pakistan over river water utilization are soaring up, and if we look into the priorities of concerned countries, different political agendas and ambitions and geopolitical realities, concluding this study has been a complex task, Hence, this conclusion is limited to the comparative analysis of issues, objections and sugge-stions which were, observed and incorporated from India, Pakistan and Jammu and Kashmir state in relations to Indus Water Treaty.There is a lot more that could be done to promote peace-building, and engaged stakeholders from within and outside the region must pursue these avenues with a renewed sense of urgency (Hill, 2013)

Indus river, a basic resource for and a powerful stimulant to economic development of the shareholders has linked the riparian countries and as well as their peoples together. On the other hand, its history reveals that it has been a ground of disputes, between neighbours/provinces or states of Indus Basin for long. Fast increasing population, expanding urbanization and fast-growing needs for irrigation and power generation have put increasing strains on the water of Indus Basin Rivers. During the British rule, there was only one political issue, i.e. to get independence from British rule, but after independence, the sub-continent faced more grave geopolitical issues, which includes the distribution of Indus Basin water as well.

The dispute over the water of the Indus Basin between India and Pakistan is notable not only for its size, significance, and complexity but also in that it was brought to an amicable resolution by a comprehensive treaty. The dispute lasted for twelve years from 1948 to 1960 but fortunately the World Bank's intervention brought the parties together and guided them towards a resolution. The resolution of dispute was made with the landmark agreement of Indus Water Treaty. This monumental treaty was the outcome of eight years of discussions and negotiations between the government of India and Pakistan under the aegis of World Bank.

The water conflict between India and Pakistan was spiraling to its critical level as the partition had left a legacy of enormous bitterness and complexities. So, it was very difficult to deal with this grave issue and institutionalise peace between the two countries. Agreements after agreements were made but no permanent solution could be reached. In 1952, the World Bank made an intervention with an intention to facilitate negotiations between India and Pakistan. The World Bank-led negotiations mainly focused on the concerned issue and all extraneous matters were kept away. The World Bank nominated a group of engineers from both countries to resolve the dispute. In 1954, the World Bank put forward a proposal embodying the main principles for dispute resolution. These principles have been accepted by both the countries, eventually signing the agreed-upon Indus Water Treaty.

The Indus Water Treaty has its origin in an international water dispute that could have led to a situation detrimental to both the parties had it remained unresolved. However, the dispute on the use of waters of the Indus Basin had its beginning during the British Empire between Punjab and Sindh (Bahawalpur and Bikaner were also involved). But, with the partition of India in 1947, the water issue became more serious as the new political boundary between India and Pakistan cut across the Indus system of rivers and disrupted its well-managed, integrated irrigation canals network. The geography of the partition was such that the headwaters of canals remained mainly with India while the land being irrigated by these canals went to Pakistan. Thus, the partitioning of the canal system has created dispute between the two countries over the share of Indus Basin water. The water dispute erupted on 1st April 1948 when East Punjab discontinued the delivery of water to West Punjab on the expiry of the Standstill Agreement. This incident exacerbated hostilities between the governments, adding more fuel to the flames. To resolve this issue, agreements and MOUs were signed but no permanent solution was found. Nevertheless, it paved the way for the process of negotiations towards the final settlement until Indus Water Treaty was signed in 1960.

The process of negotiation was so difficult and complex that the two governments virtually failed to negotiate mutually and were compelled to accept the intervention of a third party. The intervention of the World Bank's good office at the end of 1951 started communication between the two countries over water utilization. Intrinsically, the negotiation process was put in the right direction when David. A. Lilienthal, former Chairman of Tennessee Valley Authority, and a close friend of Eugene R. Black, the then President of the World Bank, presented his principal arguments over water sharing of Indus Basin.

The World Bank had earlier helped resolve such conflicts in the other parts of the globe. It wanted to help both the countries with its experience and expertise. Though the situation in sub-continent was complex but the solution had to be found— as the two contesting parties remained adamant over their basic position, the third-party mediation became necessary. Subsequently, E.R. Black called both the parties and explicitly outlined "essential principles" which ought to be followed for conflict resolution. The principles were accepted by both the countries, and after intensive discussions, modifications and negotiations, the trilateral Indus Water Treaty was finally signed on 19 September 1960 between India and Pakistan, and the World Bank was a signatory to the Treaty (Ali 2013).

Being members of the international community and the United Nations, an exceptional duty is borne by both India and Pakistan to establish the cooperation with each other necessary for the utilization of their shared Indus Basin and to avoid causing any harm to each other. However, certain Indian water storage works are harming the availability of water and, consequently, the agrarian infrastructure of Pakistan. This is because Pakistan's agricultural sector is heavily dependent on an adequate flow of water in the Indus Basin (Khan 2015) but the water in the Indus Basin reaches Pakistan after passing through Indian territory(Qureshi, 2017).

It could well be said in favour of World Bank that it addressed the water dispute with a view to redress the grievances of the common masses residing on both sides of international border between India and Pakistan. The World Bank ignored the political implications of the treaty in the best interests of the people concerned. The World Bank has not only provided technical assistance but also sufficient financial support through the Indus Basin Development Fund. The financial assistance was collected from friendly countries, which include Australia, Canada, Germany, Italy, New Zeeland, the United Kingdom, the United States; India also contributed to the fund raising. It was the magnanimity and constant efforts of the World Bank which provided financial and technical assistance for the development of two countries and its mediating role has been a successful instance of dispute resolution(Ali 2013).

Pakistan geographically is a low stream country; all rivers are coming from Jammu and Kashmir, which is the disputed area between Pakistan and India. From the day of independence both countries had some kind of issues with each other, some had been solved, but some still exist. Water issue is the one of those issues, when this issue raised both countries with the help of World Bank signed a treaty. Indus Water Treaty was the best example to solve the water issue, but after some time India made some kind of dams on the Western Rivers. It was the start of water clashes between both countries. This apart, the public in both the countries believe that historical issues have left an impact on the current relationship between India and Pakistan. It is, therefore, important that the governments of both the countries work together to solve all issues to overcome the public thinking and behaviour about the mutual understanding and relation. India-Pakistan relations always continue as a matter of anxiety and has become a subject of continuous discourse among researchers, political leaders as well as the general public globally and especially in Asia region. These suggestions can be made at this stage:

1. There is a lack of confidence between both the governments and the public, so to build up Indo-Pak Confidence measures is mandatory to fill the trust gap.

2. As all rivers are coming from Indian side so India should be more open in the aspect of sharing information with Pakistan especially about the Western Rivers. If India shares all kind of information as mentioned in the IWT, it will develop confidence between both the countries.

3. Media in Pakistan and India is free, because both the governments believe in media freedom, so media of India and Pakistan should take some positive steps to eliminate the misunderstanding between the countries.

4. To some extent IWT also needs to be revised in some aspects to bring it more in line with the current international water course law and developing concerns with water quality, environment concerns, climate change and principle of equitable sharing.

5. There is a need to develop positive thinking in the behaviour of India and Pakistan. The people of both countries had a long experience to live with each other, in some aspect they also have a same kind of cultural values,

so we should develop friendly and cooperative atmosphere through some kind of exchange program, conference, media and education. As history told us about all over the world that such kind of clashes and war leave impact on the overall situation of both countries, so it is same for both nations, so to remove the negative atmosphere and create a positive atmosphere is need of the hour among politicians and public (Muhammad Tayyab Sohail, Delin,Siddiq 2015).

Also, the success of Indus Water Treaty would not have been possible without the keen interest displayed by the then Prime Minister of India Jawaharlal Nehru and President of Pakistan Muhammad Ayub Khan, sidelining all rivalries and joining table for negotiation. They fostered a congenial environment for the third-party mediation. However, there were also some criticisms within the two nations against this. Protracted and complex negotiations were conducted between senior civil society servants, professionals, and engineers, minimising the chance of any hindrance in resolving the water dispute. Though the treaty brought peace and harmony in the sub-continent, it could not satisfy the entire spectrum of people and drew criticisms from both the countries. In both countries, critics are of the view that the negotiation of the treaty was faulty though such criticism is hardly taken into consideration when top leaderships are involved.

The distribution of rivers is actually a territorial division, and it does not specify the quantity of water for parties. The treaty merely reaffirms the territorial sovereignty of each state as the basis in the difference in water courses. It does not modify the boundary between the two countries but traces a fictitious line, East-West, which divides the basin and limits the sovereign rights of each state on half of the river system and grants quasi-exclusive rights on the other half. In fact, it is neither a territorial nor quantitative division, but a division that concerns only the use of the water. This kind of division is predominantly political and economic, but not according to prevailing water laws. Since the treaty was signed, the two parties have to deal jointly with water administration and do not have the right to interfere in the waters allocated to the other party.

The treaty established a permanent institution of Indus Commission to maintain peace and cooperation between the parties. The Commission has so far maintained peace despite the bitter political relations (three wars were fought between India and Pakistan in 1965, 1971 and 1999). In this sense it can be claimed that the treaty is a successful instance of peace and conflict resolution. It has faithfully served as a means of prevention in water-related disputes. Nevertheless, the Commission has failed to resolve certain issues. Large numbers of experts are of the view that the Commission has been politicized, and as a result could not reach any effective settlement on certain disputes.

Despite its success in water conflict resolution, there are some ambiguities in the treaty. Indus River is flowing through four sovereign countries, viz. China, India, Pakistan, and Afghanistan, including the disputed state of Jammu and Kashmir. The Indus Water Treaty protects only the rights and considerations of two countries, neglecting the other stakeholders of the Indus Basin. However, other riparian states including Jammu and Kashmir state are claiming their rights to a reasonable and equitable share of the Indus River and its tributaries flowing through their territories. It was not a deliberate omission on the part of the World Bank. It wanted to make both the countries realize the need for cooperation and compromise. No compromise, anywhere and under any condition is just or equal for the parties concerned; compromise is an opportunity to stem the further rot and utilize the time and energy thus saved to build and manage one's resources. Indus water treaty did exactly the same. Taming of waters under the respective possession and their management was given utmost priority. However, Pakistan has to address new realities and negotiate the demands of upper riparian shareholders of Indus, Jhelum and Kabul River sooner the better.

The arbitration of treaty does not create a sound mechanism to address certain issues, such as ground water use for two countries, changes in flow of water due to climatic changes, changing domestic demand due to population increase or rainfall variability and future developments. This shortcoming has created a serious chaos in the sub-continent as both the countries are facing water stress due to high population density, climate change and high-water demand. The increasing water scarcity has led to an intense water debate in India and Pakistan and the hawks on both sides are talking about water wars or abrogation of the Treaty.

Any talk of deconstruction plans on the Indus Water Treaty needs to be supplemented with alternative construction plans, otherwise whole exercise may lead to chaos and confusion. In the absence of an alternative scheme, the slogans for the abrogation of the Treaty are simply meaningless. The demand for more water, in India or Pakistan does not make the Indus Water Treaty irrelevant for the people concerned. It has to be seen from a broader perspective.

Whatever be the truth the value of the differences between the two countries have widened the trust gap between the two countries and catapulted the water issue to the top of bilateral agenda, thereby making a core issue in Indo-Pakistan relations. The reason is the lack of cooperation, distrust and poor political relationships. To address these issues there is a high need to review the viability of Indus Water Treaty as many experts from both India and Pakistan think that the treaty is outdated. It does not allow for an optimum use of the Indus water resources, and therefore, the treaty should be relooked at and modified with one which lays emphasis on joint sharing rather than territorial division of waters. This demands a common water vision by India and Pakistan that will be based on the realization of the importance of the shared rivers as being a natural resource that is integral to their survival.If climate change is to lead to a period of frequent floods, it will also be followed by a period of shortfalls in water flows. This demands a common water vision by India and Pakistan that will be based on realization of the importance of the shared rivers as being a natural resource that is integral to their survival. New and innovative areas of cooperation, inside and outside the Treaty, can be envisaged. This should include watershed management of the catchment areas of the Indus River system, especially upper catchment areas of the Western rivers. "Water should be an instrument of peace — a means to achieve human security rather than a source of discord"(Akhtar 2010).

Under IWT both India and Pakistan's abilities to face emerging realities are questionable. Both countries suffer significant power shortages. New dam construction could potentially furnish them with reservoirs to buffer prospective shortfalls, flood control against the projected rise in extreme monsoon events, and hydropower to reduce their carbon emissions. Evolving with such coordinated solutions, though, would heighten the need for enhanced cooperation as the ends of irrigation, electricity generation, flood protection, and ecosystem maintenance do not necessarily coincide. In the wake of continuing conflicts and controversies, voices in both countries have suggested revisiting the IWT terms. To be emanated from bilateral dialogues, some mutually agreed alterations to the IWT might improve the scope for effective international cooperation and integrated resource manage-ment across Indus basin (Sheik M.M 2013)

Let India, Pakistan, or any other country desist

themselves from using water as a political tool. It is, too, dangerous to handle it that way. Let us keep the interests of humanity in view, not of a group, community, or region. Water, like air, and sun, is a shared property of humanity, a gift of nature not to be vandalized for the political reasons. New and innovative vistas of cooperation- inside and outside the treaty- can be envisaged.

The discovery of a new dimension of the Kashmir conflict, based on the neo-realistic interests of riparian states in controlling vital water resources, is the hallmark of the study. It made a theory-driven case of India-Pakistan conflict and claimed with substantive empirical evidence that the control of the Indus resource has played a significant role in political thinking, strategic planning, and warfare in the region. It brings to light the competition for the control of vital water resources as an issue of high-politics in the field of international relations and explains when enduring rival nations compromise on vital concerns and why they put politico-ideological issues on the backburner.

The study argues that water is a cause of conflict or war and can also be a catalyst for cooperation or peace, depending on the geography of the resource in conflict and the nature of relations between riparian states. Both dimensions of the Indus Basin's water resources have been identified in Indo-Pakistan relations.

This reinforces the neo-realist belief that states, as rational actors, pursue policies for the maximisation of power (by acquiring control of more and more vital resources) and security (by securing vital resources and minimising perceived losses) vis-à-vis their adversaries, as well as in the international political system. These twin goals constitute their uppermost national interests, and in order to achieve them, states opt for accommodation as a security strategy when reaching a mutually hurting stalemate in their relations. The rivalry between India and Pakistan is no exception to this reality: India attempted to capture and control vital resources in Kashmir, and Pakistan responded in order to secure its resources. On reaching a mutually hurting stalemate, they accommodated each other on vital concerns and postponed the political dimension of the Kashmir issue in an effort to achieve their topmost national objectives. Nevertheless, accommodation did not act as a catalyst for peace, as the states waged a number of wars and their enduring rivalry remained intact. The conclusion is thus that accommodation may not - and did not - resolve or heal all the wounds existing between the disputants. The dispute over Kashmir still remains, and may even have intensified, since the rivers Pakistan still depends on flow through the Indian part of the disputed territory. Moreover, the infrastructure built under the IWT proved to be politically unacceptable, economically unfeasible, and environmentally unsustainable.

Plans to acquire control over the water resources in the region have their roots in the pre-partition manoeuvres of the Indian leadership. Partition of the subcontinent would not have been acceptable to the Indian leadership if the river-water control infrastructures, also containing a road link to the princely state of Kashmir, had not been placed under Indian jurisdiction. Pandit Jawaharlal Nehru's biographer, M.J. Akbar testified this fact that during a meeting in Shimla in May 1947 Nehru insisted that "Whatever the eventual nature of the post partition boundaries might be, the road link to the Kashmir valley through Gurdaspur would have been kept in Delhi's control".

Control of the Indus resource has played a significant role in political thinking, strategic planning and warfare between India and Pakistan. The decision of the Indian leadership, in referring the Kashmir dispute to the UNSC for a peaceful resolution after capturing specific parts of the state, and the later acceptance of UN proposed plebiscite by both the parties, resulted in its portrayal as an ideological and political issue. This strategy worked very well for India, since its objective was firstly, never to resolve the issue but to keep it alive as a symbol of secularism and a disproof of the two-nation theory, and secondly, to consolidate its control over real resources. Pakistan's claims to the Kashmir territory only stood to gain legitimacy through the UN resolutions, thus it had no other option but to pursue this policy, which endorsed the Kashmir conflict as an issue of identity politics. Both states have accommodated each other on vital concerns in the shape of the Indus waters treaty, and both have pursued their national interests of security and power maximisation being rational actors in the international system.

Realities on the ground have changed with the passage of time and the centrality of the control over vital water resources is emerging. Since 1989, Kashmiris have been in revolt against Indian rule. Opinion among the Kashmiri leadership is divided, with certain parts of it demanding a return to the independent Kashmir of pre-1947. Pakistan has extended 'moral support' to their cause but formally denies the provision of any material support. The conversion of the ceasefire line into an international boundary would be acceptable to India, while a further partitioning of Jammu and Kashmir would seem acceptable to Pakistan. The present standpoints of both parties are thus incompatible with the thesis of identity-politics. Since January 2004, both sides have agreed upon a number of CBMs without making any progress on the Kashmir issue, yet the matters over which both reach a diplomatic deadlock revolve around the ongoing water disputes, namely Indian plans to construct dams in the territory of Jammu and Kashmir. This testifies that the Kashmir conflict and the water disputes are intertwined in nature and the Indo-Pakistan conflict is not exclusively ideological. This fact had been overshadowed by India's unlinking of the Indus and Kashmir disputes as a precondition of accepting mediation by the World Bank, and Pakistan's conscious neglect of the linkage issue in order to secure its survival reduce its vulnerabilities and minimise its perceived losses.

Nevertheless, the Indus River resource also offers enormous potential to act as a catalyst for peace. Yet the permanent dissection and diversion of a single and geographically integrated river system under the Indus Waters Treaty, 1960 has intensified divisive politics in the region and conferred permanency upon the existing distrust between the two parties. Mediation does play a major role in smooth running of the relations between nations but any settlement which disregards natural geographical and political realities will likely lack sustainability and endurance. This constitutes a major flaw in the field of mediation and accommodation between enduring rivals and limits the viability of the science of water management and resource development. The study answers the core question, accepts the core hypothesis based on the empirical evidence, and thus achieves the research objectives.

It is concluded that the geographical dimensions of superimposed boundaries and disputed territories (such as surface features or relative locations) have played a major role in triggering water-related conflicts between India and Pakistan. If India had not succeeded in acquiring the Madhopur and Ferozepur headworks—the former also constituting the only land-link to J&K—, the crucial linkage of water and the Kashmir dispute would not have ensued. It argues that the Kashmir conflict is a product of many factors, but that the hydro-strategic nature of its territory can be identified as a major cause. Access to water resources played a significant role in the division of British Punjab and enabled India to use water as strategic, economic and socio-psychological weapon in the 1948 Indo-Pakistan war over Kashmir. India's actions instilled enormous fear into the

Pakistani public, as did its statement that it perceives itself vulnerable until the J&K territory is firmly in Indian hands. This has been of great detriment to the trust Pakistan can ever have towards India regarding its river water lifeline, should it ever opt to relinquish its claims over Kashmir territory. India's abandonment of Kashmir would result in the loss of its upper riparian status and its enormous real-political capacity to intimidate, economically strangulate, and threaten the very survival of Pakistan.

The mapping of the conflict identifies systematically the key trends in conflict and cooperation on the Indus Basin issue. An analysis of the political statements, media reports, actions of interest groups help to understand the reason behind this approach on the part of both countries. The discourse of water security that was adopted from the start and the rise of extremist political groups making maximalist demands make it virtually impossible for governments in both countries to adopt a conciliatory approach. Further, intra-State conflicts in the Indus basin, especially in Pakistan necessitate that the country secures maximum benefits from India. There is very little room for political manoeuvring on both sides. Thus, it is not a surprise that most of the cooperative interaction happens at the technocratic level or with third party support. The mapping of the conflict reveals that this is the main bottleneck that has to be resolved if constructive cooperation and sustainable development of the basin is to be achieved. Both India and Pakistan should be able to create mechanisms for joint development of the basin. This goes beyond (and even complements) the remit of the existing Treaty the purpose of which is to protect the rights and obligations of the riparian parties. Scholars and analysts agree that in the present context all decisions are likely to be politicized and securitized. This is also borne out by mapping the recent trends. Thus, the focus needs to be on strengthening trust through confidence building measures and creating platforms for diplomacy. Third party, technocratic solutions while effective in averting outbreak of violence and gross violation of the Treaty, will not yield innovative solutions for sustainable development of the basin. Similarly, it may be argued that the international actors' stake in the region is mainly averting the risk of a war between two nuclear nations, stability in the Kashmir region and protection of financial investments. Thus, for the long run it is not desirable for the international community to play a big brotherly role and for India and Pakistan to not collectively take responsibility for their own peace. While at the present moment, the feasibility of norm forming cooperative action on the Indus Basin looks bleak both countries should not abandon the long-term political vision for such measures. This in turn would require a shift from the current language of national security to a language of sustainable development and peace (Maitra 2016).

Another finding has been that a bilateral deadlock between the disputants necessitated the involvement of a mediator. Interestingly, during this period, both India and Pakistan had applied to the WB for loans with which to complete their planned irrigation projects. Fortunately, the Bank, while refusing to fund projects related to the disputed river, was willing to assist the parties in resolving their dispute. The presence of the World Bank enhanced the likelihood of accommodation since it accelerated the mutually hurting stalemate. The World Bank managed to commit India not to undertake any new projects but continue to supply Pakistan with water for irrigation until a final settlement was reached. It also linked the availability of funding with compliance. The opening of the Bhakra-Nangal Canal brought a mutually hurting stalemate for India and Pakistan. The stalemate was "hurting" or detrimental to India in two ways: firstly, India was unable to benefit despite developing huge irrigation projects in East Punjab; and secondly, the "opportunity cost of time" (i.e. the level of development India could have attained during that period) was soaring every year. Pakistan's situation, on the other hand, was even worse. It was desirous of a settlement without yielding to its legitimate claims over the "historic uses" of the eastern rivers.

The stalemate was equally hurting India and Pakistan when the World Bank offered its mediation. Pakistan accepted immediately. India though followed the suit but promptly disassociated the Kashmir issue from the water dispute.

The presence of the World Bank as a mediator towards the end of 1951, coupled with the blessing of the USA and some major powers (UK, West Germany, Canada, Australia and New Zealand as loan and funds providers), ensured that India would be restrained from using water as a military weapon against Pakistan. Although armies were deployed on both sides, primed to deal with any military eventuality, and India also attempted to infuriate Pakistan with periodic cross-border firing, Pakistan did not respond militarily. Although India took complete advantage of its upper riparian position by securing full rights to the three eastern rivers and "holding all the cards" on the western rivers, it did not bring about the destruction described in Lilienthal's article.

It is found that the assumption of mediators' impartiality is not always true because they "are best seen as self-interested actors". Actors mediating in international arenas generally pursue and work for their own set agendas. The World Bank's interest in mediating over the Indus waters dispute was rooted in establishing its credibility as an international financial institution. However, the nature of the dispute also accords specific significance: although the mediation resulted in an agreement, it only became possible in the face of the adjournment of the political dimension of the Kashmir issue. The involvement of a third party provided a technical solution to the water problem in the shape of the IWT. Despite the inherent flaws in the treaty and their repercussions, it has served as a safety valve for Pakistan's survival at times when the country's very existence was at stake. Nevertheless, the IWT did not eliminate the root-cause of Indo-Pakistan conflict over Kashmir: the issue of control over the hydro strategic territory.

The Indus Basin Treaty has given a pathway for the successful resolution of water disputes between both nations. Both countries consider the treaty a valuable document that withstood the periods of conflicts and tensions but currently due to India's hegemonic designs in the region, its survival cannot be guaranteed. Currently, the treaty is under threat owing to Pak-India tension in the aftermath of the Uri attack as some Indian commentators' advocate abrogation of the treaty while some are in favor of its revision. However, in case of its unilateral abrogation by India, Pakistan will move to the World Bank or International Court of Justice (Ahmad 2017).

The IWT, although having delivered substantial gains for both parties, has, in the long-run, engendered more complexities for Pakistan-India relations. The division of an integrated river system has given permanency to the distrust between the two states by minimizing opportunities for their interaction. It has also established the vulnerability of the lower riparian as long as the physical control of the water resources remain with India. The development infrastructure envisaged under the IWT, while temporarily alleviating the 'hurting stalemate', has proved to be unsustainable. Moreover, neither the political leadership nor the public were taken into confidence at the time of signing the IWT, giving rise to one of the major causes of Kashmiri alienation on the one hand, and inter-provincial disharmony in Pakistan on the other.

Thus, the staggering economic costs of maintaining the

264

river diversion and the infrastructure of the link-canals, together with an increasing lack of ecological sustainability in Pakistan, political losses in terms of Kashmiri alienation, and provincial dissonance over water-sharing, hindered river development in Pakistan and J&K. Moreover, the separation of the Kashmir issue from the IRS rendered the dispute purely political or ideological and also equipped India and Pakistan with enough time to consolidate their respective territorial control and harden their attitudes on the Kashmir question. As a result, accommodation may not – and, in this case, did not – resolve or alleviate the animosity felt between the rival riparian. The Kashmir dispute remains, and is likely to intensify, because the rivers Pakistan still depends on are located in, and flow downstream through, the India's J&K.The Indus Water Treaty was at its best in its time and could be effectively adapted according to the changing circumstances. However, any such modification should be in line with ecological sustainability, contemporary universal waterway, climate change, emerging concerns with water quality as well as principles of equitable water sharing. However, revision of the treaty will be possible only by the mutual consent of both countries which is presently impossible due to persistent hostilities and mistrust(Ahmad 2017).

The Indus Waters Treaty would need to be amended to incorporate changes that have taken place since its implementation and future projections of climate change, complemented by more efficient water use within each country. Increased energy demand by India and water demand by Pakistan amidst receding Himalayan glaciers will test the treaty and perhaps prompt its revision (Reddy, 2009).

IWT has been a unique compromise on the distribution of river waters in the world. Both Pakistan and India have acquired benefits from the Treaty. India secured more waters from the Eastern Rivers and Pakistan got uninterrupted supply of waters from the western rivers. The Treaty, however, bifurcated the Indus River system and ignored some important aspects relating to water issues. It requires to be updated according to environmental, ecological, climatic changes and requisites of safety from pollution. Controversial Indian projects have also underlined the need of reconsideration of the issues concerned to Indus Basin. While the shadows of nuclear war are looming over South Asia and the water issue has come up as the most dangerous, there is dire need not to insist on the continuation of differences or clinging with outdated solutions. It is also not expedient that all compromises may be rolled back but modifications in the existing IWT are indispensable for the betterment of people of Pakistan as well as of India(Kokab 2013).

Overall, the study concludes that water is a cause of conflict and/or war but can also be a catalyst for peace. Upon reaching a mutually hurting stalemate, states accommodate each other on vital concerns and postpone political issues. The rivalry between India and Pakistan is no exception to this reality. Hence the corollary of the findings is that a compromise on the issue of Kashmir is inconceivable unless a "mutually hurting stalemate" is reached. Nevertheless, the Indus River resource also offers enormous potential as a catalyst for peace. Yet the dissection and diversion of a single and geographically integrated river system under the IWT has intensified divisive politics in the region and conferred permanency upon the distrust between the two parties. Mediation does play a major role in the relations between nations but any settlement which disregards natural geographic and political realities will likely lack sustainability and endurance. This constitutes a major flaw both in the field of mediation and in accommodation (Mirza Nasrullah 2008).

It is time both the countries revisit the treaty and revise

it. A joint river basin organization should be established for sustainable and efficient utilization of Indus water resource. The organization should be independent and free to make decisions without any political pressure.The very realization of the specter of water scarcity looming large over South Asia can pave the way for peace building in this conflict torn region.

Recommendations

Keeping in view the different dynamics of the water problem, experts are talking of an Indus Water Treaty II both in India and Pakistan. One feels that this issue should be taken up seriously and negotiations on the Indus Waters Treaty II be taken up in good faith. If India and Pakistan take a political decision to restructure their relations, they will have to ensure that water serves as a link to bring them together, rather than taking them further towards conflict. Water needs to be managed as a commodity. It is essential to jointly set up an organization with representatives from both countries, whose functions would entail identifying short term and long term supply capacity of the basin and its integrated development, setting up of infrastructure and coordinating activities of the different technical agencies(Kokab 2013).

India and Pakistan should adopt a transparent approach to development problem relating to sharing water and invite interdisciplinary communications. Often, the findings of geologists escape the notice of sociologists, anthropologists and economists, but the reverse is also true. Therefore, a holistic approach is required to understand the background and functioning of highly sophisticated irrigation systems.

Besides, it is time that India and Pakistan along with other countries in the region come up with conservation policies, instead of creating more storage, that they have focused on for long. Dams are environment issues of great complexity. They are expensive to build, involve destruction of habitat and heritage, and relocation of whole communities. They also need water, and storage strategy does not consider where the water to fill dams and reservoirs will come from. It is time for the strategy to harness our water resources to change from being a large-scale capital- and technology-intensive and environmentally degrading option to management-intensive and ecologically balanced development relying on indigenous technology.

Political considerations, of course, cannot be ignored while dealing with the water issue on technical grounds, especially keeping in mind the present distrust in India-Pakistan relations and their history of antagonism. Hence, the two countries should seek international support, perhaps again with the World Bank taking the lead to negotiate a sound water sharing and usage mechanism. Mediation in case of water disputes resolution has worked between India and Pakistan in the past and would solve another great concern- financing the projects if India and Pakistan agree on something (Wasi, 2009).

Managing water distribution between India and Pakistan in an age of climate change can be adopted from the model used in the Euphrates- Tigris river basin between Iraq, Turkey and Syria. Given the conflict among these countries on military and political issues, the water settlement remains grotesque. As suggested to the Tigris-Euphrates river basin countries(Sencan G. 2023), this framework can be tried in India- Pakistan case.

Equitable and adaptive distribution of both risks and awards

It means the allocation regime should have flexibility to accommodate the needs and demands of both countries keeping in mind the rivers' ecosystem. Water allocation should not be guided by any preconceived, prejudiced and pre- set inflexible quotas or minimum requirements. The distribution shall be bound by the hydrological conditions of the rivers and the changing demands which should be genuine and not artificial.

Scientific and diplomatic transparency

It emphasizes upon objective, independent and scientific process of data collection to found the basis of water allocation process. Transparency in data and scientific methods can strengthen diplomacy by reinforcing meaningful and lasting cooperation between the two countries.

Water scarcity in the context of climate change to be accepted as the new and uncertain reality

India and Pakistan should be awakened to the new and uncertainty of water scarcity in coming decades because of climate change and its deepening impact on availability of water in the river basin. The two countries should have to reconcile with this inescapable reality. That the river basin can no longer meet the growing water demands would encourage the two nations to find out the amicable means to manage the water distribution. This would help them understand each other's demands and constraints facilitating reconciliation and cooperation.

Bilateral Organizational structure

A bilateral organizational structure should consist of (1) a high level decision making body (2) a bilateral science committee (3) a bilateral planning committee. All these three committees should work together to arrive at consensus in every decision. Once placed in the committees the members should have term limits and protections to shield them from political pressures.

High level decision making body

The delegates or cabinet ministers from both countries should be represented in the body to supervise the implementation of the management framework with equal voting power. This body should have the authority to appoint members to both science committee and planning committee. All financial involvements, salaries and budgetary allocations for data collection and scientific research shall be made by this committee from time to time as required.

Bilateral Science Committee

The members of the committee shall be public non-officials, independent, non-partisan and men of high integrity and fundamental research on this subject to be nominated by each country. It would be better if they belong to different countries other than India and Pakistan. They would provide data on all seasons like drought, flood and availability of water on lean season with updating climate change and risks. On the basis of its data and findings the planning committee would decide about the water allocation and demands of each country. The entire eco system, water level, and the conditions of endangered species in the context of climate change shall be monitored throughout the basin.

Bilateral planning committee

It would be constituted of members to be delegated equally by both countries. Its main responsibility is to translate the suggestions made by the bilateral science committee regarding annual drought tier and water availability projections into annual water allocations and planning the long-term water availability of the basin. The annual allocations would be calculated based on the science committee's independent estimates of human needs for water in each country as well as water demands from agriculture and other sectors. These demand estimates would also account for local water resources like rainfall and ground water. This would also take into account the projects like waste water treatment, recycling and ground water recharge, renewable energy-water exchanges or investments in recycling for more water allocation. It would also suggest various ecological and environmental measures to ensure preservation of water flows and more water sustainability.

The above model can be just a base for introducing more provisions into it as would look appropriate and relevant to both countries for resolution of water issues. Trying on this model with changes can lead to peace building between the two countries. Given the long history of conflict and wars in the past and deepening bitterness between the two countries on the issue of Kashmir and terrorism, the prospects for resolution of outstanding and burning issues relating to water amicably and through the various committees as suggested above would be very difficult though not impossible to carry on..

References:

- Ahmad Manzoor,Naveeda Yousaf, Muhammad Zubair,2017, "Indus Water Treaty: Threats of Abrogation, Plans for Revision and Prospects of Survivability" Vol. II, No. I (2017)
- Akhtar, Shaheen(2010), Emerging challenges to Indus Water Treaty, FOCUS, XXVIII (3).
- Ali Raja Nazakat, 2013, "Indus Water Treaty: A Geo Political Study" Thesis submitted to the university of Kashmir.
- Hilldouglas,Global Dialogue Volume 15, Number 2, Summer/Autumn 2013— Water: Cooperation or Conflict? "Water-Sharing in the Indus Basin: A Peaceful, Sustainable Future Is Possible"
- Khan Muhamad Azim et al., *Impact of Climate Change on Flora of HighAltitudes in Pakistan, in* Climate Change Impacts on High-Altitude Ecosystems361, 366 (Münir Öztürk et al. eds., 2015); *see also* 2 Encyclopedia of The Developingworld 874 (Thomas M. Leonard ed., 2013).
- KokabRizwan Ullah,Adnan Nawaz "Indus Water Treaty: Need for Review" Vol. 2 No. 2 May 2013

- *Maitra,Sulagna (*2016) "The Indus Water Treaty and Challenges to India-Pakistan Trans Boundary Water Cooperation"(page 259-284) Dr. Sanjay Kumar, Dr. Dhirendra Dwivedi, Dr. Md. Samir Hussain,First edition: 2016,Advance Research Institute for Development of Social Science (ARIDSS), Meerut,G.B. Books New Delhi.
- MirzaNasrullah M. "Water, War, and Peace:Linkages and Scenarios in India-Pakistan Relations" ,Working Paper No. 37February 2008
- Muhammad TayyabSohail, Huang Delin, Aqsa Siddiq, FarwaIdrees, Sidra Arshad, RehanMuhammad,Asia Pacific Journal of Multidisciplinary Research, Vol. 3, No. 1, February 9, 2015, "Evaluation of Historic Indo-Pak Relations, Water Resource Issues and Its impact on Contemporary Bilateral Affairs".
- Qureshi *Dr. Waseem Ahmad, 2017, "The Indus Basin: Water Cooperation, International Law and the Indus Waters Treaty."
- Reddy, R. (2009). "The Indus Water Treaty: Its Persistence and Prospects" The Northwestern Journal of International Affairs, 10(I)
- Sheik M.M, 2013, "Environmental Consciousness and Human Perception" Lap Lambert Academic publishing.
- Sencan Gokce(2023) Managing Water Scarcity in an Age of Climate Change: The Euphrates- Tigris River Basin. Environmental Change and Security Program. Wilson Center : 1-14
- WasiNausheen, sep.2009, "Harnessing the Indus Waters perspectives from Pakistan", IPCS Issue brief 128.

Bibliography

- AkhtarShaheen, "Emerging Challenges to Indus Waters Treaty: Issues of Compliance and Trans-boundary impacts of Indian hydro projects on the Western Rivers", Institute of Regional Studies Islamabad (2010).
- AlloucheJeremy, "Water nationalism: An explanation of the past and present conflicts in Central Asia, the Middle East and the Indian Subcontinent?" PhD diss., University in Geneva (2005).
- Aloys Arthur Michel, the Indus Rivers: A Study of the Effects of Partition (New Haven: Yale University Press, 1967).
- Chari PR, 2004, Indus Waters Treaty-II Optimizing the Potential, IPCS Discussion Paper.
- Climate diplomacy, report 2014, the rise of hydro-diplomacy, strengthening foreign policy for transboundary waters.
- European union 2015, Conflict and cooperation over water the role of the EU in ensuring the realisation of human rights.
- International Conference Water Environment 1992. Development issues for the 21st century. The Dublin Statement and Rep.Conf.,Dublin, Irel.,26–31Jan. Geneva: World Meteorol. Organ.
- Jason Gehrig with Mark M. Rogers Edited by Dennis Warner, Chris Seremet, and Tom Bamat, "Water and Conflict in Corporatingpeacebuilding into Water development", United States Conference of Catholic Bishops. Published 2009.
- Kameri-Mbote Patricia, January 2007, No4, "Water Conflict and cooperation: Lessons from the Nile River Basin", environmental change and security program special report.

- Khan Muhamad Azim et al., *Impact of Climate Change on Flora of HighAltitudes in Pakistan, in* Climate Change Impacts on High-Altitude EcosystemS361, 366 (Münir Öztürk et al. eds., 2015); *see also* 2 Encyclopedia of The Developingworld 874 (Thomas M. Leonard ed., 2013).
- *Maitra,Sulagna (*2016) "The Indus Water Treaty and Challenges to India-Pakistan Trans Boundary Water Cooperation"(page 259-284) Dr. Sanjay Kumar, Dr. Dhirendra Dwivedi, Dr. Md. Samir Hussain,First edition: 2016,Advance Research Institute for Development of Social Science (ARIDSS), Meerut,G.B. Books New Delhi.
- Rao, U. B. 1967. The story of rehabilitation. New Delhi, India: Ministry of Information and Broadcasting.
- SattarAbdul(2007), Pakistan's Foreign Policy(1947-2005),Karachi, Oxford University Press.
- Strategic Foresight Group, 2013, Water Cooperation for a Secure World Focus on the Middle East.
- Swain, Ashok 2013: sharing Indus River for development and peace. brussels: presentation at international council for human rights, 20 march 2013.
- UNECAFE, Multiple Purpose River Basin Development, Part 2B, p. 70.
- AdeelZafar, 2015 "Water Cooperation" United Nations University.
- Ahmad, Azhar(2012), Indus Waters Treaty A dispassionate analysis, Monthly Digest.
- AhmadManzoor,Naveeda Yousaf, Muhammad Zubair,2017, "Indus Water Treaty: Threats of Abrogation, Plans for Revision and Prospects of Survivability" Vol. II, No. I (2017)
- Ahmed, tufail(2009, July31) Water disputes between India and Pakistan, Henary Jackson Society.
- Akhtar, Shaheen(2010), Emerging challenges to Indus Water Treaty, FOCUS, XXVIII (3).

- Ali Raja Nazakat, Faiz-ur-Rehman and Mahmood-ur-RehmanWani, 2011"Indus Water Treaty between Pakistan and India: From Conciliation to Confrontation".
- Ammad Hafiz Mohammad "Water Sharing in the Indus River Basin: Application of Integrated Water Resources Management" 2000.
- Arase, D. (2010) Non-Traditional Security in China-ASEAN Cooperation. Asian Survey, 50(4), 808-833.
- Arora R.K., 2007, "The Indus Water Regime", New Delhi; Mohit publication.
- Basheer Khalil Nijim, Use in Arid Regions, (Paris: UNESCO Arid Zone Research, 1961), Vol. XVII, No. 1, pp. 143-174 op. cit., p. 28.
- Bhuttazafar(2011), Kishanganga dam: is partial stay order a comprehensive victory for Pakistan?Tribune (online), retrieved on 28 September 2011.
- Biswas A K, Hashimoto T, edsv.1996. Asian International Waters: From Ganges-Brahmaputra to Mekong. Oxford: Oxford University Press.
- Carius Alexander, Geoffrey D. Dabelko and Aaron T. Wolf, 2004, policy brief, The United Nations and Environmental Security, Water, Conflict and Cooperation.
- Chadha, G. K. 1986. The state and rural economic transformation: The case of Punjab, 1950–85. New Delhi, India: Sage Publications.
- Conca Ken, "Governing Water: Contentious Transnational Politics and Global Institution Building", 2005, Cambridge, MA: MIT press.
- Conca, K., F. Wu, and C. Mei. 2006. Global regime formation or complex institution building? The principled content of international river agreements. International Studies Quarterly 50 (2).
- Dinar Ariel, Dinar Shlomi, McCaffrey Stephen, and McKinney Daene, "Bridge over Water: Understanding Transboundary Water Conflict, Negotiation and Cooperation", 2007, Singapore: World Scintific.

- Earle, Anton; Anders, Jägerskog and JoakimÖjendal (eds.) 2010, transboundary water management: principles and practice. london: earthscan.
- Elliott, L. (2003). ASEAN and environmental cooperation: norms, interests and identity. The Pacific Review, 16(1), 29-52, 47.
- Embassy of Pakistan Let the Reader Judge, Washington, D. C., July 22, 1958; See Nijim, op. cit., p. 38.
- falkenmark, malin and andersJägerskog 2010: sustainability of transnational water agreements in the face of socio-economic and environmental change.
- Fröhlich, C. (2012), Water: Reason for Conflict or Catalyst for Peace? The Case of the Middle East, L'Europeen formation.
- Gazdar, Haris (2005). 'Baglihar and Politics of Water: A Historical Perspective from Pakistan'Economic and Political Weekly, Vol. 40, No. 9.
- Gleick, P. H. (1993). Water and Conflict: Fresh Water Resources and International Security. International Security.
- Goh, E. (2006). China in the Mekong River Basin: The Regional Security Implications of Resource Development on the Lancang Jiang. In Caballero-Anthony, R. Emmers& A. Acharya (Eds.), Non-Traditonal Security in Asia. Hamshire and Burlington: Ashgate.
- Graeger, N. (1996). Environmental Security? Journal of Peace Research.
- Gulhati N.D, 1973, "Indus Water Treaty: An Exercise in International Mediation; Bombay: Allied publishers.
- Haefner Andrea, 2013, Non-Traditional Security: The Case of Environmental Challenges in the Mekong Subregion.
- Hilldouglas,Global Dialogue Volume 15 ! Number 2 ! Summer/Autumn 2013— Water: Cooperation or Conflict? "Water-Sharing in the Indus Basin: A Peaceful, Sustainable Future Is Possible"

- Houdret, A. (2008), Scarce Water, Plenty of Conflicts? Local Water Conflicts and the Role of Development Cooperation, Policy Brief, Duisburg, Institute for Development and Peace.
- Iyer, Ramaswamy R. (2005). 'Indus Treaty: A Different View, Economic and Political Weekly', Vol. 40, No. 29.
- Kalpakian Jack, 2004, "Identity, Conflict, and Cooperation in International River System", Aldershot, UK: Ashgate.
- Kaushik k. Aditya, "Regulating Water Security in Border Regions: The Case of India and Pakistan" August 1st, 2017.
- KhagramSanjeev, 2004, "Dams and Development: Transnational Struggles for Water and Power", Ithaca: Cornell University Press.
- Khan, raja Mohammad (2011March9), Implications of US warning for a water War, The Frontier Post, (online),Kibaroglu A. 2002. Building a Regime for the Waters of the Euphrates-Tigris River Basin. Hague, Neth.: Kluwer Law Int.
- KokabRizwan Ullah,Adnan Nawaz "Indus Water Treaty: Need For Review" Vol. 2 No. 2 May 2013
- Kramer Annika, 2004, Water and Conflict, Washington, DC: Adelphi Research, Center for International Forestry Research, and Woodrow Wilson International Center for Scholars, 2004.
- Kramer Annika, 2008, Regional Water Cooperation and Peacebuilding in the Middle East.
- Libiszewski, S. (1999), International Conflicts over Freshwater Resources, in: Suliman, Mohamed (ed.), Ecology, Politics and Violent Conflict, 115-138.
- LopezA.2004.Environmental conflict sand regional cooperation in the Lempa River basin: the role of Central America's Plan Trifinio. EDSP Work. Pap. 2. Environment Development Sustainable Peace Initiat., Berlin.

- Lorenz, Frederick and Edward J. Erickson 2013: strategic water. Iraq and security planning in the euphrates-tigris basin water. Virginia: Marine Corps University press.
- Lowi, M. R. (1999). Water and Conflict in the Middle East and South Asia: Are Environmental Issues and Security Issues Linked? Journal of Environment and Development, 8(4), 376-396.
- Lowi, M. 1993. Water and power: The politics of a scarce resource in the Jordan River Basin. Cambridge, UK: Cambridge University Press.
- Malik A. Bashir, 2007 "Indus Water Regime", New Delhi; Mohit Publications.
- Manno, J. (2010), Water Issues, International Encyclopedia of Peace, Oxford University Press, Oxford.
- Manzoor Dr., Ahmad Malik, Dr. Muhammad AslamTahir and Engr. Ahmad ZeeshanBhatti ,2015, Pak-India Transboundary Cooperation on Shared Water Resources – Past and Present Perspective.
- Mehta, L.; Veldwisch, G. J. and Franco, J. (2012), Introduction to the Special Issue: Water grabbing? Focus on the (re)appropriation of finite waterresources, Water Alternatives Vol. 5(2), 193-207.
- Menon, R., and K. Bhasin. 1998. Borders and boundaries: Women in India's partition. New Brunswick, NJ: Rutgers University Press.
- M.J. Akbar, Nehru: The Making of India (London: Penguin Group, 1988), pp. 443-444.
- Michel A. Aloys, 1967, "The Indus Rivers: A Study of the Effects of Partition", New Haven and London: Yale University Press.
- Miner Mary, "Water Sharing between India and Pakistan: a critical evaluation of the Indus Water Treaty", Water International 34, no.2 (May 2009); 204-216.
- MirzaNasrullah M. "Water, War, and Peace:Linkages and Scenarios in India-Pakistan Relations" ,Working Paper No. 37February 2008

- Molle, F. and Berkoff, J. (2006), Cities versus Agriculture: Revisiting Intersectoral Water Transfers, Potential Gains and Conflicts, International Water Management Institute, Colombo.
- Muckleston K. 2003. International Management in the Columbia River System. Paris: UNESCO IHP Tech. Doc. Hydrol., PCCP Ser. 12.
- Muhammad Rashid Khan University of the Punjab, Lahore South Asian Studies A Research Journal of South Asian Studies Vol. 28, No. 1, January – June 2013, pp.213-221 Crucial Water Issues between Pakistan and India, CBMs, and the Role of Media.
- Nakayama, M. 1997. Successes and failures of international organizations in dealing with international waters. International Journal of Water Resources Development 13 (3).
- Nakayama M, ed. 2003. International Waters in Southern Africa. Tokyo: UN University Press.
- Ohlsson, Leif. (2000). Livelihood conflicts: Linking poverty and environment as causes of conflict. Stockholm: Swedish International Development Agency, Department of Natural Resources and the Environment.
- Phillips, D., Daoudy, M., McCaffrey, S., Ojendal, J.&Turton, A. (2006). Transboundary Water Co-operation as a Tool for Conflict Prevention and Broader Benefit Sharing. Global Development Studies No. 4. Ministry of Foreign Affairs Sweden.
- Qureshi *Dr. Waseem Ahmad, 2017, "The Indus Basin: Water Cooperation, International Law andthe Indus Waters Treaty."
- Ramaswamy.Iyer(2010), Water through Pakistan eyes,
- Ravnborg, HelleMunk et al.(2012), Challenges of local water govemance: the extent, nature and intensity of local water-related conflict and cooperation, Water Policy, Vol. 14.

- Reddy, R. (2009). "The Indus Water Treaty: Its Persistence and Prospects" The Northwestern Journal of International Affairs, 10(I)
- SadoffCW,GrayD. 2002. beyond the river: the benefits of cooperation on international rivers. Water Policy.
- Salman 2008. The Baglihar difference and its resolution process—a triumph for the Indus Waters Treaty? Water Policy 10:105–117.
- Sarvat N. Hanif, 2013 "Acess to water catalyst for cooperation, peace building".
- Schmeier, Susanne 2013: governing international watercourses river basin organizations and the sustainable governance of internationally shared rivers and lakes. New York: rout ledge.
- Schneider, K. (2011). Fierce competition over water threatens China's economic progress and global food, energy prices. Yale Global.
- Sheik M.M, 2013, "Environmental Consciousness and Human Perception" Lap Lambert Academic publishing.
- Siddiqui H. Iqtidar(2010), Hydro politics and water wars in South Asia, Lahore, and Vanguard Books.
- Singh Richa, "Trans-boundary Water Politics and Conflicts in South Asia: Towards 'Water for Peace" New Delhi-110016.
- Sinha K. Uttam, "India and Pakistan: Introspecting the Indus Treaty", strategic Analysis 32, No.6 (October,2008) 961-967; Sinha, "50 years of the Indus Water Treaty: An Evaluation", Strategic Analysis 34, no.5 (August,2010), 667-670; "Water a Pre-eminent Issue between India and Pakistan", Strategic Analysis 34, No.4 (June,2010) 482-485, "Will the Indus Water Treaty Survive" Strategic Analysis 36, No.5 (September,2012) 735-752.
- Siyad A. C., Muhammed (2005). 'Indus Waters Treaty and Baglihar Project: Relevance of International Watercourse Law, 'Economic and Political Weekly, Vol. 40, No. 29 (Jul. 16-22).

- Sridhar Seema, 2004, Kashmir and Water: Conflict and Cooperation.
- Sridhar seema(2008), Kashmir and Water: conflict and cooperation, In shahidimtiaz Advanced Contemporary Affairs(Ed),Lahore: Advanced Publishers.
- Swain, Ashoka. 2004. Managing water conflict: Asia, Africa and the Middle East. London: Routledge.
- Swain Ashok. 2009. The Indus II and Siachen Peace Park: Pushing the India-Pakistan peace process forward. Round Table 98 (404): 569–582.
- Tabassum, shaista(2001), the role of CBM in resolving non-military issues between India and Pakistan: A case study of the Indus Water Treaty,InAhmerMoonis(Ed), the challenge of confidence-building measures in South Asia, New Delhi, Haranand Publications.
- Tariq, MuhammadSardar(2009), The Indus Water Treaty and emerging water management issues in Pakistan, Problems and Politics of water sharing in Pakistan, Islamabad, Policy Research Institute.
- Tariq Sardar Muhammad, 2014, "Managing the Indus Waters: Alternative Strategies" Institute of peace and Conflict Studies.
- *Qureshi Dr. Waseem Ahmad, Mich. St. Int'l L. Rev., 2017 –HeinOnline*The Indus Basin : Water Cooperation, International Law and The Indus Waters Treaty
- Verghese, BG, "Water issues in South Asia," ORF Discourse, Vol. 5, Issue 8, April 2011.
- Vaid Manish &MainiTridivesh Sing, "Indo-Pak Water Disputes: Time for Fresh Approaches" Chapter-4, peace print: South Asian Journal of peace building, vol.4, no-2, 2012.
- Voutira, E., and B. Harrell-Bond. 2000. "Successful" refugee settlement: Are past experiences relevant? In Risks and reconstruction: Experiences of resettlers and refugees.

- WasiNausheen, sep.2009, "Harnessing the Indus Waters perspectives from Pakistan", IPCS Issue brief 128.
- Waseem, A. (2007). Irrigation Engineering II. Pinto, Jeffrey K. (2009). Project Management - Achieving Competitive Advantage (Custom Edition). Upper Saddle River, New Jersey: Pearson. ISBN 978-0-558-20289-7 (Dulhasti HE Project).
- Waslekars, "The Final Settlement: Restructuring India-Pakistan Relations, Strategic Foresight Group Mumbai (2005).
- Waterbury, J. 1990. Dynamics of basin-wide cooperation in the utilization of the Euphrates. Paper presented at the conference "Economic Development of Syria: Problems, Progress, and Prospects," Damascus, Syria.
- Wolf Aaron T, Annika Kramer, Alexander Carius, and Geoffrey D. Dabelko, 2006, Water Can Be a PathWay to Peace, not war.
- Zawahri, N. 2008a. Designing river commissions to implement treaties and manage international rivers: The story of the Joint Water Committee and Permanent Indus Commission. Water International 33 (4): 464–474.
- Ali H Saleem, MeheraMalini, September 2014, "flood in India and Pakistan offer a chance for peace-building."
- Basheer Khalil Nijim, The Indus, Nile and Jordan: International Rivers and Factors in Conflict Potential (Thesis submitted to Indiana University, 1969).
- Dawn (2010). The daily Dawn 20th February, 2010. An article by Ahmad Bilal Sufi.
- Bokhari, Ashfak. "Kishanganga verdict a tilt in India's favor." The Dawn, February 13, 2013.
- B.G. Verghese, "Fuss Over Indus-I: India's Rights Are Set Out in the Treaty," The Tribune (Chandigarh), 25 May 2005.
- ChandranSuba, "Indus Waters Governance-II: From 'Letter and Spirit' to 'Letter vs Spirit", Institute of Peace and Conflict Studies (19 July 2010).

- Chellaney Brahma. 30. Dec.2016. "India can solve its water scarcity by correcting Indus Water Treaty".
- ChitrakarNavesh. 2018. "India's Modi inaugurates hydro project in Kashmir, Pakistan protests", Reuters Staff.
- Dawn, dawn.com. January 04, 2017, 10.27 pm. "Indus Water Treaty made peaceful cooperation possible between India, Pakistan."
- Finance Express, June 5, 2018, 11.17 am. "Kishanganga Dam dispute: Stand down, accept India's offer, World Bank tells Pakistan."
- Free press Kashmir, May 23, 2018. "Seeking an 'amicable solution' to water dispute between India, Pakistan: World Bank.
- Gill, M.S. "Water crisis of east and west Punjab." The Hindu, May 28, 2010.
- HaidarSuhasini, The Hindu, September 27, 2016, "India suspends talks on Indus Water Pact".
- HaidarSuhasini, The Hindu. 3rdmarch 2017.
- Hali M Sultan, 2018, "Pak-India Water War", Pakistan Today.
- India Tv. June 5, 2018, 11.34. "Kishanganga Project: World Bank backs India, asks Pakistan not to take the matter to ICA".
- Kaushik k. Aditya, "Regulating Water Security in Border Regions: The Case of India and Pakistan", August 1st, 2017.
- Madhana, Niharika. "Water Wars: Why India and Pakistan Are Squaring Off Over Their Rivers," Time, April 16, 2012.
- Muhammad TayyabSohail, Huang Delin, Aqsa Siddiq, FarwaIdrees, Sidra Arshad, RehanMuhammad,Asia Pacific Journal of Multidisciplinary Research, Vol. 3, No. 1, February 9, 2015, "Evaluation of Historic Indo-Pak Relations, Water Resource Issues and Its impact on Contemporary Bilateral Affairs".

- NayarKuldip, January 9, 2017, "Pakistan, India and the Indus Water Treaty".
- ParvaizAthar, September 25, 2016, "Indus Water Treaty rides out latest crisis".
- Qureshi Dr. Waseem Ahmad, 2017, "The Indus Basin: Water Cooperation, International Law andthe Indus Waters Treaty".
- Sarvat N. Hanif, 2013 "Acess to water catalyst for cooperation, peace building".
- Stone R. David, "The United States and the Negotiation of the Indus Water Treaty", U.S.I. Journal 140, no.579 (January-March, 2010):75-87.
- Swain Ashok. 23September 2016. "Withdrawing Indus Waters Treaty is not a solution to punish Pakistan as it will only bring global condemnation."
- Swain Ashok, September 30, 2016, "The Indus Water Treaty, not for revenge but for development and peace".
- The Hindu, September 27, 2016, "Will approach U.N. if India violates Indus Water Treaty."
- United Nations Educational, Scientific and Cultural Organization (UNESCO), 2009, "Valuing Water", UNESCO World Water Assessment Programmers.
- Veilleux, Jennifer C. (2013), Water: Cooperation or Conflict?, The Human Security Dimensions of Dam Development: The Grand Ethiopian Renaissance Dam, Global Dialogue, Vol. 15(2).
- Verghese B. G., "It's Time for Indus-II." The Tribune 26 (May 25, 2005).
- Wolf T. Aaron, 2007, "Shared Waters: Conflict and Cooperation" Annual Review of Environment and Resources Volume 32, 2007.
- Khan, S.M. (2008). Economics of Indus Basin Treaty, www.cssforum.com.pk.
- Sharma, Rajeev (2007), Uri Project, Pakistan threatens to approach WB, TribuneThe Express Tribune, January 12th, 2012. An article published.

- The Indian Express, September 30, 2016.
- TikhonovaPolina. November 4, 2016. "India vs. Pakistan water Conflict Poses Global Threat."
- Transboundary Water Cooperation, July 2006, A BMZ Position Paper.
- Waterbury J. 1979. Hydropolitics of the Nile Valley. New York: Syracuse Univ. Press.
- Waterbury J. 2002. The Nile Basin: National Determinants of Collective Action. New Haven/London: Yale University Press.
- Wolf T Aaron; Yoffe, Shira B. and Giordano, M. (2003), International Waters: Indicators for Identifying Basins at Risk, Unesco,Paris.
- Wolf T. Aaron, Kramer Annika, Alexander Carius, and Geoffrey D. Dabelko, Managing Water Conflict and Cooperation, The Worldwatch Institute,2005,
- Wolf T. Aaron, 2003, "Transboundary Water Conflicts and Cooperation.
- Zaheerul Hasan. "Indo-Pak Dispute over Kishanganga Project." Pak Tribune, October 30, 2012.
- Zee News, june 05, 2018, 03.59pm. "Kishanganga dam dispute: World Bank asks Pakistan to accept India's demand".
- Ali Raja Nazakat, 2013, "Indus Water Treaty: A Geo Political Study" Thesis submitted to the university of Kashmir
- Hafiz Saeed blames India for Pakistan floods, calls it ... (n.d.). Retrieved October 23, 2016, from http://timesofindia.indiatimes.com/india/Hafiz-Saeed-blames-India-for-Pakistan-floods-calls-it-waterterrorism/articleshow/42116443.cms.
- Pacific Institute (2015), Water Conflict Chronology, availableat:http://www2.worldwater.org/chronology.html.
- India suspends Indus commissioners' meetings. The Third Pole. (n.d.). Retrieved October 23, 2016 from

https://www.thethirdpole.net/2016/09/26/india-suspends-indus-commissioners-meetings/.

- Pakistan approaches International Court of Justice, World ...(n.d.). Retrieved October 23, 2016, from http://www.dnaindia.com/india/report-pakistan-approaches-international-court-of-justice-world-bank-overindus-waters-treaty-225943.
- United Nations. 2002. Report of the World Summit on Sustainable Development.Doc.A/CONF.199/20,SalesNo.E.03.II.A.1. NewYork:UN.http://www.un.org/jsummit/html/documents/summit docs/131302 wssd report reissued.pdf.
- UNW-DPAC, 2013a. Water Cooperation in Action: approaches, tools and processes http://www.un.org/waterforlifedecade/water_cooperation_2013/.
- Pdf/water cooperation in action approaches tools processes.pdf.
- https://www.lawteacher.netzthe-India-Pakistan.
- Wirsing and Jasparro, 2006 and Sridhar, 2005)Wirsing, R.G and Jasparro, C., (2006) "Spotlight on Indus River Diplomacy: India, Pakistan, and the Baglihar Dam Dispute". Asia-Pacific Center for Security Studies. Available from http://www.apcss.org/Publications/APSSS/IndusRiverDiplomacy.Wirsing.Jasparro.pdf).gq

www.ingramcontent.com/pod-product-compliance
Lightning Source LLC
Chambersburg PA
CBHW050213270326
41914CB00003BA/387